Candidates '76

Timely Reports to Keep
Journalists, Scholars and the Public
Abreast of Developing Issues, Events and Trends

January 1976

CONGRESSIONAL QUARTERLY

1414 22ND STREET, N.W., WASHINGTON, D.C. 20037

760031

Congressional Quarterly Inc.

Congressional Quarterly Inc., an editorial research service and publishing company, serves clients in the fields of news, education, business and government. It combines specific coverage of Congress, government and politics by Congressional Quarterly with the more general subject range of an affiliated service, Editorial Research Reports.

Congressional Quarterly was founded in 1945 by Henrietta and Nelson Poynter. Its basic periodical publication was and still is the CQ *Weekly Report,* mailed to clients every Saturday. A cumulative index is published quarterly.

The CQ *Almanac,* a compendium of legislation for one session of Congress, is published every spring. *Congress and the Nation* is published every four years as a record of government for one presidential term.

Congressional Quarterly also publishes paperback books on public affairs. These include the twice-yearly *Guide to Current American Government* and such recent titles as *Presidential Elections Since 1789* and *The Middle East: U.S. Policy, Israel, Oil and the Arabs, second edition.*

CQ Direct Research is a consulting service which performs contract research and maintains a reference library and query desk for the convenience of clients.

Editorial Research Reports covers subjects beyond the specialized scope of Congressional Quarterly. It publishes reference material on foreign affairs, business, education, cultural affairs, national security, science and other topics of news interest. Service to clients includes a 6,000-word report four times a month bound and indexed semi-annually. Editorial Research Reports publishes paperback books in its fields of coverage. Founded in 1923, the service merged with Congressional Quarterly in 1956.

Editor: Mercer Cross

Contributors: Rhodes Cook, Alan Ehrenhalt, Edna Frazier, Bruce F. Freed, Al Gordon, Barry Hager, Ed Johnson, Rochelle Jones, Warden Moxley, Mary Neumann, Matt Pinkus, Ted Vaden. Art director: Howard Chapman. Production manager: I.D. Fuller. Assistant production manager: Kathleen Walsh. Editorial assistant: Susan Henry Davis.

Book Service editor: Robert A. Diamond

Library of Congress Catalog No. 75-37211
International Standard Book No. 0-87187-084-3

TABLE OF CONTENTS

Presidential Outlook: Post-Industrial Politics: A Guide to 1976 1

Ford: Sharpening the 2-Edged Sword of Incumbency 5

Reagan: A Strong Challenge from the Republican Right 12

Bayh: Appealing to the Old Democratic Coalition 17

Bentsen: Tribulations of a Little-Known Candidate 22

Carter: Translating Charm, Determination into Votes 27

Church: An '80 Per Cent Certainty' of Running 31

Harris: Again, A Thundering 'New Populism' 35

Humphrey: The Last Long Wait for Lightning to Strike 40

Jackson: Marketing a Record of Effective Legislating 44

Kennedy: The Non-Candidate Everybody Talks About 51

Muskie: Four Years After Defeat, Lingering Interest 56

Sanford: Making an Asset of Distance from Washington 60

Shapp: Persistently Working at Being Taken Seriously 64

Shriver: In Energetic Pursuit of the 'Kennedy Legacy' 68

Udall: A House Reformer Pressing for Presidency 72

Wallace: A Fourth Straight Drive for the White House 78

McCarthy: A Solitary Call to Abolish the 2-Party System 84

Other Prospects: No Shortage of Hopefuls Awaiting the Call 89

Campaign Finance Law: Paying for Elections: New Law Under Attack 95

Reference Bibliography 103

Explanation of CQ Vote Studies on Members of Congress 107

Index 108

Introduction

If the past few presidential election campaigns contain a lesson for 1976, it is this: early in the year, the only predictable commodity is uncertainty; any guess is hazardous.

And 1976 is even more treacherous than its predecessors. For the first time ever, an unelected President who was elevated from an appointive vice presidency is running for a full term. The uniqueness of the situation has contributed to one announced challenge to President Ford in the Republican primaries, with others a possibility. In the Democratic primaries, at least 10 and probably more candidates will compete for the nomination. At least one presidential candidate will run as an independent in the November election, and he may have company before it is all over.

Because of the surfeit of aspirants, the names of the eventual major-party nominees may be clouded in confusion far longer than usual—perhaps until the national conventions. Contributing to the delay will be 30 or more state presidential primaries, a record. The trail from New Hampshire in February to California in June will be long, exhausting and expensive.

The expense of campaigning is a critical factor in the emerging confusion of 1976. In another first, as a result of a post-Watergate campaign finance law, candidates have had to plan their strategies around restrictions both in their contributions and in their spending. The constitutionality of the law has been challenged, and after an initial decision upholding it, an appeal is pending before the Supreme Court as this book goes to press. A decision is expected before the first primary; even if all or part of the new law is thrown out, its provisions will have a significant residual impact on the campaign.

Republican Surprises

Seldom does an election season go by without a few surprises, and this year's has had one already. In November 1975, Vice President Nelson A. Rockefeller came up with the unexpected announcement that he would not be President Ford's running mate in 1976. Rockefeller acknowledged that his decision was a response to dissatisfaction among his old foes on the Republican right. He stepped aside to make the going easier for the man who had appointed him a year earlier. But, even while declaring his support for Ford, he kept all his options open for a possible role of his own later in 1976.

Ford, meanwhile, has been campaigning early and energetically. He has made clear in his early speeches that he will espouse conservative themes in his campaign. He has a serious challenge for the nomination from Ronald Reagan, long-time hero of party conservatives. Reagan and his substantial following would like to hand the incumbent President the biggest disappointment of all by eliminating him from the race in the early primaries.

Ford and friends state emphatically that they are not about to let that happen. But their campaign has suffered from dissension that has led to the departure of two important election committee officials. As if that were not trouble enough, Ford is hearing increasingly loud grumbling from Republican moderates in the Senate over his rightward rhetoric. The Rockefeller move only intensified their antagonism. Should Reagan eliminate Ford, a challenge from the moderates, not to mention Rockefeller, would be a strong possibility.

Then there is John B. Connally. The suave Texas Democrat-turned-Republican is talking about a possible candidacy, either as a Republican or, under certain conditions, as an independent.

Democratic Divisions

Everybody expected a crowded Democratic field, and they were not disappointed. The Republicans can find some gratification, however scant, in the bulging roster of ambitious Democrats. Despite all the campaigning by the Democrats, none of them can yet claim anything close to an apparent plurality of party support. All are acutely aware of the abrupt evaporation of past apparent pluralities as the early primaries felled the erstwhile giants.

The Democratic overcrowding and the swollen number of state primaries—at least seven more than in 1972—are directly attributable to some new changes in party procedures for selecting candidates. The changes, with their emphasis on proportional representation at all levels in the selection process, have made running seem attractive to a range of Democrats from the liberal to the conservative. The conventional wisdom is that the list will be shortened dramatically by the early primaries.

Absent from the Democratic list is the one man who has outshone all the others as the popular choice of his party in public-opinion polls: Massachusetts Sen. Edward M. Kennedy. With Kennedy out of the race by his own emphatic declaration of non-candidacy, the front-runner in many polls has been Democratic Gov. George C. Wallace of Alabama. Close behind Wallace in some polls (and ahead in others) has been Minnesota Sen. Hubert H. Humphrey, the Democratic nominee in 1968, who is not a candidate in 1976 but would be more than willing to accept the challenge if it came his way. In a similar category, although not mentioned as often, is Maine Sen. Edmund S. Muskie, Humphrey's 1968 running mate.

The names of Humphrey, Muskie and others come up in any talk of a "brokered" convention—the kind of convention that could, in a reversion to the days before primaries became so important, work out a slate chosen by party powers behind closed doors. Most Democrats would go a long way to avoid such a convention. Wallace is the man who frightens them most, because he could come into the convention with a big bloc of delegate votes and be in a position to exert strong influence on the choice of the nominee.

The assumption of most Democrats is that George Wallace will not, no matter how well he runs in the primaries, be the Democratic presidential nominee. If he is rejected, however, he is considered a likely third-party candidate. And if he runs on his own, one of the critical questions of election year 1976 will be about which party, the Democrats or the Republicans, will lose more votes to Wallace.

Another pull for votes, although much diminished from what it would have been eight years earlier, will come from Eugene J. McCarthy, the former Minnesota senator and 1968 Democratic peace candidate who drove the late Lyndon B. Johnson into early retirement. McCarthy is running as an independent this time and is one of the plaintiffs in the suit challenging the new election law.

Inside This Book

These and other figures—the candidates and the potential candidates—are the central characters in the drama of the 1976 election campaign. The principal purpose of this book is to provide background on the characters and what they are doing. Some chapters deal with politicians—Kennedy of Massachusetts, for example—who probably will not become presidential candidates this time around but who will, nonetheless, play prominent parts in the year's events.

The book does not deal with prospective favorite-son candidates, but only with those whose appeal extends beyond the boundaries of their home states. Although many informed observers might consider Pennsylvania Gov. Milton J. Shapp a favorite-son candidate for the Democratic nomination, he insists that he is a national candidate, and he is treated as such, with a chapter devoted to him alone.

Also purposely omitted is a chapter on vice presidential possibilities. Clearly, some of those ostensibly running for the number-one position would be satisfied to settle for number two. But that list is not only conjectural but endless, and the vice presidential nominees will not be known, if past tradition is followed, until they have been chosen by the presidential nominees and nominated by the conventions next summer.

The book begins with a chapter discussing the general political milieu of bicentennial America. From there it goes into the candidates and key figures, starting with incumbent Ford and challenger Reagan and continuing, in alphabetical order, through the Democrats to independent McCarthy. There is a chapter containing brief profiles of other, less likely prospects in both parties, including Nelson Rockefeller, John Connally and a number of other Democrats and Republicans. The last chapter discusses in some detail the campaign finance reform law of 1974 and its effect on 1976.

Mercer Cross
November 1975

POST-INDUSTRIAL POLITICS: A GUIDE TO 1976

The 1976 presidential election will be a new experience in American politics—an event likely to depart from form as few elections before it ever have.

Much of the change is procedural. A new campaign finance law limits what citizens may donate and candidates may spend. Presidential primaries have proliferated to the point where they all but eclipse traditional delegate selection methods. The Democrats are experimenting with proportional representation throughout the pre-convention process.

Beneath the structural change, however, lie deeper changes that are taking place in the American economy and society. Scholars are reaching a remarkable consensus about their nature. The procedural changes of the past few years will dramatize their effect.

The changes coalesce around the term "post-industrial society," developed by sociologist Daniel Bell and expanded, sometimes under other names, by political scientist Zbigniew Brzezinski, economic consultant Herman Kahn and election scholar Kevin P. Phillips.

A post-industrial society, these men say, is one in which knowledge and technology replace manufacturing and physical labor as the dominant facts of economic and social life.

"Since World War II," Phillips wrote in his 1975 book, *Mediacracy*, "the United States has been in the vanguard of a new, post-industrial economic era increasingly built around the sale of services and knowledge rather than manufactured products."

"The post-industrial society," Brzezinski wrote similarly in 1970, "is becoming...a society that is shaped culturally, psychologically, socially and economically by the impact of technology and electronics—particularly in the area of computers and communications."

The post-industrial changes affect politics most dramatically through their creation of a new class, a college-educated elite whose livelihood and culture are tied to knowledge—and who vote accordingly.

Trying to define membership in the new class is a slippery task, but Phillips points to government bureaucracies (which now include one in six U.S. employees), colleges and universities, communications empires, think tanks, charitable foundations, consultants, journalists and assorted other professionals. About 35 per cent of the U.S. gross national product is accounted for by the production, consumption and dissemination of knowledge, a percentage which is thought likely to reach 40 by 1980.

Books and Tennis Balls

In his 1970 book, *The Emerging Republican Majority*, Phillips argued that the development of the new class and its stake in expanded government and research would generate sharp class conflict. He said this would enable the Republican Party to reach majority status by exploiting the anti-new-class resentments of those still tied to the older society and values.

By 1975, Phillips had changed his mind on much of his earlier view, saying the growth of the post-industrial society was more likely to result in the destruction of the existing two-party system, possibly leading to a new populist-conservative coalition attacking the new class but cutting across traditional party lines to do so.

The outlines of the new class have been emerging within the Democratic Party for most of the 1970s, identifiable in movements to stimulate federal government action on civil rights, women's rights, consumerism and the environment. Scholars also link this class to the anti-war movement and the growing drive to limit industrial growth.

The post-industrial class is seen as less interested in material acquisition and consumption, more interested in reading and leisure activity. The wife of Rep. Michael J. Harrington (D Mass.) may have summed it all up unwittingly the day Harrington was elected to the House as an anti-war representative in 1969. "All our wealth," Mrs. Harrington said, "is in books and tennis balls."

The Counter Reformation

Arrayed against the books and tennis balls are the values of millions of Americans for whom the post-industrial class is still distant and uncomfortable. Herman Kahn refers to this phenomenon as the "counter reformation"—the attempts to reaffirm old virtues, mainly among "the lower middle class, hard-pressed financially but hoping to move upward, unsophisticated in literary issues but otherwise practical and commonsensical, also patriotic and religious, and embracing perhaps two thirds of America," as Kahn put it in a copyrighted interview in *U.S. News & World Report* in 1973.

This class struggle began to appear in the civil rights and Vietnam war struggles of the 1960s, reached general consciousness in 1970, when advisers urged Democratic congressional candidates to avoid divisive "social issues," and flowered in 1972, when George McGovern was successfully portrayed as the candidate of "abortion, amnesty and acid."

In 1976, however, post-industrial politics is likely to reach a new level, aided by the procedural changes that will force it to the surface. The new rules of 1976 are readymade to serve those whose feelings about social issues are most intense, and who are most willing to work to dramatize them. For it is intensity that has become the key element in a candidate's trek through the election year.

In almost every instance of change in the American political process, there has been a premium on intensity, activism, ideology, and even demagoguery; most recently, the campaign finance reform act of 1974. The law places a $1,000 upper limit on presidential campaign contributions by individuals. In addition, the federal government will

Party Affiliation of Voters

	Rep.	Dem.	Ind.
June-Aug. '75	21%	44%	35%
March-May '75	22	44	34
Nov. '74-March '75	22	46	32
July - October '74	23	47	30
March-June '74	23	44	33
Sept. '73-Jan. '74	24	42	34
May-Aug. '73	24	43	33
March-May '73	26	43	31
Nov. '72-Feb. '73	27	42	31
June-Oct. '72	28	43	29
June-Sept. '71	25	44	31
Jan.-March '71	26	45	29
(18-year-old vote enacted)			
Sept.-Oct. '70	29	45	26
July-Aug. '69	29	44	27
May-June '69	28	42	30
Jan.-June '68	27	46	27
Aug.-Oct. '67	27	42	31
Jan.-Feb. '67	27	46	27
Nov.-Dec. '66	27	48	25
March-May '65	27	50	23
Jan.-Feb. '64	25	53	22
Aug.-Nov. '60	30	47	23
Aug.-Oct. '50	33	45	22
Jan. '40	38	42	20

SOURCE: The Gallup Opinion Index

provide matching funds for all contributions up to $250. (The law's constitutionality has been challenged in the courts, and the Supreme Court is expected to rule on it by early 1976.) At a stroke, the law gives an advantage to candidates who can generate the enthusiasm and dedication of true believers, the ones who are motivated to give small contributions.

These are the emotional candidates—Gov. George C. Wallace of Alabama, former Gov. Ronald Reagan of California and, in theory at least, liberals like Sen. Birch Bayh of Indiana or former Sen. Fred R. Harris of Oklahoma. The rules work against the centrists, such as Sen. Edmund S. Muskie of Maine in the Democratic Party and Sen. Charles H. Percy of Illinois among the Republicans.

Reinforcing this premium upon emotional appeal is the rapidly diminishing significance of political parties. The mass media—centerpiece of post-industrial power for many observers—has also become the centerpiece of the modern political campaign.

For the past decade, candidates have depended increasingly on direct personal contacts with voters through the media, and decreasingly on party organizations. Moreover, presidential candidates build their own ad hoc organizations to seek out voters favorable to their candidacy and get them to the polls. Here again, enthusiastic volunteers are needed to replace the traditional party organizations. The candidate with the most fervent style, platform or personality is likely to attract them most effectively.

And finally, the proliferation of presidential primaries makes it very difficult to sustain a campaign without the enthusiasm and excitement created by a radical or ideological approach. Drawing increasingly independent

and skeptical, even cynical, voters to the polls is likely to require moral incentives. Those incentives usually come not from the compromising, consensus-seeking center of politics, but from the fringes, from those candidates with a radical program or with simple solutions.

Wallace can provide some of those moral incentives with his attacks on big government and its social welfare bureaucracy. The Democratic left provides the incentives with parallel criticism of big business. The rules intensify the argument and polarize both constituencies.

The Nomination Paradox

All of this leads, however, to a basic paradox of modern politics: the divergence of strategy between winning primaries and winning a general election. Maneuvering for the primaries demands a strong, even a belligerent stand on the issues, but the general election campaign requires a broad, issue-straddling appeal. Any candidate who goes out on a limb with a controversial issue is likely to suffer for it.

In 1972, McGovern made dramatic headway in the Democratic primaries by taking strong stands on such issues as Vietnam, minority rights and a guaranteed income. But these positions, while helping him in the primaries, came back to haunt him in the fall campaign after he had received the Democratic presidential nomination. Many conservative Democrats forsook the ticket to vote for the winner, Richard M. Nixon.

The move to the fringes is already beginning in both parties for 1976, dictated by the changes that place a premium on the intensity of a candidate's following. Bayh stepped close to the McGovern trouble areas of 1972 when he told a convention of the National Organization for Women in October that he favors legal rights for homosexuals. President Ford, under pressure from Reagan, has begun to sound increasingly conservative, to the distress of the Republican left. By the end of October, liberal Republican Sen. Charles McC. Mathias Jr. of Maryland was prepared to describe Ford as "a captive of the Reagan right."

Still another factor changing the decision-making process in 1976 is the proportionality rule adopted by the Democratic Party. Under this system, statewide winner-take-all primaries are barred. Instead, delegates selected on a statewide basis must be apportioned in roughly the same way as the percentage of the popular vote each candidate receives. States may circumvent this rule if they elect delegates on a district basis, where the winner of the popular vote in each district would get all that district's delegates. Even so, one presidential candidate is unlikely to sweep all of a state's districts; thus a state's delegation would still be divided. And some states which have adopted the district system have even provided for proportionality within each district's delegation; California is the most notable example.

Supporters of proportionality argue that it allows greater representation for all views and prevents one candidate from winning all of a state's delegation with only a plurality of the vote. Critics protest that proportionality risks creating a chaotic situation in which no candidate can accumulate a majority of the delegates. It encourages candidates to stay in the race in the hopes of accumulating enough delegates to be a factor at the convention. The purpose of primaries is to make a decision, but proportionality works against that purpose. Here again, the new rules are a step toward conflict, not old-fashioned consensus.

Bread and Butter

To a great extent, the role of post-industrial and new class issues in 1976 will depend on the condition of the economy. The worse it is, the easier it will be for economic issues to crowd the new class issues out of the discussion.

Democrats hope to capitalize on the issues of inflation and unemployment. It is hard at this stage to tell whether they will be able to. In an optimistic report following the third quarter of 1975, government spokesmen declared the recession "definitely over" with a rise in the gross national product of 11.2 per cent, the fastest pace in 20 years.

At about the same time, however, leading experts on public opinion were testifying before the Joint Economic Committee that Americans are pessimistic about their personal lives and disbelieve the Washington pronouncements that the recession is over. "The public does not expect any substantial improvement in economic conditions in the foreseeable future," testified Washington pollster Peter D. Hart. Pollster Louis Harris added, "There is a deep suspicion across this land that inflation is making a comeback, that current measures to stem inflation may just not be working, and that even double-digit inflation is not so remote."

Generally speaking, the primacy of the economic issue should tend to unite the Democrats and give them a theme which most party members can agree on. But here, too, there is the lurking danger of a class issue that could divide post-industrial Democrats from blue-collar Democrats. One of the fastest-growing issues of the new class has been the argument that too much growth is harmful, that biggest is not always best. In a number of cases, this issue has already divided labor from environmentalists.

Some argue that the anti-growth movement runs directly counter to the interests of blue-collar Democrats, dependent on expanding factories and production. The "growth backlash" among some liberals may create its own counter-movement and add to the split within the Democratic Party.

This cleavage has already made its appearance within the Democratic pre-nomination struggle, dividing Rep. Morris K. Udall of Arizona on the left from Sen. Lloyd Bentsen of Texas on the growth-minded right.

"We need leaders who promise less," Udall has written, "who discourage wasteful throwaway products, big gas-guzzling cars and electrical gadgets...and other extravagances with no redeeming social values."

Bentsen sounded a different note recently in one of his campaign speeches. "Isn't it funny," he said, "that the people who argue against economic growth are the kind of people who already have enough?"

It is doubtless in the Republicans' interest to get the economy into good shape by election day—or at least on an upward swing. This would blunt the major unifying theme the Democrats have and bring social issues to the front.

Cutting Edge

The cutting edge of most social issues seems to favor the Republicans. Feeling among millions of voters runs strongly against school busing, welfare expenses, the high crime rate and what many consider the "permissive" and "irreligious" lifestyle of the new class. The Republicans successfully harnessed these feelings in 1972 and used them against McGovern. They could easily be used again against a liberal Democratic nominee in 1976.

1976 Presidential Primary Dates

State	Date
New Hampshire	Feb. 24
Massachusetts	March 2
Florida	March 9
Illinois	March 16
North Carolina	March 23
New York	April 6
Wisconsin	April 6
Pennsylvania	April 27
Texas	May 1
Alabama	May 4
Georgia	May 4
Indiana	May 4
District of Columbia	May 4
Tennessee	May 6
Nebraska	May 11
West Virginia	May 11
Maryland	May 18
Michigan	May 18
Idaho	May 25
Kentucky	May 25
Nevada	May 25
Oregon	May 25
Mississippi	June 1
Montana	June 1
Rhode Island	June 1
South Dakota	June 1
Arkansas*	June 8
California	June 8
New Jersey	June 8
Ohio	June 8

Arkansas is expected to change its presidential primary date to May or March.

Polls show that some of the new class issues are more volatile than others. In some cases, the opinion of a minority of ideologues is intense enough to blunt a more passive majority.

In testimony before the Senate Government Operations Committee on Oct. 24, pollster Harris asserted that Americans favor some form of gun control by proportions ranging up to 73 per cent. Yet, so emotional and determined are opponents of gun control that most observers conclude that there is little likelihood of any legislation passing during the 94th Congress.

The reason is that those who feel strongly about gun control legislation—or certain other social issues—are likely to vote on the basis of a candidate's stand on that issue alone. Although they may represent only a small percentage of voters, if they vote as a bloc they have a credible opportunity of swinging an election in one direction or another. This influence is increased in a multi-candidate field where each vote may mean victory. No candidate is going to win the 1976 presidential election on the issue of busing or gun control or abortion. But someone might lose it on one of these issues.

Education may be growing in importance as a class issue. It is not just busing for racial purposes, or the type of textbooks that are involved. Many traditionalists see the public schools as dominated by the new class—by unions that work primarily in the interests of teachers instead of pupils, and by courts which impose sociological experiments on the children and ban prayer or other religious devotions from the schools. The anger and resentment inherent in this situation could express itself politically if candidates began to use it.

The Chessboard

It is within the framework of these factors in play for 1976 that the candidates and their advisers are planning campaign strategy. The Democratic primary field promises to be a large one—10 declared candidates by December, and several more in prospect. The Republican field may expand from the expected two-man confrontation.

With the Democratic field stretching all the way from right to left—from Wallace to Harris—the central questions surrounding the party's 1976 struggle are these: Can the center of the party hold and produce a nominee who can unite the party, or will one of the wings predominate and expose simmering class conflicts? Will the nominee emerge from the primaries or be a compromise candidate selected at the convention? Can the party win back disaffected elements from among southerners and blue-collar workers?

Those who believe that the Democratic nominee will emerge from the primaries see the primary process as a sorting procedure, with various candidates eliminated along the way. Democratic National Chairman Robert Strauss, for one, predicted on Oct. 7 that the primaries would settle the Democratic race.

According to this theory, the early primaries, through New York and Wisconsin on April 6, will shake out the field, leaving four or five major contenders. This group will be further reduced by the later primaries, with a climax among the leaders on June 8, when California, Ohio and New Jersey will hold simultaneous presidential primaries. *(Primary schedule, table p. 3)*

But others have their doubts. They contend the field is so full that different candidates may win different primaries, establishing no over-all trend or lead. This may in turn invite favorite-son candidates into the race, further mixing the field. And even if some candidate emerges victorious in the primaries, critics argue that the new proportionality rule still can prevent him from getting enough votes to win the nomination at the convention.

Thus, some see the prospect of a brokered national convention, or at least a multi-ballot convention, with the likelihood of a dark horse or someone who has not competed in the primaries emerging as the eventual nominee. The name of Sen. Hubert H. Humphrey of Minnesota keeps emerging in this regard. Humphrey has stated repeatedly that he will not compete in the primaries or seek the nomination, but would accept a draft.

And looming over the field of Democrats sits the figure of Wallace, the quintessential foe of the new class and everything it stands for. Just how his appeal will hold up through the primaries and what he will do after the national conventions are questions which worry the Democrats perhaps more than any others.

On the Republican side, the main questions surround the future existence of the party itself, and the incumbent President: Will Gerald R. Ford become the first Republican President to be denied the nomination since Chester A. Arthur in 1884? Will the Republican Party be able to hold together, or will it go the way of the Whigs and Federalists? Can the Republicans, now constituting only 21 per cent of the electorate, successfully attract independents and disaffected Democrats to overcome the party's minority status?

What at first looked like a two-man fight between Ford and Reagan could disintegrate into a melee similar to the Democratic one. It depends on whether Ford can establish credibility as the moderate candidate able to take on and defeat Reagan. If he cannot, other contenders may jump in and open up the race.

Ford's preoccupation with the Reagan challenge has given the President trouble with Republican liberals. Like Mathias, they charge that Ford by moving to the right is forfeiting support at the center needed for a November victory. However, the liberals have the problem of splitting the moderate-to-liberal Republican primary vote if they enter a candidate while Ford is still in the race.

With the abrupt departure of Ford campaign aides Lee Nunn and David Packard, as well as the November cabinet reshuffle, there was increasing talk of a collapse of both the Ford administration and the Ford candidacy. There was also a consensus developing that Ford was in danger of losing two early primaries—New Hampshire on Feb. 24 and Florida on March 9—losses that would be difficult for even an incumbent President to overcome.

Polls taken in October still showed Ford with a comfortable lead over Reagan among Republican voters nationwide—58 to 36, according to a Gallup Poll. But the Reagan primary campaign will have the intensity factor on its side. Dedicated conservatives will almost certainly turn out in greater proportion than moderates. And if Ford's problems are compounded by an image of weakness at the center, his lead could change rapidly.

Party Survival

Whether the Republican Party can survive all these strains is a question being increasingly debated. Already a new conservative organization has been formed combining both Wallace and Reagan supporters. Called the Committee for the New Majority, its efforts will be directed toward giving some candidate a third-party option if neither of the two major parties nominates a candidate acceptable to conservatives.

There seems to be an increasing likelihood of a multi-candidate general election campaign. Former Sen. Eugene J. McCarthy (D Minn. 1959-71) has already launched his independent candidacy. And besides the possible candidacies of Reagan and Wallace, additional names are being mentioned as potential independent candidates in November—among them John B. Connally of Texas, a former Democratic governor of Texas (1963-69) and a convert to Republicanism.

The continued growth of the independent segment of the electorate *(table p. 2)* gives support to those who believe that the political parties may be of declining relevance to presidential politics. Once candidates realize that they can avoid divisive primaries by entering the general election as independents, the theory goes, the political parties will have lost one of the last of their main functions. With federal compensation provided for independent candidates who receive more than 5 per cent of the vote, such candidacies may bloom, if not in 1976 then certainly by 1980.

The economic and social revolution of postwar America, combined with structural and procedural reforms, is radically altering the political landscape. The beneficiaries will be those who foresee the opportunities and pitfalls of the new conditions.

—By Warden Moxley

SHARPENING THE 2-EDGED SWORD OF INCUMBENCY

The coming collision of Gerald R. Ford and Ronald Reagan will match the "inside strategy" of an incumbent President and party leader against the "outside strategy" of a challenger determined to bypass the party structure in many states and appeal directly to the voters.

For President Ford, the inside strategy already has produced endorsements from key Republican officials in nearly every large state—officials such as U.S. Rep. Louis Frey Jr. in Florida, Sen. John G. Tower in Texas and all but one of the 12 Republicans in the congressional delegation from Illinois.

Ford strategists insist that a Republican nomination fight in 1976 remains exactly what such contests have been in the past: an argument over control of the party machinery. "It's a highly professional in-house struggle," said one of the President's advisers. "A primary is an organizational fight; a general election is an issue fight."

"The key to it," agreed Ed Terrill, Ford's coordinator in the non-primary states, "is having the right people on the Ford committee in each state. You try to get the people that know everyone and will do the work."

Reagan's people are not so sure of that. They note what happened in the Democratic nomination contest of 1972, when Sen. Edmund S. Muskie of Maine had the important people but Sen. George McGovern of South Dakota won the delegates.

"We've never been in the business of trying to gain endorsements," said John P. Sears, director of Citizens for Reagan and strategist for the former California governor. "At the presidential level, I don't believe you get very far by getting politicians to come out in behalf of your candidate. Endorsements are not of much value these days."

The different styles are evident in Florida, where Frey is heading the Ford campaign and seeking to line up as many endorsements as possible from party leaders at the local level. "The people that I want," said Frey, "I've got 80 per cent of them."

"I wouldn't doubt that Lou Frey has talked to more people in Florida than we have," Sears admitted, adding that contacts alone mean little at this point. "I'm a great believer in organization," Sears said, "but only when you have the votes."

Some of the older Ford strategists entered national Republican politics in 1952, the last year the party had a contest that lasted throughout the pre-convention season. Gen. Dwight D. Eisenhower and Ohio Sen. Robert A. Taft competed for the nomination in a match that ended only with Eisenhower's victory on the convention floor in Chicago. At that time, the Republican nomination process was still largely a closed affair, with most of the delegates selected at state caucuses and conventions dominated by party insiders.

Some of the younger generation of Ford advisers think it may be dangerous to underestimate what Reagan can do outside the party structure, especially now that three-fourths of the delegates are chosen in primaries and Reagan can use television to make his case. "Reagan doesn't need an

organization," said Norman (Skip) Watts, Ford's coordinator for the primary states. "He's one of the world's greatest salesmen. He'll come sweeping through with his oratorical flair. If he does catch fire, he could steal a lot of potential helpers away from us. We have to use incumbency and organization to match his oratory."

The Intensity Factor

It is not just oratory that worries Ford strategists, but the intensity of Reagan's followers. It has become a truism in presidential politics that primaries and caucuses are won by the candidate whose supporters are zealous enough to attend the meetings, make the telephone calls and staff the precincts. The "intensity factor" is used to explain both the nomination of Sen. Barry Goldwater (R Ariz.) in 1964 and the success of the McGovern campaign in 1972.

"We don't have any specific strategy to counter the zeal of the Reagan people," said Howard H. (Bo) Callaway, Ford's campaign chairman. "But we are getting a lot of zeal from a lot of people. We think we're getting more precinct workers in New Hampshire and Florida than Reagan is."

Ford's claims of strength are disputed by Reagan organizers. His Florida chairman, for example, predicted late in November that "we will beat Jerry Ford 2 to 1" in the March 9 primary there.

Some Ford strategists who have watched Reagan in the past say he has limitations that so far have escaped national notice. "I don't discount Reagan," said one. "He's the most formidable candidate in either party. He's the best orator in either party. But he's a miserable campaigner. Sooner or later he's going to have to get another speech. He won't shake hands with more than three people. He's great at walking into an auditorium 10 minutes late, giving a stirring speech and then walking out without talking to anybody."

The Ford people insist that the President will not personally criticize Reagan's style in the campaign. "The President's style is to campaign for what he believes in," said a senior official. "But you can be sure there will be people who will attack Reagan. He's had a free ride, and the free ride will be over." But the same official acknowledged that there would have to be restraints on these criticisms, lest the President win the nomination and find Reagan supporters unwilling to help him.

Some at the President Ford Committee—the incumbency-emphasizing name of Ford's national campaign organization in the capital—see the press as a temporary Reagan ally, seeking to dethrone the President in the interest of bringing about Republican chaos and a Democratic victory. "Obviously we've got a hostile press," said one Ford official. "There's an alliance of the press, the Democrats and the hostile Congress to help Reagan....

Ford's Interest-Group Ratings

Americans for Democratic Action (ADA)—ADA ratings are based on the number of times a representative voted, was paired for or announced for the ADA position on selected issues.

National Farmers Union (NFU)—NFU ratings are based on the number of times a representative voted, was paired for or announced for the NFU position.

AFL-CIO Committee on Political Education (COPE)—COPE ratings reflect the percentage of the times a representative voted in accordance with or was paired in favor of the COPE position.

Americans for Constitutional Action (ACA)—ACA ratings record the percentage of the times a representative voted in accordance with the ACA position.

Following are Ford's ratings since Congressional Quarterly began publishing them in 1960:

	ADA[1]	COPE[3]	NFU[3]	ACA
1973	0	22	15	83
1972	6	11	20	68
1971	8	25	27	79
1970	12[4]	0	54	68
1969	7	33	40	53
1968	17	50	56	74
1967	13	8	11	85
1966	0	0[2]	22	74
1965	11	0[2]	19	81
1964	15	9[2]	21[2]	79
1963	0	9[2]	21[2]	89
1962	13	0[2]	10[2]	82[2]
1961	10	0[2]	10[2]	82[2]
1960	33	10[2]	20[2]	60
1959	22	10[2]	20[2]	88[5]

1. *Failure to vote lowers score.*
2. *Scores listed twice indicate rating compiled for entire Congress.*
3. *Percentages compiled by CQ from information provided by groups.*
4. *ADA score includes some votes from December 1969.*
5. *ACA score covers year 1957, 1958, 1959.*

Evans and Novak [syndicated newspaper columnists] won't write anything John Sears doesn't tell them."

Semi-Incumbency

All sides agree that Ford's incumbency will help, but the advantage may be slight. An elected President running for re-election can call upon party regulars who worked for him four years earlier. Ford has no such political base; local Republicans owe him no more than they owe Reagan.

The real advantage of Ford's incumbency, his advisers say, is the way he can use it to make the kinds of decisions conservative Republican voters like. "Any time Reagan gins up a hell of an issue," said one of the President's strategists, "Ford can defuse it whenever he wants to with the power of decision. But at the same time Reagan can whack him hip-and-thigh with a new issue."

The power of incumbency, in other words, carries with it the obligation to deal with problems Reagan can avoid. Reagan may criticize; Ford must act. So the Ford people see incumbency as a two-edged sword.

Many of those on Ford's side say that he did not use his incumbency particularly well during the fall of 1975, when he spent most of his weekends on political journeys into various states, giving speeches, shaking hands and escaping two attempted assassinations—but rarely stopping for serious political talk with his allies. The trips left many people wondering what Ford could possibly learn from shaking hands that was worth risking his life.

Ford advisers who approved the trips say that his speeches before party audiences helped the state organizations financially and gave the rank and file a reason to owe him something in 1976. "He kept his word," one source explained, "and raised a whole chunk of dough for the party—instead of for himself. A lot of the party people are indebted to him now."

But other Ford supporters disagree. "It's been nonproductive, for the most part," said Sen. Robert Dole of Kansas, a member of the Ford advisory committee and a former Republican national chairman. "Ford is so amenable to everything—you can talk him into nine meetings in one day, even if he only has two scheduled.... But if Ford's going to confront the Congress, he should do it here, not in Wyoming. This is the arena. If I were advising him, I'd set aside a certain amount of time to talk about politics, and zero in on politics, and build some organization.... Four hours with a group of people in New Hampshire or Florida would be more productive than flying to Kansas or California to make a speech."

An official at the President Ford Committee said handshaking and speaking tours are simply part of the President's political style. "He likes it," the official said. "I won't debate on how much he learns shaking hands—although I think he learns something. When he's in an airport, and people want to see him, he enjoys that."

Will Bo Go?

Many of those disappointed with the Ford campaign have been focusing their criticism on Callaway, particularly after the resignations in October of Lee Nunn as political director and David Packard as chief fund-raiser of the President Ford Committee. One Ford ally reported that during the Kissinger-Schlesinger shakeup, Reagan aide Lyn Nofziger called him to urge that Callaway not be included among those fired.

But there were indications by mid-November that the issue was quietly being resolved, with Callaway remaining as spokesman and titular head of the campaign while more of the day-to-day decisions fall to his deputy, California campaign consultant Stuart Spencer.

Callaway is philosophical about the criticism he took in the news media after Nunn and Packard left. "I expected it," he told Congressional Quarterly. "I think it's finally going to disappear.... There's never been a campaign that got started that didn't have problems. The campaign is far ahead of where Nixon's Committee to Re-elect the President was—and they spent a lot more money. And we're doing it under the restrictions of the new law."

Dole worries, however, that even with a change in responsibilities at the President Ford Committee, Ford himself is still taking too much advice from White House aides with limited political experience. "There's always a tendency to tell the President nothing but goodies," said Dole. "But the time is almost come to have a hair-down conversation with him. He's never run for President before. If he's only talking to White House people who haven't run for anything either, I don't know how they're going to get anything done."

Nuts and Bolts

Much of the campaign planning, of course, can be done without the President's direct involvement, and it is the nuts and bolts work that was accelerated with the arrival of Spencer in October. In addition to his over-all role as deputy campaign director, Spencer is taking personal charge of the New Hampshire and Florida campaigns. He considers them more crucial than the later primary states, which are under the direction of Watts.

Leaders of the President Ford Committee insist, however, that the real control in each state belongs to the state campaign chairmen—Frey in Florida, Tower in Texas and Rep. James C. Cleveland in New Hampshire. Watts said the 1976 Ford campaign had to be decentralized to undo the damage done by Nixon's Committee to Re-Elect the President (CREEP) in 1972. "The Republican organization and workers [at the state level] suffered under the heel of CREEP last time," Watts said. "CREEP battered the organization. They browbeat them into strategies and mechanics and personnel, and directed campaign policy from here."

Frey declared that he is the boss in Florida. "I'm completely in control," he said. "We tell them what we want to do, and they help us. You can't have thousands of people coming in and changing things."

The issue of local control is more troublesome in New Hampshire, however, where former Gov. Hugh Gregg (R 1953-55) refused to take the Ford chairmanship on the grounds that he would not be able to run the campaign in any way he chose. Gregg then endorsed Reagan and became his chairman in New Hampshire.

At the Washington end of the campaign, the President Ford Committee also has the services of an advisory committee of Republican notables and Ford friends. Its members include three former national party chairmen (Dole, Dean Burch and Ray C. Bliss), the two Republican leaders in Congress (Sen. Hugh Scott of Pennsylvania and Rep. John J. Rhodes of Arizona), one governor (James E. Holshouser of North Carolina) and one former governor (William W. Scranton of Pennsylvania).

Ford's Background

Profession: Attorney.
Born: July 14, 1913, Omaha, Neb.
Home: Grand Rapids, Mich.
Religion: Episcopal.
Education: University of Michigan, B.A., 1935; Yale University Law School, LL.B., 1941.
Offices: U.S. House of Representatives, 1949-73; chairman, House Republican Conference, 1963-65; minority leader, 1965-73; Vice President, 1973-74; President since Aug. 9, 1974.
Military: U.S. Navy in World War II.
Memberships: Interparliamentary Union, U.S.-Canadian Interparliamentary Group, American Legion, VFW, AMVETS, Masons, Elks, Rotary.
Family: Wife, Elizabeth Bloomer; four children.
Congressional Committees: Appropriations, 1951-65; Public Works, 1949-50.

But the advisory committee has done little advising. "We met twice," Dole said. "The first time we each drank a Coke, and they gave us a report. We haven't been asked to make any policy. I think we're honorary pallbearers.... It's ornamental, and I don't know how long I want to participate in something like that."

Callaway concedes that the role of the advisory committee in making policy has been minimal. But he says he talks to many of the members individually on the telephone.

If the advisory committee did gather to give advice, many of its members would express concern about the Ford fund-raising operation. Under Packard's direction, the Ford committee raised slightly more than $700,000 in July, August and September, compared with a Reagan total of about $400,000 in only 2½ months during the same period. Even more disturbing to Ford supporters, more than 90 per cent of the contributions to Ford were in amounts greater than $250 and therefore ineligible for federal matching subsidies in 1976. Most of the contributions to Reagan were in the smaller, matchable sizes.

Ford campaign officials say that fund-raising went slowly during the summer, because Packard could not devote sufficient time to the job. "We'll get small contributions when we go after them," one official said. The Ford campaign will seek certification of eligibility for matching payments, but the President has not decided whether or not he will actually take matching money.

Ford advisers insist that the November cabinet shakeup eventually will benefit the President, despite early fears that the departure of Defense Secretary James R. Schlesinger would become a sore point for national-security-minded conservatives. "The Schlesinger firing is a negative politically," a Ford adviser conceded. "It's being perceived as a victory for the folks who want to give away the country and against those who want to defend the country. But it's dwindling very fast. When people understand the depth of the change in Kissinger's role, that will help."

Vice President Rockefeller's removal of himself as Ford's prospective running mate in 1976, on the other hand, has "been a plus everywhere," the adviser continued. "It takes away the biggest issue Reagan had."

At Reagan headquarters, Sears was not willing to concede on either point. "We've never made an issue over Rocky," he said. "I don't notice a large stream of people say-

Congressional Quarterly Vote Study Scores...

	1973	1972	1971	1970	1969	1968	1967	1966	1965	1964	1963
Presidential											
support	80	70	89	89	76	63	50	40	46	38	35
opposition	16	8	7	8	18	28	41	46	46	56	54
Voting Participation	89	84	87	90	92	90	85	81	86	88	84
Party											
unity	75	73	81	69	57	66	74	69	70	84	69
opposition	17	16	12	26	35	24	18	10	16	10	17
Conservative Coalition											
support	75	73	87	64	61	63	70	70	73	67	67
opposition	13	17	8	18	34	25	17	16	18	33	20
Bipartisan											
support	77	75	83	85	85	82	74	74	78	71	72
opposition	9	7	2	3	7	7	7	9	7	12	10

† Explanation of studies, p. 107.

ing that now that Rockefeller is off the ticket, they'll support Ford." Sears said that Reagan would not be likely to drop the Schlesinger issue either, "if it becomes apparent during the next few months that there is no debate in the Ford administration over detente."

The Primaries

New Hampshire

The Feb. 24 New Hampshire primary will be crucial for Ford, and not only because it comes first. A victory for the President in New Hampshire would insulate him from some of the damage he might suffer if he lost in Florida March 9 and in North Carolina March 23. A Reagan victory in New Hampshire would allow the challenger to shoot for three victories in the first five primaries—assuming Ford won in Massachusetts March 2 and in Illinois March 16.

Ford does not have the full party structure behind him in New Hampshire. Republican Gov. Meldrim Thomson is for Reagan, although the controversial governor is not in formal charge of Reagan's effort. Publisher William Loeb and his *Manchester Union-Leader* will be loud voices promoting Reagan's cause.

Some observers in New Hampshire think that help from Thomson and Loeb may be a mixed blessing. The governor is thought to be politically weak himself as he looks to a third two-year term, and Loeb proved conspicuously ineffective in his attempts to persuade people not to elect Democrat John A. Durkin to the Senate in a 1975 special election.

On the Ford side is most of the moderate wing of a state party that has been angrily divided since the death of Sen. Styles Bridges (R 1937-61) nearly 14 years ago. Reagan scored some impressive defections from this group, notably Gregg and former State Sen. Stewart Lamprey, but most of it remains intact and is on Ford's side.

Massachusetts

One week after the New Hampshire voting, Ford is likely to win a victory in Massachusetts. But it may not be an overwhelming victory. The Massachusetts Republican Party voted in October to elect its 43 convention delegates by proportional representation. This decision, made over the strenuous objections of Republican Sen. Edward W. Brooke, means that Reagan will be guaranteed a reasonable proportion of the delegation—possibly enough to embarrass Ford in a state where no one is expecting anything but an easy Ford victory.

"I think Republican conservatives are underestimating Reagan's strength," said Massachusetts Republican chairman John Sears (no relation to the Reagan campaign's John Sears). "Surely he'll get at least one-third of the vote," added Sears, who is neutral. Reagan supporters in Massachusetts, led by the state Republican committeeman, Edward King, are urging the former governor to campaign there.

Ford's people believe they have support in the most important places. "Cleveland's got a favorable rating of about 80 per cent," said Watts. "That's better than Gregg, who hasn't been around politics since the 1950s." Ford advisers believe New Hampshire is one state in which they can win a clear victory with organization, and Reagan cannot counterattack through the media. There are only two commercial television stations in New Hampshire.

Florida

The Florida primary is increasingly being seen as the decisive one, the one in which Reagan must defeat Ford to win the nomination. Frey agrees. "If we stop Reagan in our state, it's over," Frey said. "We can save money, time, bloodshed and effort, and elect a Republican President." Moreover, Frey is publicly confident that will happen. "We've got the issues going for us, we've got the momentum and we've got the people," he boasted.

...Covering 21 of Ford's Years in House †

	1962	1961	1960	1959	1958	1957	1956	1955	1954	1953
Presidential										
support	52	42	84	63	76	73	94	88	89	94
opposition	40	51	12	13	24	23	6	12	11	6
Voting Participation	90	82	97	75	99	98	100	97	96	99
Party										
unity	72	76	84	77	70	83	84	68	*	*
opposition	21	9	14	0	27	17	16	32	*	*
Conservative Coalition										
support	37	83	84	100	*	*	*	*	*	*
opposition	44	4	16	0	*	*	*	*	*	*
Bipartisan										
support	78	71	84	64	91	83	90	82	*	*
opposition	8	8	11	8	9	12	10	13	*	*

* No ratings in these years.

But it may not be that simple. Some of the issues are not liable to help Ford, such as his administration's moves toward closer ties with Cuba and his cooperation with Congress on legislation permitting common-site picketing by labor unions at construction sites. The Miami area has a high percentage of Cuban voters who are exiles from Fidel Castro, and prominent Republicans throughout the state are close to the construction industry.

Like the one in New Hampshire, the Florida Republican Party has been badly split in recent years. Both factions are conservative. One grew up in the 1950s in the Pinellas County (St. Petersburg) area, built largely by former Rep. William C. Cramer (R 1953-71), a close personal friend of Ford. Most of this group is for Ford. The other grew up later, attracted votes from converted Democrats in north Florida and other areas and at times included former Sen. Edward J. Gurney (R 1969-74) and former Gov. Claude R. Kirk Jr. (R 1967-71). This group is more favorable to Reagan.

Frey, although Gurney's former law partner, has worked with both sides at various times in his career. "My ability to stay out of it and then get in it is what attracted people's attention," he said in explaining why he became head of Ford's Florida campaign. "That's why I've got credibility." Like Cleveland in New Hampshire and Callaway at the national level, Frey is a former colleague of Ford in the House.

No one doubts that there is potential for a Reagan victory in Florida. The state's delegation nearly went for Reagan at the 1968 Republican convention, holding for Nixon only after pleas from Sen. Strom Thurmond (R S.C.), Sen. Tower of Texas and Barry Goldwater, the 1964 party nominee. If Reagan does not win in Florida, the Ford people believe they will be a lot closer to the nomination.

Illinois

Ford's campaign organizers are also optimistic about the primary in Illinois March 16. Although Illinois is Reagan's home state—he grew up in Tampico and attended tiny Eureka College, near Peoria—Ford aides believe the President's midwestern roots and style will go over well there. The respected former Gov. Richard B. Ogilvie (R 1969-73) is Ford's chairman. "The Illinois President Ford Committee is very well organized," said State Republican Chairman Don Adams, who professes neutrality.

Reagan's key supporters are Republican Rep. Philip M. Crane, the lone holdout from Ford in the congressional delegation, and State Rep. Don Totten of Hoffman Estates.

A recent poll in two heavily Republican downstate districts, the 18th and the 21st, showed Ford with a 2-1 lead. But local observers are wary of those results, if only because Reagan has not yet been visible in Illinois as a campaigner.

North Carolina

The North Carolina primary March 23 is a potentially serious trouble spot for Ford. Like Florida, the state's delegation went for Nixon at the 1968 Republican convention only after intense persuasion. And the Reagan effort in North Carolina has the help of Republican Sen. Jesse A. Helms, a longtime critic of the moderate Republican governor, Holshouser, who is for Ford.

A poll of county chairmen in North Carolina Nov. 12 indicated a close race, even though Holshouser is placing much of his political reputation on the line as Ford's chief supporter and as a member of Ford's national advisory committee. The poll showed that 31 county chairmen backed Ford, and 26 were for Reagan. The rest were undecided or did not answer.

Convention States

There are few tangible clues about the campaign in the non-primary states, but Ford got off to a slow start in many of them. Ed Terrill, his national coordinator for these states, did not begin work until Nov. 10. A quick check of the non-primary states turned up little formal action on Ford's behalf. "As far as organizing any committee in the state, I'm not aware of it," said the Missouri Republican chairman, Lowell McCuskey. Things were equally slow in Minnesota, where no Ford chairman had been named by mid-November.

Nevertheless, there are indications that Ford strategists are beginning to think about a longer campaign and are dropping the idea that Reagan can be disposed of quickly with knockout blows in New Hampshire and Florida. "We're settling in for the long haul," Callaway said, "because it's only prudent."

Up From the House

Ford has never sought office beyond Michigan's 5th Congressional District, which he represented from 1949 until he became Vice President in 1973. In 1948, the year of his first election, he was a young attorney in Grand Rapids.

He challenged the renomination of isolationist Bartel J. Jonkman (R 1940-49) in the Republican primary. Ford won the nomination and went on to swamp a Democrat by the first of his regular 60-per-cent-plus margins.

In later years, Ford at various times considered running for Michigan governor or senator, and in 1960 he was talked about as a possible running mate for then Vice President Richard M. Nixon. But in each case, he decided to retain his safe political base in Grand Rapids.

After his arrival in the House, Ford attracted little attention as he joined dozens of other conservative Republican back-benchers. He first rose to prominence in 1963, when he became a candidate for the chairmanship of the House Republican Conference, an honorific post but one that provided him a platform within the party leadership. With the support of Republican "young Turks" in the party, he defeated veteran conservative Charles B. Hoeven (R Iowa 1943-65). In another leadership challenge two years later, Ford defeated House Minority Leader Charles A. Halleck (R Ind. 1935-69).

To his colleagues in the House, Ford built a reputation for being solid, dependable and loyal—a man more comfortable carrying out the programs of others than initiating things on his own. In his weekly appearances with the late Senate Minority Leader Everett McKinley Dirksen (R Ill. 1951-69)—dubbed "The Ev and Jerry Show" by reporters—he usually receded into the background, leaving most of the publicity to the colorful, sonorous Dirksen.

Ford's Campaign Staff

Manager: Howard H. (Bo) Callaway, former secretary of the Army and former U.S. representative (R Ga. 1965-67).

Deputy manager: Stuart Spencer, a California political consultant.

Deputy manager: Robert Marik, former associate director of the Office of Management and Budget.

Press secretary: Peter Kay, a California television news reporter.

Coordinator for primary states: Norman (Skip) Watts, former advance man and aide to California Gov. Ronald Reagan (R 1967-75).

Coordinator for non-primary states: Ed Terrill, on leave as campaign director of the National Republican Congressional Committee.

Voting Record

Ford's conservative philosophy showed up in the thousands of votes he cast in the House. He was not associated with the passage of any significant legislation. During the 1950s and 1960s, he voted against most legislation expanding the federal role in solving modern social problems. He opposed federal aid to education, voted against the creation of the Office of Economic Opportunity and against Medicare and opposed federal help for state water pollution programs.

Ford took a basically negative view toward civil rights legislation. He voted for some bills, such as the Civil Rights Act of 1964 and the Voting Rights Act of 1965, but he backed weaker substitutes for these bills before their passage. He also endorsed a Nixon proposal, eventually defeated, to weaken the Voting Rights Act when it came up for renewal in 1970. Ford opposed federal open housing legislation in 1966, but backed it in 1968.

Ford's suspicious attitude toward federal spending did not extend to national defense. On the Defense Appropriations Subcommittee, he was a consistent supporter of Pentagon budget requests. As a vocal anti-Communist and a firm believer in a bipartisan foreign policy, he used his post as minority leader to marshal Republicans behind President Johnson's Vietnam policies even as many Democrats became increasingly hostile to them. Ford criticized Johnson for not pursuing victory there vigorously enough.

With a Republican President back in the White House, Ford supported Nixon's policy of gradual "Vietnamization" and endorsed the 1973 peace accord. Through the end of his House career, he continued to oppose any legislation to end the war faster than Nixon wanted to move.

The Presidency

The qualities Ford exhibited in the House made him a good choice for Vice President when Spiro T. Agnew resigned in disgrace in October 1973. He could be partisan without evoking the passionate hostility Agnew had drawn at a time when Nixon was fast running out of defenders in the Watergate investigations. And, as a veteran House member well liked by his colleagues, Ford was certain to be confirmed. He was, in December.

Ford's accession to the presidency in August 1974 was greeted with relief by the nation generally. But when the pardon of Nixon was announced Sept. 8, after Ford had barely completed a month in office, he eliminated much of the national goodwill and contributed to the growing cynicism over the integrity of the political process.

When the 94th Congress convened in January 1975 with a top-heavy Democratic majority, Ford began to move to the right on a variety of fronts. He vowed to veto attempts to increase expenditures for social programs and to resist the development of new layers of government bureaucracy. This newly aggressive stance presented a clear challenge to the New Deal-style programs that had been enacted and nurtured by Democrats—and acquiesced in by Republican administrations—over a 40-year period.

In place of federal funds for the nation's problems, Ford stressed the virtues of free enterprise and the dangers of overregulating the economy. He proposed a tax increase to combat inflation, a normal position for a conservative Republican, but was forced to reverse himself when unemployment increased to levels unmatched since the Depression and to accept a Democratic plan for a stimulating tax cut.

In energy policy, he revealed an array of proposals designed to increase the price of oil and reduce public consumption, a policy vigorously denounced by critics as a windfall for the major oil companies. Congress adopted a position of dogged resistance to Ford's economic programs, as the Democrats prepared to push through bills providing a massive influx of public funds for jobs and housing.

But Ford's veto brought them up short. He used it repeatedly—and nearly always successfully—in 1975 to enforce his vision of limited government. Ford frequently refers to the veto in his campaign speeches as a major reason to retain a Republican in the White House.

Ford's vigorous reaction to the Cambodian government's May 12, 1975, seizure of the merchant ship Mayaguez went a long way toward re-establishing his credibility with conservative Republicans. Public approval of Ford's decisiveness was reflected almost immediately in the opinion polls.

Positions on Issues

These are some of the positions Ford has taken on other important issues during his presidency:

Spending

In addition to his vetoes of Democratic programs, Ford as President has consistently condemned the size of government bureaucracy and called for cutbacks in existing federal activities. He has asked Congress for a tax cut combined with a limit on federal spending, without recommendations for reductions in specific areas.

"The American people want a $28-billion tax cut and a $28-billion reduction in the growth of federal expenditures," he said at a press conference. "They know that that is the right way to meet the problem of getting our long-term reform in tax legislation and to achieve a responsible program in spending limitations."

New York City

Ford in October 1975 strongly rejected pleas by New York City officials that the federal government act to prevent the city from defaulting on hundreds of millions of dollars in debts due in December. In an October 29 speech to the National Press Club, the President said he would veto any bill providing federal aid as a "terrible precedent" that would only postpone the day that New York City would have to live within its own resources.

Instead, Ford proposed a revision of federal bankruptcy laws that would make it easier for the city to maintain basic services after a default. His plan would allow New York City, with state approval, to file a petition of bankruptcy without the agreement of its creditors. He appeared ready to make his opposition to a "bailout" a major issue in 1976.

However, as New York moved closer to a deadline for coming up with sufficient funds to pay its debts, the administration's opposition appeared to weaken. In November, Ford said he would look at the steps New York state had taken to raise revenues and change the city's fiscal practices before considering whether to sign whatever aid legislation Congress might finally enact.

Energy

In San Francisco Sept. 22, 1975, Ford announced a plan for a $100-billion government corporation to stimulate commercial development of new energy sources. He said he expected the agency to begin a crash program that would spur "dramatic action to produce oil and gas from coal, safe and clean nuclear and coal-generated electric power, harness the energy of the sun and the natural heat within the earth."

Food Stamps

One of the first major proposals of the Ford administration would have drastically increased the cost of food stamps. Congress rejected the idea, but Ford has periodically revived plans for an overhaul of the nation's food policies for poor Americans. A new plan to cut 3.4 million persons out of the food stamp program and reduce benefits for 5.3 million others—at a saving of $1.2-billion a year—was sent to Congress Oct. 20.

In his message, Ford said that his recommendations "follow a fundamental principle on which I stand: The federal government should help, within the limits of national resources, those who are in need; but we should not give one dollar of federal assistance to those not in need."

Busing

Long an opponent of school busing to achieve racial balance, Ford early in his presidency injected himself into the busing crisis in Boston by criticizing busing orders of federal judges. He later said he would enforce federal court orders as the law of the land even though he disagreed with them.

In 1975, the President had little to say about busing. He reportedly opposes a constitutional amendment to ban busing "at this time," but has ordered the Departments of Justice and Health, Education and Welfare to review alternatives to it.

After a meeting with Ford in October 1975, Sen. Tower of Texas said that Ford did not support the amendment proposal, because "the President didn't feel there had been an adequate test in the Supreme Court to determine the validity of legislative or administrative remedies short of a constitutional amendment." Tower added that Ford did not oppose a constitutional amendment outright and suggested that he might support one if the Supreme Court overturned legislative moves to end busing.

—By Alan Ehrenhalt and Matt Pinkus

A STRONG CHALLENGE FROM THE REPUBLICAN RIGHT

Conservatives have been chafing for a long time for a genuine electoral duel between their limited-government philosophy and the big-government reflexes of the liberals. If the well-laid plans of former California Gov. Ronald Reagan do not go awry, 1976 may be the year.

Other years seemed more propitious, yet they disappointed the conservatives. A true choice between governmental theories was expected in 1964, but the assassination of President Kennedy placed Arizona Sen. Barry Goldwater in an impossible electoral situation. The 1972 Nixon victory still is claimed by some as a clear conservative mandate, but to most minds an inept McGovern candidacy and Watergate nullified the claim. In 1976, with a lifelong Republican Party loyalist in the White House, the time should seem wholly unripe for a challenge to that incumbency from the right—a challenge that is the necessary prelude to the ideological shootout conservatives desire.

By Reagan's reckoning, however, the time is in fact quite ripe. As one of his chief backers, Sen. Paul Laxalt (R Nev.), put it in an interview with *Congressional Quarterly*, "Much of the Ford support is soft, lukewarm. He was unelected. He was blessed by the Congress, because he got along with it, and Congress is not in great shape as an institution. He is identified with Congress and with Washington.... He is perceived by conservatives as having a tendency to compromise, not to act on principles."

That view of the Ford strength is supported both by opinion polls and by the results in elections where Ford has laid his presidential prestige on the line. An August 1975 Gallup Poll showed that while 52 per cent of Republican voters approved of Ford as President, an embarrassingly low 19 per cent expressed strong approval. In the 1974 general election, Ford was markedly unsuccessful in helping stem the expected Democratic tide. And nearly a year later, in the key 1976 state of New Hampshire, Ford's stumping for Republican Louis C. Wyman against Democrat John A. Durkin in a replay of their 1974 Senate contest apparently had little effect. Durkin handily won the race that had been a draw the previous year.

If Ford's support is as lukewarm as Reagan partisans believe, the early primaries should provide the proof. Thus New Hampshire and Florida loom as even more important in the electoral scheme than they usually do. Laxalt and other Reagan strategists already are proclaiming that a 35 per cent showing in New Hampshire would be considered a Reagan victory, since they will be confronting an incumbent, if unelected, President. In the past two campaigns, such defeats were hailed as victories by bad-odds Democratic candidates, Eugene J. McCarthy in 1968 and George McGovern in 1972. The media-abetted ploy may be feasible again.

But the Reagan forces entertain greater ambitions. They do not rule out the possibility of winning outright in New Hampshire and Florida. If they do, Laxalt predicts that "there is a strong probability that Ford would withdraw in the manner of Johnson. The ball game would be over." Alternatively, Reagan backers foresee mixed but

positive results leading up to a Reagan victory in his home state June 8, clinching the nomination for their man.

Early Maneuvering

As early as 1973, Reagan was preparing the way for a presidential bid. That year, he mounted a campaign to convince California voters to place a constitutional ceiling on state taxation and expenditures. Before the November vote was held, he was touting it as a potential model for other states and the federal government to employ in grappling with what Reagan views as the overgrowth of government and the dangerous level of taxation.

The measure was heavily criticized as unworkable and was roundly defeated, but no steam appeared to go out of the Reagan drive. In 1974, he resisted the implorings of California Republicans to run for a third term as governor. He headed out instead onto what he called the national "mashed potato circuit" to give speeches and promote his role as conservative spokesman.

For most of 1974, Reagan appeared to cling to the hope that President Nixon could remain in office. Should that have occurred, the reasoning went, Reagan probably would have been a solid choice over Vice President Ford. Ford's ascent to the presidency at first balked Reagan's steady march toward the Republican nomination. In just over a year of Ford's tenure, however, Reagan has come to the view of the incumbent's position that Laxalt articulated.

Reagan's announcement Nov. 20 brought to an end an anxious period for his supporters. As early as summer

1975, some backers were pressing Reagan to declare quickly, in light of Ford's unprecedented early declaration. Their fear was that the President would pre-empt the Reagan candidacy by effectively pressuring local party officials to join the incumbent's team before a vacillating Reagan jumped into the race. Both Laxalt and John Sears, the operational head of the Washington-based Citizens for Reagan, now insist that little has been lost through delay.

Sears discussed at length with Congressional Quarterly what he views as the mistakes made by Democratic candidate Edmund S. Muskie in 1972, when he relied on party endorsements to carry him through. Playing down the value of endorsements in both parties now that the nomination process is largely one of winning primaries rather than searching for delegates, Sears argued that "Reagan's success or failure will depend on the primaries...We are going to the people. We'll rise or fall based on that," not on party line-ups.

Reagan's official announcement also will end a rather lucrative period of activity for the syndicated columnist and commentator and former governor. As a former movie and television actor long familiar to Hollywood, it was natural for Reagan to turn to the media for his living once he was out of office. In January 1975, he began both a syndicated news column and a syndicated radio commentary. Both have been ideal vehicles for spreading his conservative gospel, for expanding public awareness of Reagan as a political thinker and for making money.

Some observers have suggested that Reagan's delay in announcing was a result not of uncertainty but of a calculated decision that the delay represented the most profitable way of pursuing his unannounced candidacy through this initial phase. The Federal Election Commission had even been requested to consider whether Reagan ought not to be declared a candidate earlier, and whether the sums that he had raised and spent in the weeks preceding his announcement should be made subject to the limitations of the new campaign finance law. To date, the commission has not indicated how it may rule on that request.

'Very Real Threat'

There was a time when Reagan the politician was not taken seriously. His adult life until 1966 had been spent largely in the entertainment field—sportscasting, acting in unexceptional movies and on television. He had also been a stump speaker of some note on the conservative lecture tour, especially during the 1964 Goldwater campaign. As Laxalt recalled, Reagan was viewed at first by his fellow governors as "tinsel, somehow not quite real" until they began to deal with his programs and abilities. Edmund G. (Pat) Brown, the incumbent Democrat whom Reagan trounced by nearly a million votes in 1966, later admitted in his book, *Reagan and Reality*, that "I greatly underestimated Reagan.... We thought the notion was absurd" that this political novice could be governor.

That time is past. Moderates such as Sen. Charles Mc. Mathias Jr. of Maryland have begun to warn their fellow Republicans of a "very real threat" from the right wing of their party. Such concerns have even led to murmurings about centrist third parties, should the Republicans be captured by the Reagan right. Vice President Rockefeller publicly dismissed the magnitude of the Reagan threat, yet his own withdrawal from the electoral sweepstakes was induced by White House distraction over that threat and the resultant concern over Rockefeller's presence on a Ford

ticket. Moreover, opinion polls indicate that Reagan, at age 64, is capable of mounting a serious challenge, both to Ford in the primaries and, if he wins the Republican nomination, to the Democratic candidate.

Reagan supporters feel their candidate's strengths are his distance from what voters see as the federal morass of Washington and his record in Sacramento, essentially the first major governorship in a growing trend of statehouse fiscal conservatism.

One Reagan aide argued that "the conservative thinkers in Washington are too theoretical and too prone to 'pseudo-realism.' That is, they have a tendency to say, 'We can't do anything, much as we'd like to.' They excuse their inaction and go on just playing goalie against all the new liberal programs. It's not enough for conservatives just to stop every new idea that comes along. We've got to do something, or we'll be swamped by the programs already on the books. Reagan proved he is not too theoretical and that he won't sell out to the bureaucrats. He has a record you can look to."

Laxalt emphasizes Reagan's administrative performance. "We now have basically the same problems at the national level as he did in California," he said. "There he acquired a surplus position through his welfare reforms and holding the state government work force down. The proof of how well he did is that Jerry Brown [Edmund G. Brown Jr., Pat Brown's son and now governor of California] is trying to out-Reagan Reagan."

Anti-Government Candidate

Even if Reagan was not universally successful in cutting back the size and cost of government in California, there is no question that he tried. And there is no question about his desire to try at the national level as well. His principal stump speech is replete with analysis of the errors of big government—Congress is his chief target—and suggestions about how a Reagan administration might avoid them. As he warns, at the current pace of growth, "the per cent of GNP [gross national product] government consumes will be 66 per cent—two-thirds of all our output—by the end of this century."

This growth in big government has, in Reagan's view, "created our economic problems...it has created the horrendous inflation of the past decade." Far worse, the "collectivist, centralizing approach" has "threaten[ed] the freedom of individuals and families. The states and local communities have been demeaned into little more than administrative districts, bureaucratic subdivisions of Big Brother government.... Thousands of towns and neighborhoods have seen their peace disturbed by bureaucrats and social planners, through busing, questionable education programs and attacks on family unity."

The basic Reagan prescription for the ills of big government is to transfer the responsibility and the money back to the states. Welfare, education, housing, food stamps, Medicaid, community and regional development, and other programs should revert to state control. "Transfer of authority in whole or part in all these areas would reduce the outlay of the federal government by more than $90-billion," he has said. "...With such a savings, it would be possible to balance the federal budget, make an initial $5-billion payment on the national debt and cut the federal personal income tax burden of every American by an average of 23 per cent."

Under Reagan's program, only those functions of government that are truly "national," such as defense, space, veterans' affairs, energy and environment, should remain vested in Washington. In addition to the massive transfer of authority back to the states, Reagan proposes to:

• "Set a date certain for an end to federal price fixing and an end to all federal restrictions on entry" by regulatory agencies in non-monopoly industries.

• "Put a statutory limit on the growth of our money supply, so that growth does not exceed the gain in productivity. Only in this way can we be sure of returning to a strong dollar."

• Simplify the method of tax collection so that all taxpayers can understand the forms quickly, and enact tax reform that "makes it more rewarding to save than to borrow and encourages a wider diffusion of ownership to America's workers."

Reagan's anti-government, anti-Washington pitch strikes a chord with many voters. It is the same chord, as some Reagan supporters concede, that Democratic Alabama Gov. George C. Wallace successfully exploits.

There are a few elements of Reagan's platform that have a populist ring. His desire to end the rate-setting, or price-fixing, authority of government agencies, for example, will not sit well with the captains of transportation. As one of his advisers put it, "Big government and big business are not precisely blood enemies; a huge, complicated system of regulation is harder on little businesses than on the behemoths."

Reagan backers privately press the view that only a Reagan candidacy could, because of the overlap of their constituencies, prevent Wallace from launching an independent effort. Such a third-party Wallace move, although technically a defection from Democratic ranks, would quite possibly hurt the Republican nominee more than the Democrat.

Vulnerabilities

Despite the promise of being an anti-government candidate in a time when voters are suspicious of politicians and government, Reagan has liabilities that he must overcome if he is to achieve national office for the first time. The first has already begun to emerge from Republican party ranks.

As any candidate becomes a serious prospect for success, he engenders opposition that lay dormant when he was not taken so seriously. In Reagan's case, the liberal and moderate elements of the party have begun to realize that he is indeed a genuine contender.

They have begun to complain publicly that the party must not narrow its base of appeal if it is to succeed electorally. Any initial successes of Reagan against Ford would bring the threat of a moderate-liberal challenge. Even if that section of the party proved incapable of denying him the nomination, it could reduce his general election prospects.

A second problem for Reagan may prove to be his penchant for hyperbole, which can be lethal for a national figure. Some examples:

• On the occasion of the distribution of free food to the poor people of the San Francisco Bay area by the Hearst family just after Patty Hearst's kidnaping, he said, "It's just too bad we can't have an epidemic of botulism."

• He once argued that the Watergate burglars should be treated kindly because they were not criminals "at heart."

Reagan's Background

Profession: Actor.
Born: Feb. 6, 1911, Tampico, Ill.
Home: Pacific Palisades, Calif.
Religion: Christian Church.
Education: Eureka College, Peoria, Ill., B.A., 1932.
Office: Governor of California, 1967-1975.
Military: Army Air Corps, 1942-46; discharged as captain.
Memberships: Tau Kappa Epsilon fraternity, Screen Actors Guild.
Family: Wife, Nancy Davis; four children, two by previous marriage to Jane Wyman.

Later, he reacted to the news of former President Nixon's phlebitis condition with, "Maybe that will satisfy the lynch mob."

• He was widely quoted as commenting while governor on means of quelling student protests: "If there is to be a bloodbath, let it be now." But he since has maintained that the quote was unfairly taken out of context.

Personal Background

If Reagan does overcome those liabilities and emerge as a successful candidate, his will have been an unusual path to national political office. Born to a poor Illinois family, he went to a small, little-known college in that state and there focused his interests in traditional ways—sports (football and swimming) and a fraternity. He also developed an interest in radio. Upon leaving college, he became a radio sports announcer, covering Iowa football and Chicago Cubs baseball games. Soon he was one of the better-known sportscasters of the Midwest.

In 1937, Reagan landed a Hollywood contract with Warner Brothers and began a movie and television career that spanned more than two decades. He is usually not given much credit as an actor, but one biographer concluded that the second world war and some bad breaks with his contract arrangements stymied what otherwise might have been a more substantial cinematic life.

An additional factor that may have held back Reagan's acting career was his political activism. In the pre-war years, he was a liberal, active in the Screen Actors Guild and working for benefits for his fellow actors. His preoccupation with such matters was great enough that his first wife, actress Jane Wyman, cited it as one of the sources of her estrangement from him and her consequent desire, in 1948, to divorce him.

By the time Reagan remarried in 1952, his politics were no less active, but they had begun to turn more conservative. That year he was still a Democrat, but he voted for Eisenhower. Later in the 1950s, he meshed his television acting career with a position making conservative speeches for General Electric. By the early 1960s, he had joined the Republican Party. In 1964, he sealed his image as an effective conservative spokesman with his speeches in support of presidential nominee Barry Goldwater. Reagan's most famous appeal for Goldwater, near the end of the campaign, elicited more contributions than any other speech in political history.

Two years later, acceding to encouragement from wealthy California Republicans, he entered his first political race—for the highest office of what was just becoming the most populous state in the union. His success then over a veteran politician said something about Reagan's potential in a business not long his own. Now politics is more fully his business, and the ultimate limit of his potential in it is about to be tested.

Positions on Issues

Reagan's incessant attacks on the federal bureaucracy are a consistent sequel to his programs as governor. Three issues dominated the Reagan tenure in the California statehouse: welfare cutbacks, educational change and attempts to limit over-all governmental spending and grant relief to California taxpayers.

Welfare

Of the three, welfare reform is considered by Reaganites as the most successful endeavor. It was also the most controversial aspect of Reagan's record as governor.

Welfare reform did not emerge as a high-profile Reagan issue until his second term. Just after a solid re-election victory over the folksy Democratic assembly leader, Jess Unruh, Reagan began in 1971 to publicize the complex of existing welfare programs as the number-one problem of both California and the nation. His contention was that, unless checked, these programs would eventually lead the state to bankruptcy. He noted that the number of Californians receiving welfare benefits had risen from 620,-000 in 1961 to 2.4 million in 1971, or one in nine state citizens, and that by mid-1972 the projected number was three million, with some 25,000 to 40,000 persons being added to the rolls each month.

Reagan's response was a 70-point welfare and Medi-Cal reform package. (Medi-Cal is California's liberalized version of Medicaid.) The proposals were designed to reduce the welfare rolls, eliminate fraud, put employable welfare recipients to work and lower the costs of Medi-Cal.

Observers differ in their assessments of the ultimate results of the Reagan welfare reform campaign. The Democrat-dominated legislature forced him into a compromise package thought to be liberalizing in many ways but constricting in others. The liberal California Supreme Court balked at some of the Reagan moves. Bitter disagreement remains over whether the Reagan approach denied benefits to the truly needy or to chiselers only.

In any event, the welfare caseload growth was stemmed. The drop began early when Reagan issued some new regulations but before any remedial legislation had been passed. Toward the end of Reagan's second term, in late 1974, the total number of welfare recipients on the rolls had dropped by 400,000 people from the level in early 1971, when he began his effort.

A national health care program has been second only to welfare on Reagan's list of objectionable governmental programs that he has denounced in his campaigning for 1976. In an argument published by a medical magazine, *Private Practice,* he dismissed the need for such a program as an illusion, asserting that "Virtually all Americans have access to excellent medical care today."

Education

Reagan's first term had begun with fireworks over the highly regarded California system of public universities. Such campus ferment as the Berkeley "free speech movement" of 1964 and the growing student distaste for the

Vietnam war were new phenomena then, and Reagan did not approve. He has been explicit in his feeling that the student activists with whom he tangled were outright revolutionaries whose demands ought to be quashed before they infected the entire political system.

Within a week after Reagan became governor, the University of California regents, at Reagan's urging, fired the president of the university, Clark Kerr, whom he perceived as having been too compliant with student protesters. Reagan slashed the higher education budget by 27 per cent in his first two years, and cut faculty salaries. He made numerous saber-rattling statements, which alienated students and many others. He called in the National Guard to expel students forcibly from the vacant tract of Berkeley land that had been dubbed "People's Park."

Kerr later was quoted as saying that Reagan "helped turn public opinion against the university. In fact, the left wing liked Reagan's policies—they both used confrontation to their advantage." Reagan himself has insisted that he never intended to make the campuses an issue, but that popular irritation with students made it one.

By the end of his second term, Reagan's stances against students were receding from the picture. The level of activism and campus violence was down dramatically. The higher education budget actually had risen substantially. Reagan had pointed out in 1971: "State aid for public schools has gone up more in the last four years than in any four-year period in California history. From 1958 to 1967, teachers' salary increases averaged 4.5 per cent a year. Since 1967, they have averaged 7 per cent." By 1975, teacher turnover had declined in the system, and scholarship monies had gone up.

For some critics, however, the Reagan record in education is symptomatic of a reckless style that may bode poorly for his discretion in other fields. It is also thought that this aspect of his administration may hurt him with more youthful voters.

Economics

The Reagan record on cutting the governmental budget and obtaining tax relief for citizens is likely to be of much greater relevance than education to his presidential hopes. His intention and ability to do just that at the federal level are at the heart of his message. Here, too, the final scorecard is ambiguous.

Facing an imminent deficit when he first assumed office, he was forced to raise taxes by some $900-million, and state taxation actually rose more under Reagan than it had under his predecessor. Moreover, Reagan ultimately failed to control the total size of the state budget. From 1967 to 1974, it doubled, from $4.6-billion to $10.2-billion.

Yet Reagan managed to control the growth of the state bureaucracy itself. It was no larger (some 100,000 employees) when he left than when he had arrived eight years before, a far cry from the upward national trend. He also obtained tax relief for Californians by occasional single-shot tax rebates (an estimated $1-billion worth) and by local property tax relief (another billion). Finally, he did arrive, albeit with the help of increased federal revenue-sharing, at a projected surplus budget position in his last year as governor. That same year, he also was able to soften his budgetary stringency with state employees, recommending substantial pay hikes for many of them.

The gem in Reagan's fiscal crown was to have been the constitutional limitation on government expenditures and taxation which a low turnout of California voters rejected in 1973. The principal behind the proposed constitutional amendment is simple: Reagan feels that the upper limit of government spending, hence government taxation power, ought to be pegged to the size of personal income. Proposition 1 would have put the ultimate ceiling on state expenditures and taxation at 7 per cent of total personal income in the state, but that limit would have been reached by gradual reductions, not all at once.

Despite the simplicity of the principle, the referendum item was enormously complex, some 4,500 words long and poorly understood. Many who did understand it opposed it as being out of step with the growing desire for government involvement in the solution of society's problems.

As indicated in his speeches, Reagan thinks that excessive federal spending is more than an objectionable drain on taxpayers' resources. It is also, to him, the single substantive factor that causes inflation: "The federal deficit provides the chief motive for the debauching of our dollar." Reducing spending, he says, will end the pressures in the capital markets, result in greater consumer purchasing power and reduce the burden of interest payments on outstanding federal debt.

Defense, Foreign Policy

Reagan has been quite outspoken on foreign policy questions. His principal theme is anti-communism. The Soviets and the Chinese leaders are viewed as cynical, power-aware negotiators who are not to be trusted too easily. Thus detente is viewed with suspicion. Reagan feels the United States has been on the short end of the specific deals that have been completed in the fledgling detente era and has been lulled into a dangerous misconception of the intentions behind the sustained Soviet military buildup.

In related foreign policy questions, Reagan is suspicious of the Ford administration stance on the strategic arms limitation talks. He would move carefully and exact adequate reciprocal concessions from Cuba before bettering formal relations with Fidel Castro. He opposes any U.S. troop withdrawals around the world (Korea, western Europe) except in the context of mutual, balanced withdrawals by the opposing Communist powers. He argues for retaining tight control over the Panama Canal. He is a firm supporter of Israel, viewing that nation as an enclave of democracy in the Middle East.

Crime

Reagan favored the reinstitution of the death penalty in California after the state supreme court revoked it. He took a dim view of the U.S. Supreme Court rulings that restricted the range of police powers of search and inquiry of citizens. In praising the work of police officers, he has used the rhetoric of law and order, talking about the "barbarians" and the "clearing in the jungle" which is civilization.

He has been outspoken in his attack on drugs and has opposed the legalization of marijuana with such remarks as this: "They have found a substance in marijuana which is very close to the female hormone. Some men find they are developing feminine characteristics." Referring to suggestions that drugs be decriminalized, that prostitution be legalized and that pornography be tolerated, Reagan said in 1974: "The virus of permissiveness spreads its deadly poison.... In too many cases the permissive philosophy has allowed guilty offenders to go free, to continue to prey on

Reagan Staff, Advisers

Chairman, Citizens for Reagan: Sen. Paul Laxalt (R Nev.), 53.

Campaign manager: John Sears, 35, a Washington attorney and a former aide to President Nixon and Vice President Agnew.

Press liaison: Lyn Nofziger, 51, a political consultant and former journalist (Copley News Service) who joined Reagan's staff in 1966 as his press secretary; head of the Nixon re-election campaign in California in 1972.

Research and issues adviser: Jeff Bell, 31, a political activist and journalist who has worked on the staff of the American Conservative Union, in the Nixon campaign of 1968 and on Gov. Reagan's political staff in California.

Scheduling and writing: Peter Hannaford and Michael Deaver, both public relations consultants in Los Angeles.

the innocent citizens who look to our legal system for protection."

A Reagan task force recommended stronger laws against drug dealing, opted for mandatory jail sentences for the use of weapons in crimes, suggested using six-person juries for some crimes and proposed several other alterations in the California criminal justice system.

Civil Rights, Civil Liberties

Reagan opposes busing to achieve racial integration. He has viewed it as misconceived, and his backers indicate that he would support a constitutional amendment to end its use if the courts do not reverse their reliance on it.

Energy, Environment

Reagan believes that the federal government has a legitimate role in the research and development aimed at adequate energy supplies. Yet he is skeptical of the Rockefeller-Ford proposal for a massive energy corporation supported by the government; he feels that would simply preempt the private market, with the attendant ills that he sees in all big-government solutions.

He is in favor of the development of nuclear energy, and despite the famed Santa Barbara oil spill which first brought the issue to light in his state and in the nation, he favors offshore drilling.

As governor, he took some actions that were viewed with favor by environmentalists. He once canceled construction of a highway after a horseback visit to a wilderness area that would have been damaged, and he signed into law an act requiring environmental impact statements for new construction in California. He also agreed with the principle of the elimination of air and water pollution, but he tempered that agreement with a traditional concern for industrial and economic growth. "The voices of reason are being drowned out by the prophets of calamity," he complained in 1973. "A strange sort of no-growth, no-development syndrome is proposed without regard for the consequences this might have on the lives of our people or the vitality of our economy...it is time to remember that we are ecology too."

Reagan has accosted the federal Environmental Protection Agency for making hasty and erroneous judgments that hurt the states and their economies—in advocacy of the catalytic converter for automobile emission control, for example.

—By Barry Hager

APPEALING TO THE OLD DEMOCRATIC COALITION

In a Democratic campaign year with an abundance of liberal candidates, each one must go to some pains to distinguish himself from the others if he expects his chances to last beyond the spring. Sen. Birch Bayh of Indiana is attempting to prove that he is the candidate best able to re-establish the coalition of divergent interests that carried the Democratic Party to its greatest power, during the era of Franklin D. Roosevelt.

Bayh believes that the old concert of interests can be rebuilt. His supporters insist that his legislative record and his established vote-gathering ability in Indiana amply prove that he is the man who can bring it about. One adviser distinguished Bayh from the other liberals in these words: "The difference with guys like [Fred R.] Harris and [Rep. Morris K.] Udall is that Birch Bayh has actually been in leadership positions in struggles that have been of immense importance to these groups, rather than simply being able to show up and say that he voted right. That makes for a very different relationship with these groups, especially with their leaders."

Particularly important to the Bayh campaign theory is his cozy relationship with the old guard of union leadership. Since the reported disaffection of AFL-CIO President George Meany and other labor leaders with Washington Sen. Henry M. Jackson, formerly their favorite contender, over his support of the 1974 trade bill, Bayh's stock appears to have risen. He was the only candidate who attended the regional conferences of liberal Democrats in the fall of 1975 who also was invited to an AFL-CIO gathering in San Francisco in October.

Nor is Bayh's relationship with labor a recent one. From his earliest days in the Senate, he has received strong labor support. He has been graced by healthy contributions from union-affiliated political action groups.

Perhaps the most prominent role ever played by Bayh, one that pleased labor as well as blacks and other minorities, was his leadership of the Senate's rejection of two Nixon appointees to the Supreme Court. Both were federal judges from the South, Clement F. Haynsworth Jr. of South Carolina and G. Harrold Carswell of Florida. Both failed to win Senate confirmation after bitter battles that Bayh spearheaded, against Haynsworth in 1969 and against Carswell in 1970.

As he led the attack on Haynsworth's sense of propriety, the White House countered with charges against Bayh for taking union contributions and then voting for legislation benefiting the unions. Had more members of the Senate been free of the same alleged conflict, the criticism might have been more telling. As it was, Bayh was unhurt by the charges, and he has seldom been inclined to apologize for his labor support.

Despite his alliance with labor, Bayh has deftly retained his ideological freedom of movement. His position on the Vietnam war was in dovish contrast to the "hard hat" approach. Like many other ultimate doves, Bayh stood by the Kennedy and Johnson policies in the early years. But in 1968, he returned from a Vietnam inspection tour clearly

opposed to the war effort. He was then active in the prolonged struggle by Congress to reassert control over the warmaking powers. He sponsored amendments that established Congress' power to review and reduce the manpower levels of the military, and he supported the 1970 Cooper-Church amendment to curtail the use of American ground forces. He now states his belief that "Vietnam ranks among this country's greatest and most tragic mistakes."

Bayh also manages to balance the conflicting positions of labor and blacks in some instances. The controversial "Philadelphia plan," which set black employment quotas on federally contracted construction, was opposed by the unions but supported by Bayh. He also differed with the unions by giving support to Richard Hatcher, the black mayor of Gary, Ind.

Bayh's support for black causes has been consistent. He has supported the major civil rights bills throughout his Senate tenure, including the voting rights, public accommodations and fair housing laws. He has been an advocate of federal funding of community and urban development programs and other efforts to relieve inner-city distress.

Nor has Bayh overlooked the Hispanic population. He fought for the 1975 expansion of the Voting Rights Act to embrace non-English-speaking minorities such as Spanish-Americans. He has cosponsored a proposal for more bilingual proceedings in federal district courts.

Still another group with whom Bayh has political credit is women. Bayh floor-managed the Equal Rights Amendment in the Senate and successfully fended off the attempts by Sen. Sam J. Ervin Jr. (D N.C. 1954-75) to dilute the constitutional proposal. He also headed the fight for the prohibition of sex discrimination in educational establishments, including military installations, receiving federal funds.

Bayh has a solid record of support for welfare, Social Security, Medicare and the total range of other governmental programs that affect the poor of all ages.

The Primary Strategy

The test of Bayh's strength with the coalition will be in the early primaries. His strategists readily concede that those elections will be crucial, for it is their contention that one candidate will emerge from the liberal cluster and develop the momentum to become the party nominee. As Bayh's press secretary, Bill Wise, stated it, "By the time we reach the New York primary [April 6], the field should be narrowed to one liberal candidate. The others aren't going to disappear, but in terms of real effect, only one will be important. He will face Jackson and [Alabama Gov. George C.] Wallace for the nomination."

Wise, reflecting the thinking of his boss, is confident of the hypothetical liberal leader's prospects at that point, for he feels the hawkish record of Jackson on Vietnam will irrevocably hurt him with the 1972 McGovern element still influential in the party. He views Wallace as out of the question for the Democratic nomination.

Bayh's Interest-Group Ratings

Americans for Democratic Action (ADA)—ADA ratings are based on the number of times a senator voted, was paired for or announced for the ADA position on selected issues.

National Farmers Union (NFU)—NFU ratings are based on the number of times a senator voted, was paired for or announced for the NFU position.

AFL-CIO Committee on Political Education (COPE)—COPE ratings reflect the percentage of the time a senator voted in accordance with or was paired in favor of the COPE position.

Americans for Constitutional Action (ACA)—ACA ratings record the percentage of the time a senator voted in accordance with the ACA position.

Following are Bayh's ratings since he entered the Senate in 1963:

	ADA[1]	COPE[3]	NFU[3]	ACA
1974	62	100	100	6
1973	85	91	100	4
1972	80	88	100	6
1971	96	80	90	14
1970	72[4]	100	100	11
1969	78	100	94	7
1968	50	100	50	38
1967	62	90	89	4
1966	80	92[2]	93	11
1965	94	92[2]	85	8
1964	86[2]	80[2]	76[2]	3[2]
1963	86[2]	80[2]	76[2]	3[2]

1. Failure to vote lowers score.
2. Scores listed twice indicate rating compiled for entire Congress.
3. Percentages compiled by CQ from information provided by groups.
4. ADA score includes some votes from December 1969.

Thus, Bayh's plan is to become the front-runner before the New York primary. To achieve this, the campaign is concentrating on New Hampshire, Massachusetts, New York and Iowa. In each of those states, Bayh has what his staff calls broad-based steering committees studded with experienced local politicians. Wise suggests that they learned from the abbreviated Bayh campaign in 1971 that less staffing at the national level and more work at the state level is a better tactic. That is how the effort is being structured, with the small Washington staff not yet fully in place.

In his 1971 campaign, the junior senator from Indiana was still relatively little-known and had to convince the press and others that he was a serious candidate. Now his name recognition is comparatively high, and he is viewed by most observers as a serious contender.

Yet his early withdrawal in October 1971, after a cancer operation on his wife, Marvella, precluded any test of his ability to test his popularity with the voters outside Indiana. His actual vote-getting ability still remains in question. Even where local leaders of the groups for whom Bayh has worked in the Senate favor him, that popular vote test still must be met.

A second potential problem is that, in several campaign appearances before sophisticated audiences, Bayh has received low marks from some listeners for his casual, down-home style. Others who have met him during his campaign travels have complained of his failure to deal with the complexities of some issues. Still others were critical of the sanctimonious tone they perceived in Bayh's Oct. 21, 1975, announcement of candidacy in his hometown of Shirkieville, Ind., where he said: "Those of you who have known me the longest know I have never had a burning desire to be President of the United States. You know I feel closer to my God right here."

A third potential problem is simply timing. Bayh did not enter the race until comparatively late in the year, and admittedly he has to play catch-up with the earlier contestants. His staff is confident that he can do so, pointing to the rapidity with which he qualified for federal matching funds under the new election law as proof of the range of his support and his ability to tap it.

Senate Elections

One way of assessing Bayh's potential for reaching the voters is to look at his past campaign successes. His first campaign for the Senate, in 1962, was against a three-term Republican incumbent, Homer E. Capehart (1945-63), and Bayh was given little chance. A former speaker of the Indiana House, Bayh was then obscure enough that one of the principal features of the Bayh campaign was a radio jingle that explained how to pronounce his name ("bye"). Capehart presented a bellicose image during the Cuban missile crisis that overshadowed the 1962 election season, while Bayh ran a campaign marked for its energy and for his willingness to meet the people. Bayh won his upset, 50.3 to 49.7 per cent, and went to the Senate at age 34.

In 1968, Bayh was challenged by Republican William D. Ruckelshaus. Despite Ruckelshaus' later familiarity as a result of his role in the 1973 "Saturday night massacre" of Watergate, he was the one who had the obscurity problem then. Ruckelshaus was helped by presidential candidate Richard M. Nixon, who carried Indiana that year by more than a quarter million votes, his best showing in any state. Still, Bayh escaped the coattails and won a second term, 51.7 to 48.1 per cent.

In 1974, Bayh was challenged by Republican Indianapolis Mayor Richard Lugar. At one time, Lugar was seen as a substantial threat to Bayh, but then the title accorded Lugar of being the Watergate-damaged Nixon's favorite mayor began to lose its appeal. Bayh again won, 50.7 per cent to 46.4 per cent.

Those results, although all close, generally are read as an indication of Bayh's campaigning ability; he is widely regarded as an anomaly because he is so much more liberal than his customarily conservative Indiana constituency. Yet Bayh runs successfully in Indiana also because he is careful to serve the state well in traditional ways that are outside ideological categories.

As a member of the Public Works Committee during his earlier days in the Senate, he was successful in significantly enlarging the amount of "pork barrel" public works funds that came Indiana's way. He worked for relief, in Indiana and elsewhere, in the wake of natural disasters. He successfully fought to have the Indiana Dunes area designated as a national lakeshore. When traumas to the economy, such as the closing of factories, have occurred, he has attempted to reach solutions that moderate the impact on his constituents

Personal Background

Bayh, still boyish-looking at age 47—he will be 48 on Jan. 22—is very much an Indiana product. Born near Terre Haute, he comes from German stock. He grew up on a farm and attended the Purdue University School of Agriculture, where he demonstrated his athletic ability by becoming the state Golden Gloves light-heavyweight champion. He had been too young for the wartime Army, but served in the U.S. occupation forces in Europe after high school, in 1946-48, before settling in for his Purdue degree.

In 1955, at age 27, Bayh began eight years of service in the Indiana Assembly. He gained the esteem of his party colleagues, who made him minority leader in two sessions, and he was assembly speaker for one term when the party obtained temporary dominance. His relations with the press in those days were sufficiently solid for newsmen to vote him Indiana's "most able representative" in 1961.

Bayh's success in the legislature did not come at the expense of his other development. He also was working during this period to obtain his law degree. He received it from Indiana University in 1960. A little more than two years later, he abandoned private practice to run for the Senate.

Positions on Issues

Bayh's best-publicized and most substantive legislative work has been related to his chairmanship of the Constitutional Amendments and Juvenile Delinquency Subcommittees of the Senate Judiciary Committee.

Constitution

He has shown a gift for identifying issues on which a positive contribution can be made without alienating any particular interest group. His involvement with constitutional amendments is the most significant example of this. Bayh has led the battles for several amendments since he came to the Senate and took his place on the Judiciary Committee. He has made his chairmanship of the Subcommittee on Constitutional Amendments an important post. The proudest Bayh achievement in the constitutional realm is his authorship of the 25th Amendment, which spells out

---

Bayh's Background

Profession: Attorney, farmer.
Born: Jan. 22, 1928, Terre Haute, Ind.
Home: Shirkieville, Ind.
Religion: Methodist.
Education: Purdue University, B.S., 1951; Indiana State College; Indiana University Law School, J.D., 1960.
Offices: Indiana General Assembly, 1955-63; minority leader for four years, and speaker for two years; Senate since 1963.
Military: Army, 1946-48.
Memberships: Junior Chamber of Commerce; American Farm Bureau Federation; National Farmers Union; American, Indiana and Vigo County (Indiana) Bar Associations.
Family: Wife, Marvella Hern; one son.
Committees: Appropriations: chairman, Subcommittee on Transportation and Related Agencies; Subcommittees on Agriculture, Labor-HEW, Treasury and HUD and Independent Agencies; Judiciary: chairman, Constitutional Amendments Subcommittee; chairman, Subcommittee on Juvenile Delinquency; Subcommittees on Administrative Practice and Procedures, Antitrust and Monopoly, Constitutional Rights, Internal Security, and Penitentiaries.

---

procedures for dealing with presidential disability.

Bayh and many others had been led by the illnesses that afflicted President Eisenhower, and much more by the assassination of President Kennedy, to have strong concern over the mechanism of succession to the presidency in the event of temporary disability or death. Bayh raised the Senate's awareness of the issue, pushed his bill through Congress and ultimately saw it ratified and added to the Constitution in 1967. Since then, the amendment has been brought into use twice—first in the appointment of Gerald R. Ford as Vice President and then in Ford's choice of Nelson Rockefeller to succeed him.

Bayh's subcommittee work also involved him in the move to extend the vote to 18-year-olds. Voting patterns since have indicated that the young tend to vote neither more frequently nor in a significantly different ideological pattern from other voters. Whatever its impact, the franchise extension allows Bayh to present himself as being concerned with allowing youth a fair share of the political process.

The Equal Rights Amendment has met stiff opposition and has not yet been ratified. Another proposed constitutional amendment of substantial concern to Bayh has not met with legislative success. Since 1966, he has been convinced that the electoral college method of electing Presidents should be replaced by direct election.

Youth and Crime

The second area to which Bayh has devoted a large amount of his energies is juvenile crime. His record for legislation here is impressive; the record on results is not, and the blame in the eyes of Bayh's committee aides belongs squarely on the Republican administrations of Nixon and Ford. Bayh juxtaposes two figures: the percentage of crimes committed by juveniles and the proportion of federal crime money being spent on juveniles. He finds the divergence between the two—far more crime than money—most disturbing.

Bayh had fought for more than a year to create a special federal office designed to address the problems of

Bayh's CQ Vote Study Scores*

	1974	1973	1972	1971	1970	1969	1968	1967	1966	1965	1964	1963
Presidential												
support	28[1]/26[2]	30	30	22	26	47	45	64	64	70	59	76
opposition	42[1]/28[2]	53	54	46	33	35	24	17	15	14	7	6
Voting Participation	69	86	83	59	68	77	64	75	80	84	79	82
Party												
unity	61	81	71	58	65	73	60	65	74	73	68	70
opposition	8	5	8	5	5	9	7	14	8	8	6	5
Conservative Coalition												
support	13	7	7	2	3	9	20	16	14	10	12	9
opposition	58	83	76	63	60	71	49	57	74	74	65	56
Bipartisan												
support	59	77	70	37	55	62	51	59	69	73	59	78
opposition	9	9	16	19	11	12	13	14	9	13	8	9

1. During President Nixon's tenure in 1974.
2. During President Ford's tenure in 1974.   * Explanation of studies, p. 107.

juvenile offenders and to administer the flow of federal funds to programs dealing with those problems when he finally saw a bill signed into law, the Juvenile Justice and Delinquency Prevention Act (PL 93-415), in 1974. Even then, the bill had been badly pared down. There were further delays in funding the program, for which he blames Ford. Bayh thus can be expected to dwell on the failure of "law and order" advocates to finance and implement legislation aimed at curbing a significant portion of the crime problem.

Other Bayh efforts in the youth and crime area have included:

● Sponsoring, in 1974, a runaway youth program, which provides funds for the sheltering and counseling of runaways.

● Highlighting the problem of school vandalism and violent assault within schools by holding subcommittee hearings in the summer of 1975 and sponsoring legislation to respond to the problem.

● Working to curtail the diversion of legitimately manufactured drugs to illicit users by placing tighter controls on the production of amphetamines and barbiturates.

● Supporting a number of measures to curb drug abuse and to provide more adequate and accessible treatment for drug offenders.

● Sponsoring a successful proposal to ban the incarceration of youthful offenders with hardened criminals.

Bayh has been particularly active in the movement for gun control, having sponsored a ban on the sale of "Saturday night specials" and having proposed a Violent Crime and Repeat Offender Act which would feature stiff, mandatory punishment for a variety of crimes related to the possession or use of a weapon.

Energy

Bayh's committee work has not led him into the energy field to the extent that he would like as a candidate, and he is moving into that area aggressively. His principal effort is his bill (S 2387) to end the vertical integration of the major oil companies. Bayh aides say there is a good chance that his bill may pass.

The thrust of the bill is to break the control that oil companies now have over all aspects of oil production, from wellhead to automobile tank. The assumption behind the bill is the classic antitrust belief that such vertical integration is anti-competitive and hence raises prices.

Bayh has shown particular interest in the need for adequate funding of research into ways in which sulfur can be removed from coal so that the country's most abundant fossil fuel can be used in an environmentally satisfactory way. He also embraced the goal of U.S. energy self-sufficiency within a decade back in 1973 by cosponsoring a bill allocating $2-billion a year for 10 years for energy research and development.

Economy

Bayh has highlighted the economy as a fundamental issue. If unemployment figures remain high, he can be expected to hit hard on the failure of the Republican administration to give the working man a job. Bayh has acted in the past to cushion the impact of hard times by drafting legislation extending the scope and length of unemployment benefits. He favors a more aggressive federal role as a public service employer in order to reduce unemployment.

Bayh has joined numerous other critics of the policies of the Federal Reserve Board. He has argued that the high interest rates and the tight money policies of the Republican administration and the Federal Reserve are responsible for the inflation and unemployment the economy has suffered. He has also made other fiscal recommendations, including his support of countercyclical revenue-sharing to cities hit by particularly high levels of unemployment. Bayh has cosponsored legislation to create an economic planning board.

Tax reform is also a priority for Bayh. He has supported tax relief for small taxpayers and for the elimination of loopholes for preferred incomes, exporters, business depreciation and the oil depletion allowance.

Environment

Bayh has been concerned with noise pollution. He has opposed the supersonic transport for that reason as well as for its possible impact on the ozone layer. He supported the Environmental Noise Control Act.

Bayh drafted legislation opposing the use of pesticides on wild animals on public lands. He sponsored legislation banning the use of such allegedly cruel trapping devices as the leghold trap in hunting done on public lands.

Health Care

Bayh supports the principal of a comprehensive national health insurance program. He has favored additional funding for maternal and child health programs, for nutritional programs for the elderly, nurse training, home health care and hospital modernization. He cosponsored the Black Lung Benefits Act of 1972 (PL 92-303). He also cosponsored a bill to provide for coverage of one preventive checkup a year for Medicare recipients.

Defense, Foreign Policy

Bayh has been a strong supporter of Israel, voting consistently for the necessary military aid to preserve the integrity of the nation. In his support for or opposition to other governments, Bayh invokes what he calls the requirement of mutuality of responsibility. Governments that the United States aids should, in those terms, recognize that they have the obligation to nurture democratic institutions and refrain from racial or religious discrimination. They should also contribute to their own defense in accordance with their means. In light of these general principles, Bayh has urged NATO to take over more of the U.S. defense burden in Europe, allowing the United States to reduce its troops there. He advocated cutoffs of aid to Sukarno's In-

donesia and to the former junta in Greece. He opposed the importation of chrome from Rhodesia.

On "third world" issues, Bayh chides the Republican administrations for essentially ignoring the questions posed by the developing nations. He argues that "there can be no real long-term peace unless the United States joins in the effort to improve living conditions for all human beings."

Bayh has generally taken the stance that the limitation of the U.S. arms race with the Soviet Union is appropriate. He has, in the past, supported agreements between the two countries which would reduce the levels of armaments and curb the development of additional missile technology. However, he expresses some concern about what he has called the "tendency of two Republican Presidents and Secretary of State Kissinger to overstate the meaning of detente in its present context."

—By Barry Hager

Bayh Staff, Advisers

Chairman, Committee for Birch Bayh in 1976: Matthew E. Welsh, Indianapolis attorney and former governor of Indiana (D 1961-65).

Campaign manager: Jayson Berman, a 10-year veteran of Bayh's Senate staff.

Deputy campaign manager: Ann Lewis, a former aide to Mayor Kevin White of Boston.

Press secretary: Bill Wise, a former journalist (*Life* magazine) who has been Bayh's Senate press secretary for six years.

Finance chairman: Myer Feldman, an attorney and former White House counsel to Presidents Kennedy and Johnson.

TRIBULATIONS OF A LITTLE-KNOWN CANDIDATE

Five years into his first term, Lloyd Bentsen, the well-tailored junior senator from Texas, called the ritual news conference to announce his candidacy for the Democratic presidential nomination in 1976. "The paramount issue is economic recovery," said the millionaire former insurance executive, offering himself as the best-qualified candidate for solving the nation's economic problems.

That was in February 1975. Bentsen had laid the groundwork for the campaign the previous year, when, as chairman of the Democratic Senatorial Campaign Committee, he had visited 36 states and traveled 200,000 miles. In the first half of 1975, his all-out campaign took him to 40 states and logged another 300,000 miles.

But the frenetic travels and the well-modulated message of the 54-year-old Texan did not reap the response he had hoped for. By autumn, he was short of money and low in name recognition.

An analytical, pragmatic man, he took a practical alternative. He retrenched. "If I had the money, if I were permitted by the law to raise it and if I were permitted to spend it, I'd go into the big industrial states and buy massive TV," he said. "I don't, so I think it's smarter to husband my resources and stay the course."

In short, if the 1976 Democratic nominee is chosen on the first convention ballot, his name will not be Lloyd Bentsen. Bentsen's ultimate success may depend on a stalemate in the primaries that results in a multi-ballot convention and the eventual selection of a compromise candidate. His modified strategy is to concentrate on selected areas, hoping to go into the convention with a sizable bloc of delegates and thus a strong bargaining position.

"I am beginning to think that no one will go into the convention with a commanding lead," Bentsen said in a September interview with *The Houston Chronicle.* "It means a better chance for me. Things might break my way."

The campaign finance reforms of 1974 are the reason for Bentsen's money shortage. But they may also be his salvation in keeping some semblance of a campaign alive in 1976. He has raised the necessary funds in small contributions from the required minimum of 20 states to qualify for matching campaign money from the federal treasury.

The Troubled Campaign

Despite the travels, the speeches and the slogan—"A Roosevelt Democrat for the '70s"—Bentsen has remained unknown to most Democrats. A Harris Survey in the summer of 1975 found that his name was recognized by only one-third of those surveyed nationwide, nearly the same percentage as in a similar poll taken two months earlier. He was favored for the nomination by only 1 per cent of the Democratic respondents. Bentsen, though, has shown little concern with low poll figures, noting that when he kicked off his senatorial campaign in 1970, he was known by only 2 per cent of the Texas voters.

In addition to his fund-raising difficulties, Bentsen cited his Senate responsibilities as a major reason for scaling down his campaign. "My first commitment is in the Senate," he said. "If I were out of a job like some of the candidates, then I could run in most of the primaries."

Staff disagreements over campaign strategy were played up by the press after the Sept. 5 resignation of Benjamin L. Palumbo, Bentsen's campaign manager and former aide to Democratic New Jersey Sen. Harrison A. Williams Jr. Palumbo's departure spurred reports that this represented an abandonment of his proposed "go-for-broke" approach. Palumbo reportedly favored a strong campaign in the northeastern primaries—liberal strongholds where Bentsen is not well known—hoping that the Texan could be dramatically successful, as John F. Kennedy was in West Virginia in 1960.

But Bentsen opted for a lower-risk strategy, one which would concentrate his time and resources on areas where he expects the best results. Bentsen commented that he would "play his strengths" in the primaries and caucuses and "go into those congressional districts where the voters favor more moderate candidates, independent thinkers rather than ideologues."

Bentsen has since announced that he will enter a "representative number of primaries" across the nation, with the qualification that the exact ones will be determined after all states complete their delegate selection rules. He does not plan to enter the first-in-the-nation New Hampshire primary Feb. 24, but probably will enter several other northern primaries. Ohio, Pennsylvania and Illinois are considered likely targets.

Bentsen has spent considerable time in the vote-rich states of New York and California. But, because of the cost of running statewide campaigns, he will likely concentrate on targeted districts in these states.

The Bentsen campaign is particularly well organized, his aides say, in four southern states: Virginia, Louisiana, Texas and Oklahoma. In Virginia, he executed a coup of sorts by getting endorsements from some of the state's top Democrats. In Louisiana, Bentsen has the endorsement of Democratic Gov. Edwin W. Edwards.

Texas, though, is the keystone of the Bentsen campaign. He must win the Texas primary May 1, not only to demonstrate his home-state popularity but to assure himself of a sizable bloc of delegates. His chances in Texas are complicated by the fact that he will be on the ballot twice—as a candidate both for President and for re-election to the Senate.

Not only must Bentsen wage two campaigns, but the Federal Election Commission has ruled that he may spend only $640,000 in the Texas primary, the Senate maximum. His presidential opponents, however, each may spend $1.3-million in the state. The commission concluded that Bentsen "is already the senator from Texas and thus, within Texas, begins with a significant exposure advantage over his rivals." Bentsen campaign tacticians are confident that, in spite of spending limitations, he can win both races.

Bentsen's Interest-Group Ratings

Americans for Democratic Action (ADA)—ADA ratings are based on the number of times a senator voted, was paired for or announced for the ADA position on selected issues.

National Farmers Union (NFU)—NFU ratings are based on the number of times a senator voted, was paired for or announced for the NFU position.

AFL-CIO Committee on Political Education (COPE)—COPE ratings reflect the percentage of the times a senator voted in accordance with or was paired in favor of the COPE position.

Americans for Constitutional Action (ACA)—ACA ratings record the percentage of the times a senator voted in accordance with the ACA position.

Following are Bentsen's ratings since he entered the Senate in 1971:

	ADA[1]	COPE[2]	NFU[2]	ACA
1974	38	45	59	41
1973	55	64	71	41
1972	35	30	67	45
1971	33	55	73	33

1. Failure to vote lowers score.
2. Percentages compiled by CQ from information provided by groups.

They expect him to win at least a plurality of the delegates in the presidential voting because of the controversial primary law passed by Bentsen supporters in the 1975 state legislature. The law will expire after the 1976 primary. It permits Bentsen to win all the delegate votes in a state senatorial district if his delegate candidates receive a plurality of the vote.

Wallace supporters and Texas liberals unsuccessfully opposed the primary. Billie Carr, the Democratic national committeewoman from Texas and a long-time liberal adversary of Bentsen, filed a challenge with the Democratic National Committee's Compliance Review Commission. The challenge, though, was dismissed by the commission at its October meeting, and Carr may file a court suit against the primary. She has called it the "godawful primary written for and by Bentsen."

With new Democratic delegate selection rules and the long list of candidates splintering the vote, Bentsen is convinced that his position near the philosophical center of the party is the right place to be in 1976. As he commented to an interviewer in July: "The other [Democratic] candidates are trying to move into the middle. I don't have to. I'm already there."

Still, while Bentsen has intensively courted a wide range of groups, there is little evidence that he has attracted deep support from any segment of the party. Texas Democratic Chairman Calvin Guest observed in a September 1975 interview with *Time* magazine: "The problem is to communicate his great leadership ability. Groups he has spoken to often go away without understanding what he really said." A Bentsen Senate aide concurred: "His ability is more managerial than inspirational. It's difficult to communicate this in a campaign." Although Bentsen is not a speaker who influences his audiences, most close observers of his campaign remark that he comes across as calm and knowledgeable. His supporters believe that this campaign style will be an asset in 1976. Commenting on the generally unemotional response to the lengthy roster of Democratic contenders, a Bentsen aide observed: "There'll be no little girls screaming and tearing cuff links off this time around."

The Bentsen campaign staff claims inroads among minority and interest groups; the most impressive, an invitation to speak to the AFL-CIO national convention in early October. Bentsen was one of only four senators invited to appear (Henry M. Jackson of Washington, Birch Bayh of Indiana and Hubert H. Humphrey of Minnesota were the others). However, this inroad with organized labor could be jeopardized by Bentsen's announced intention to vote against the common-site picketing bill, a measure of particular importance to the building trades unions.

Early Years, House Career

Liberalism has not been a characteristic of Bentsen and his family. His paternal grandparents were from Denmark. They migrated to the lower Rio Grande Valley early in the 20th century. Bentsen's father and uncle became wealthy in real estate, at the end of World War II owning 100,000 acres of ranch and farm land. Although accused of land fraud by several customers in the late 1940s and early 1950s, the Bentsens were never convicted. In 1974, the fortune of Bentsen's father was estimated to be about $50-million.

After graduation from the University of Texas Law School and service in the Army Air Corps in World War II, Lloyd returned to the Rio Grande Valley and moved quickly into politics. With wealth and military fame, he made an attractive candidate, and in 1946 (at age 25), he won his first election—for county judge in Hidalgo County, Texas. Although a member of the county's powerful land-owning class, Bentsen was considered a brash newcomer and ran on the slogan, "Beat the Machine." *(Background box, opposite)*

Two years later, he ran for the U.S. House of Representatives. Using the same slogan, Bentsen challenged incumbent Democrat Milton H. West (1933-48). Anticipating a difficult campaign and suffering from ill health, West bowed out of the primary race, and Bentsen defeated his remaining three opponents. He was unopposed in the general election and, at age 27, became the youngest member of Congress. His district, the 15th, was a large one, situated north of the Mexican border and west of the Gulf of Mexico. More than half of the residents were Mexican-Americans, and Bentsen's fluency in Spanish was an asset.

Bentsen served three terms in the House, winning re-election each time without Republican opposition. He compiled a basically conservative voting record and was a strong supporter of public works and veterans' legislation.

He was rarely in the limelight, although in 1949 he was one of only two Texas House members to support an anti-poll-tax bill, and in 1950 he suggested that President Truman threaten the North Koreans with use of the atomic bomb if they did not withdraw from South Korea within a week.

Bentsen was mentioned as a gubernatorial candidate in 1954. But, citing his inability to support his wife and children on his congressional salary of $12,500, he chose instead to retire from the House at age 33 and enter private business.

Business Career

Borrowing $7-million from his family, Bentsen moved to Houston, where he established the Consolidated American Life Insurance Company. In 1958, Bentsen merged his company with Lincoln Liberty Life Insurance Company of Lincoln, Neb., and gained controlling interest. Bentsen headed the company's investments section, headquartered in Houston. In 1967, a holding company, Lincoln Consolidated Inc., was formed, which controlled the insurance company, a banking operation and several mutual funds. Bentsen became president of Lincoln Consolidated and chairman of the board of Lincoln Liberty Life.

The Texas Observer reported that in 1969, Bentsen's last full year as president of Lincoln Consolidated, the insurance firm alone, Lincoln Liberty Life, had assets of more than $75-million. In addition to his leadership of the holding company, Bentsen was on the board of directors of several companies, including Lockheed Aircraft Corporation, Continental Oil Company and Bank of the Southwest.

While declining to discuss his personal finances during his 1970 Senate race, Bentsen disclosed in March 1971 that his net worth was $2.3-million ($3.6-million in assets). His leading assets were $1.8-million in real estate and nearly $1.3-million in stocks and bonds. In 1972, Bentsen sold his active interest in Lincoln Consolidated Inc., and in 1974 he placed his assets in a blind trust.

Although immersed in the business world for 15 years, Bentsen and his wife, Beryl Ann, kept their hands in Democratic politics. In 1960, Bentsen was the Texas finance chairman for the Kennedy-Johnson campaign. Four years

---

Bentsen's Background

Profession: Financier, attorney.
Born: Feb. 11, 1921, Mission, Texas.
Home: Houston, Texas.
Religion: Presbyterian.
Education: University of Texas, LL.B., 1942.
Offices: House, 1948-55; Senate since 1971.
Military: Army Air Corps, 1942-45; discharged as major.
Family: Wife, Beryl Ann Longino; three children.
Committees: Finance: chairman, Subcommittee on Financial Markets; Public Works: chairman, Subcommittee on Transportation; Joint Economic: chairman, Subcommittee on Economic Growth.

---

later, he expressed interest in Democrat Ralph W. Yarborough's (1957-71) Senate seat, but was dissuaded from running by President Johnson, who wanted to establish harmony in the Texas party. From 1966 to 1969, Bentsen's wife served as Texas' Democratic national committeewoman.

1970 Senate Campaign

"I want to be known or remembered for something other than my financial statement," Bentsen announced on his return to elective politics in 1970. At the urging of former Gov. John B. Connally (1963-69) and other leaders of the state's conservative Democratic hierarchy, Bentsen abandoned his business career to oppose Yarborough for the party's Senate nomination. Yarborough, a three-term incumbent, had a liberal voting record and a maverick organization independent of the party structure. He enjoyed strong support from organized labor and the state's chief minority groups, blacks and Mexican-Americans.

An early underdog, little-known statewide, Bentsen relied on an extensive advertising campaign on television and in the newspapers to gain recognition and throw Yarborough on the defensive. The ads labeled Yarborough as an ultraliberal who was out of step with the more conservative Texas electorate. They helped to produce a campaign that was bitter even for the wide-open style of Texas politics.

Bentsen won with 53 per cent to Yarborough's 47 per cent. His victory was attributed to his advertising campaign, his inroads among the conservative, poorer voters in rural eastern Texas and a light turnout that was particularly noticeable among minority groups.

Money was also a factor. Bentsen outspent Yarborough nearly 3 to 1, reporting expenditures of $800,000 to $275,000 for Yarborough. More than a quarter of Bentsen's expenditures were for broadcast advertising. The purse strings of wealthy, conservative Texans were opened to defeat Yarborough, and Bentsen collected more than 40 individual contributions of more than $2,500 each.

In the general election, Bentsen's Republican opponent was Rep. George Bush (1967-71). Like Bentsen, Bush was a millionaire businessman with a conservative image. There were few major policy differences between the two, and the distinctions that developed were more of style than substance. Against Bush, Bentsen's rhetoric moved back toward the center. Despite the active support of Bush by the Republican administration, Bentsen won with 53.5 per cent.

Senate Career

Although disappointed by Bush's defeat, the White House, expecting Bentsen to vote conservatively in the Senate, hailed Bentsen's election as a "philosophical victory" for the Nixon administration. But the new senator was quick to emphasize his Democratic credentials. Speaking to a group of Democratic women in January 1971, he remarked: "If the Republicans were ready to claim me as a soul brother, why did they send the whole first team down to Texas to campaign and spend millions trying to beat me?"

Aware of Bentsen's conservative campaign against Yarborough, a number of Washington observers were equally surprised by the moderate voting record the new senator compiled. "A lot of people expected Bentsen to be a dinosaur," an informed Texas source told Congressional Quarterly in a 1975 interview, "but one of his first votes was against the SST." Bentsen also showed in early 1971, on a move to change the cloture rule, that he would not be as conservative as most other southern senators. He supported the effort to reduce the majority required to invoke cloture from two-thirds to three-fifths. Throughout his first term, Bentsen's special-interest-group ratings have stayed near the center. *(Box, p. 23)*

Bentsen's Senate staff believes his moderate voting record has helped solidify his Texas political base. One aide commented: "Sen. Bentsen has captured the broad center of Texas almost perfectly," and cited a poll taken for the senator's office in the late spring of 1975. It showed that 59 per cent of the Texas voters approved of Bentsen's performance in the Senate, and indicated that he would defeat Yarborough by better than 2 to 1 if they met in the 1976 Democratic senatorial primary.

But Bentsen's centrist position has its detractors. Billie Carr told CQ: "I don't think he's presidential material or qualified. He brags that he votes with liberals part-time, conservatives part-time. But he's without commitment. He's a poll-taker."

Members of Bentsen's Senate staff disagree. Administrative Assistant Gary Bushell described his boss as a pragmatist who brings a "fact-finding, problem-solving approach" to decision-making. Another Senate aide

described Bentsen as a "cool, deliberative, analytical guy, not calculating for himself. Otherwise, frankly, he would have voted with the Democrats on the attempt to override President Ford's oil decontrol veto [Sept. 10, 1975]."

According to many Senate observers, Bentsen's office is one of the most efficient in the Senate. After his election, Bentsen hired a management consultant firm to review the efficiency of other Senate staffs and to make recommendations for the operation of his own. The result was a detailed organizational manual drawn up to pinpoint the responsibilities of each staff member and guide the management of the office. Bentsen has freely delegated responsibility to his aides, and staff rapport is reportedly good. "It's an excellent operation, no two ways about it," observed a Washington correspondent for a Texas newspaper. A former Bentsen assistant stated that two leading reasons for the office's successful operation are the senator's personal accessibility and managerial expertise: "He has no hesitation to listen to someone normally not in the councils of the office. He's very well organized."

While Bentsen has won praise as an intelligent, well-organized senator who does his homework, he has neither sought nor attracted much public attention. He has allied himself with the Democratic leadership of the Senate, gaining compliments from Majority Leader Mike Mansfield (Mont.) as a man of presidential stature. But Bentsen has won few headlines. "He plays close with the leadership and strains to be moderate," said one source. "He's cautious in what he says, careful not to snipe at colleagues or fellow hustlers for the nomination."

Bentsen's legislative specialty is the economy. He is a member of the Finance, Public Works and Joint Economic Committees and chairs a subcommittee of each. His first extensive national media exposure was in July 1974, when he was chosen by Senate Democrats to deliver the party's televised rebuttal to President Nixon's economic message. It was a prestigious assignment for a Senate freshman. It gave him a forum in his area of expertise. And it may have given momentum to his presidential aspirations.

Positions on Issues

Following is a summary of the positions taken by Bentsen on some major issues since he has been in Congress:

Economy

Bentsen's economic proposals combine New Deal-type public employment programs with tax reforms to help both business and wage-earners. Bentsen's proposals to revive the economy stress the creation of more jobs. He has proposed the creation of a youth-oriented conservation work program similar to the Civilian Conservation Corps of the 1930s, and the establishment of an employment tax credit. Designed to stimulate hiring in the private sector, the latter proposal would give businesses a 10 per cent tax credit on the first year of every new employee's salary.

To spur greater business investment, Bentsen has proposed several measures to increase the available investment capital: principally, a reduction in the interest rate, a decrease in the capital gains taxes for long-held assets, a 400 per cent increase in allowable capital-loss tax deductions and a 10 per cent investment tax credit. In January 1975, Bentsen introduced the Stockholders Investment Act (S 443), designed to increase competition in the stock

CQ Vote Study Scores*

	1974	1973	1972	1971
Presidential				
support	53¹/18²	44	57	61
opposition	28¹/43²	47	35	37
Voting Participation	74	89	90	89
Party				
unity	48	59	55	57
opposition	32	35	38	36
Conservative Coalition				
support	43	57	56	73
opposition	38	36	34	18
Bipartisan				
support	60	80	80	78
opposition	8	6	9	9

* Explanation of studies, p. 107.
1. During President Nixon's tenure in 1974.
2. During President Ford's tenure in 1974.

market by encouraging the participation of small and medium-sized businesses.

In addition to substantial tax breaks and assists for business, Bentsen has advocated permanent personal income tax cuts totaling $13-billion, and a 20 per cent tax credit for families saving up to $250 yearly for their children's higher education. The tax credit proposal, known as the educational savings plan, was introduced in bill form (S 666) in February 1975.

Bentsen supported the 1975 Tax Reduction Act (PL 94-12), which, in the Senate version, called for a $30-billion tax cut and the repeal of the oil and gas depletion allowance. Both features were modified in a House-Senate conference committee. A permanent depletion allowance exemption for independent oil and gas producers, for which Bentsen had fought, was preserved.

Energy

Bentsen has opposed President Ford's plan to reduce oil imports by one million barrels a day, contending that this would put 500,000 more Americans out of work.

In early 1975, he outlined his own energy plan. It had four basic aspects:

● A rebatable gas tax, starting at 5 cents a gallon in 1976 and increasing to at least 20 cents a gallon four or five years later; tied in would be a reduction in withholding taxes for people of low and middle income.

● An excise tax on bigger cars, coupled with a tax credit for automobiles with good gas mileage.

● The creation of an energy development bank to guarantee loans for developing new energy sources.

● A five-year tax amortization for converting industries from oil to coal.

National Defense

When Bentsen entered the Senate in 1971 he was assigned to the Armed Services Committee. He was expected by many Washington observers to be one of the Nixon administration's regular supporters on defense issues. But in 1972, Bentsen led the unsuccessful Senate fight against the accelerated construction and deployment of the Trident submarine.

Although far from an opponent of the defense establishment, Bentsen has said that the American military could be run more efficiently for less money. In 1973, he cosponsored legislation to create a Defense Manpower Commission designed to eliminate waste.

Foreign Policy

Bentsen has been a strong proponent of increased congressional involvement in foreign policy. In both the 93rd and 94th Congresses, he sponsored bills (S 1472, S 632) requiring the submission of executive agreements to Congress for approval. In 1973, he cosponsored the War Powers Act (PL 93-148), which limited authority to commit U.S. forces abroad without congressional approval.

While asserting that he favors detente, Bentsen has taken a hard line toward the Soviets. He suggested that Ford not attend the summit meeting in July 1975 unless the Soviets promised to comply with the principles of the Helsinki agreement, which prohibits interference in the internal affairs of other nations, and Bentsen charged that there was a possibility that the Soviets were providing financial assistance to Communists in Portugal's civil disturbances.

Bentsen Staff, Advisers

Campaign director: Bob Healy, a former legislative assistant and speechwriter for Sen. Hubert H. Humphrey (D Minn.) and an aide to Bentsen while chairman of Democratic Senatorial Campaign Committee in 1974.

Associate campaign director and director of organization: Ron Platt, a native of Oklahoma who was executive assistant to former Virginia Lt. Gov. J. Sargeant Reynolds (D 1970-71) and a campaign consultant before joining Bentsen in January 1975.

Finance director: George L. Bristol, deputy treasurer of the Democratic National Committee from 1969 to 1972. In private business in Dallas before joining Bentsen as executive assistant in Austin office in 1974.

Administrative assistant: Gary Bushell, a lawyer who served on the staff of the Federal Power Commission before joining the Bentsen Senate staff in 1972.

Senate press secretary: Jack Devore, a veteran El Paso, Texas, television-radio newsman who joined the Bentsen Senate staff in 1972.

Bentsen's dissatisfaction with administration foreign policy has centered on Secretary of State Henry A. Kissinger, who Bentsen feels exercises too much power. In February 1975, Bentsen described U.S. foreign policy as "dangerously constricted...with an undemocratic emphasis on secret diplomacy, personal negotiations and one-man authoritarianism." In May, he introduced a bill (S 1667) to prohibit one person from simultaneously holding the positions of secretary of state and assistant to the President for national security affairs—dual roles held by Kissinger.

Other Issues

Pension reform: Bentsen considers one of the highlights of his legislative career to be his sponsorship in 1973 and 1974 of a pension reform law (PL 93-406). Bentsen's initial bill was worked into the final version, which established federal standards for private plans.

Transportation: Bentsen is chairman of the Public Works Subcommittee on Transportation. In 1973, he was Senate floor manager of the $20-billion Federal Aid Highway Act (PL 93-87).

Campaign reform: The Texan introduced an amendment to the campaign finance reform bill in 1973, setting a $3,000 limit on individual contributions to a single presidential candidate during each primary and general election campaign. The bill passed the Senate but not the House. When the Federal Election Campaign Act (PL 93-443) became law the next year, a Bentsen amendment was included banning contributions by foreign nations. But the new bill reduced the individual contribution ceiling to $1,000 per election. Bentsen voted for most of the public financing provisions of the bill.

Crime: In July, Bentsen introduced a bill (S 2151) prohibiting possession of a handgun by anyone previously convicted and drawing more than a one-year sentence for a crime involving a handgun. However, Bentsen has opposed tighter gun-control legislation, instead favoring stricter punishment and faster trials for criminals.

Civil Rights: He has opposed school busing. In August, he voted for a seven-year extension of the Voting Rights Act with expanded protection for Spanish-speaking and other language minorities.

—By Rhodes Cook

TRANSLATING CHARM, DETERMINATION INTO VOTES

It is a long way from Plains, Ga., to the White House, but former Georgia Gov. Jimmy Carter (D 1971-75) insists he can make it. The 51-year-old Carter announced his candidacy for the 1976 Democratic presidential nomination Dec. 12, 1974, unveiling his campaign slogan: "For America's third century, why not our best?"

Since his term as governor ended in January 1975, Carter has been on the road campaigning nearly full-time. His tentative plans called for 250 days of campaign travel in 1975, and his spokesmen in Atlanta said he would surpass that goal by a wide margin. In an article in *The New York Times* Sept. 5, Carter said he had been in 42 states and more than 200 cities and towns so far.

People who have seen Carter stumping give him good marks for personal charm, moral fervor and determination. He will need all the assets he can muster. An October Gallup Poll said that nearly three-fourths of the voters had never heard of Jimmy Carter and that he could claim the support of less than 3 per cent of the nation's Democrats. The key question is whether his determination will translate into votes.

Simple Strategy

His strategy for rising from nowhere in the polls to the Democratic nomination, as George McGovern did in 1972, is fairly simple—exploit what strengths he has and try to turn weaknesses into advantages. Thus the fact that he is out of office gives him an opportunity to be a full-time candidate; his lack of Washington experience gives him a chance to run against federal incompetence; the small audiences he has been speaking to allow him to use his talents for one-to-one campaigning; his low name recognition permits him to construct a campaign image of his own choosing.

In terms of winning delegates, Carter has devoted a lot of attention to the states which hold early caucuses and to the early primaries in New Hampshire and Florida.

Probably the biggest encouragement to his struggling campaign occurred in Iowa, whose Jan. 19 precinct caucuses, starting the process of selecting the state's 47 delegates to the Democratic national convention, are the first in the nation. Carter was one of seven Democratic presidential aspirants who spoke at a Jefferson-Jackson dinner in October at Ames, Iowa.

His active campaigning in the state paid off, to the surprise of many, in a survey conducted by *The Des Moines Register* of those attending the dinner. Among the 1,094 persons surveyed, Carter led the Democratic field with 23 per cent. His closest rival was a man who was not even a candidate, Minnesota Sen. Hubert H. Humphrey, who had a distant 12 per cent.

In addition to Iowa, Carter is said to be developing unexpected strength in New Hampshire, where the country's first primary will be held Feb. 24. Reports from Florida say he is doing well there, too, but not yet well enough to beat Democratic Gov. George C. Wallace of Alabama.

Finances

Hamilton Jordan, Carter's campaign manager, says Carter expects to meet his fund-raising goal of $750,000 for 1975. According to the Oct. 10 filings with the Federal Election Commission (covering the period Jan. 1-Sept. 30), Carter had raised $504,587 and spent $506,518. Since he became a candidate, he had raised $551,300, spent $536,800 and had a net balance (allowing for cash-in-hand, unpaid debts and pledges outstanding) of about $15,000. Carter said Aug. 14 that he had qualified for federal matching funds in 1976 by raising the requisite $5,000 in 20 states through contributions of $250 or less. He was one of the candidates offered Secret Service protection on the basis of having met the public financing threshold.

At the start of his campaign, Carter said he would not accept contributions larger than $1,000 from individuals, although bigger contributions were permissible under the federal campaign finance law until Jan. 1, 1975. He criticized other candidates for accepting large contributions before the deadline. According to the election commission filings, Carter has had few large contributors and has received little special-interest money.

Prospects

Jordan admits that if Carter does not win in the early going, he could be out of the race as early as April. "If we lose, we have no success story to sell," he said.

If, on the other hand, Carter is successful in the initial primaries, Jordan believes the momentum will carry the ex-governor through the rest of the primaries. "We are not trying to pick up delegate support for a brokered convention," he said. "Our strategy is based on winning the nomination."

By conventional standards, Carter has to be regarded as a long shot. But few of his opponents have more than a toehold either. In an October 1975 Gallup Poll, Carter was one of several candidates who was the first choice for the Democratic nomination among less than 3 per cent of those surveyed.

Carter's effort is attuned to some of the nation's post-Vietnam, post-Watergate and post-oil-embargo moods. A centrist candidate divorced from the Washington establishment could win some support, he reckons.

The former governor has impressed people who have met him in face-to-face situations, and has been able to win the support of people who do not fully agree with him on issues. For instance, an influential midwestern Democrat who planned to back another candidate was sufficiently impressed by a meeting with Carter that the midwesterner now favors Carter.

Admiration for Carter has not been universal, though. Some political leaders who have had private meetings with him complain that some of his ideas are unrealistic. A prominent New England Democrat who attended such a session thinks that Carter greatly underestimates the influence of interest groups and the bureaucracy in Washington and has failed to realize the extent to which a President must delegate authority.

Carter has recruited sufficient support in the early caucus states to give his campaign the potential for a good start. His cause has been aided in the New Hampshire primary by the prospect of at least a four-way split of votes for more liberal candidates. The presence on the ballot of Washington Sen. Henry M. Jackson, however, is seen as a threat to Carter's chances in New Hampshire.

Florida's March 9 primary remains the critical test for the Georgian. He has to put a dent in George Wallace's vote there. Texas Sen. Lloyd Bentsen has dropped out of the Florida race, giving Carter a clear shot at Wallace.

Carter's Staff, Advisers

Campaign director: Hamilton Jordan, formerly with the International Voluntary Service in Vietnam, former executive secretary to Gov. Carter and director of the Democratic National Committee's 1974 campaign committee.

Deputy campaign director: Marc Cutright, a former aide to Jordan on the campaign committee.

Fund-raising director: Frank Moore, a former executive secretary to the governor and former executive secretary of the Middle Flint (Georgia) Area Planning and Development Authority.

News media coordinator: Jody Powell, formerly Carter's gubernatorial press secretary.

Delegate selection coordinator: Rick Hutcheson, formerly with the Democratic National Committee.

Issues coordinator: Steve Stark, a former reporter for *The Boston Globe.*

Nevertheless, Wallace remains the front-runner in the Florida primary. For that matter, Wallace is given a good chance of overturning Carter in the Georgia primary.

Success against Wallace could make Carter an attractive choice as the Democratic vice presidential candidate. But to win the top spot, he will have to show a broad national appeal. He does not seem to be particularly strong in northern and western states, and his prospects for success in the key late primaries appear to rest on whatever momentum he can generate in the early going.

None of this appears to have shaken Carter's confidence. He continues to deny any interest in the vice presidency and continues to predict victory. "I'm going to run in every primary, and I'm going to win," he told one interviewer. And Jack Germond of *The Washington Star* reported: "Carter gives the impression that the only decisions still to be made are those about his running mate and his cabinet."

The Wallace Problem

Despite all this ebullience, Carter—and other southern candidates as well—has to live with one stark fact: He has no chance to win the Democratic presidential nomination unless he can beat Wallace in the South. Carter has denied that his strategy is directed specifically at Wallace.

Carter also denies that there has been any change in his attitudes about the Alabama governor. But some newsmen and political figures felt that Carter tried to align himself with Wallace during the 1970 gubernatorial campaign in Georgia, and throughout the 1972 presidential campaign he kept warning other Democrats that the party had to pay attention to Wallace. Now Carter emphasizes that he has never endorsed George Wallace and is portraying himself as a moderate southern alternative.

One distinction he makes is on civil rights. Carter has been endorsed in his presidential campaign by Rep. Andrew Young (D Ga.), one of the principal black political leaders in Georgia. Carter also has the endorsement of the Rev. Martin Luther King Sr., an Atlanta minister and father of the late civil rights leader.

This new-found popularity among black leaders in contrast to Carter's overwhelming lack of support in 1970 is attributed to a number of factors, some symbolic and some substantive. In the former category are his inaugural address as governor in 1971 and his decision to hang a portrait of Martin Luther King Jr. in the capitol. In the substantive category are his social service budget increases and his appointment of blacks to state jobs.

Carter incorporated his inaugural "the time for racial discrimination is over" passage into his presidential announcement declaration, and he defines his position on civil rights as moderate to liberal. But he has consistently opposed forced busing. One reason he has the support of Atlanta black leaders is that his position on busing is not a problem for them. They back the so-called "Atlanta plan" under which blacks have pushed for the appointment of blacks to key administrative positions in the Atlanta school system rather than for busing.

Black support for Carter is not unqualified. An aide to Young noted that the representative was backing Carter as the best southern alternative to Wallace. If circumstances change, so could Young's view.

Personal Background

Carter often is referred to as a "peanut farmer and nuclear physicist"—an intriguing description, but not an entirely accurate one. The family's enterprises in Plains include warehouses, a peanut-shelling plant and a cotton gin in addition to the peanut farm. He is as much an executive as a farmer.

His connection with nuclear physics came in his Navy days, when he was assigned to Admiral Hyman G. Rickover's atomic submarine program. He did graduate work at Union College, but did not get a degree.

Carter was the pre-commission commander of the U.S.S. *Sea Wolf,* the nation's second nuclear sub. He resigned from active duty in 1953 because of his father's death, returned home and built the family farm into the prosperous business it now is.

He was active in community affairs and politics. He served as chairman of the school board, was a church deacon and gained some local notoriety by refusing to join the segregationist White Citizens Council.

He was elected to the Georgia State Senate in 1962 and was re-elected in 1964. As a legislator, he was considered a moderate in the mold of Gov. Carl E. Sanders (D 1963-67).

1966 Race

Carter ran for governor in 1966, joining a crowded field of Democrats hoping to succeed Sanders, who was ineligible to run. (The Georgia constitution bars governors from serving consecutive terms.)

Historically, former Georgia governors have not had much success regaining their office later. Nevertheless, two former governors had entered the 1966 race and were considered the front-runners—Ernest Vandiver (D 1959-63) and Ellis Arnall (D 1943-47). Vandiver had to drop out after suffering a heart attack. That made Arnall the early favorite in the Democratic race. Also running was Atlanta restaurant owner Lester G. Maddox, a militant segregationist who had received national publicity for closing his restaurant rather than serve blacks.

Carter's themes of fiscal caution, governmental restructuring and planning have been essential elements of his political platform in subsequent campaigns, including his presidential effort.

The 1966 campaign also established Carter's willingness to spend long hours stumping for votes. Although Carter was not given much chance at the outset, his intensive efforts yielded him a strong third place in the Democratic primary—50,000 votes behind Arnall, who was first, but only 6,000 behind Maddox, who was second. Maddox went on to become governor.

1970 Race

With Maddox unable to succeed himself and forced to run for lieutenant governor (he won), the 1970 gubernatorial race was expected to be a battle between two moderates—Carter and former Gov. Sanders—in marked contrast to the 1966 election. Sanders was given an edge by most observers. Private polls gave the former governor a substantial lead but also indicated that Carter was rapidly closing the gap.

The 1970 campaign was one of the most controversial chapters of Carter's political history. Carter had been expected to position himself slightly to the right of Sanders in order to capture some of the state's conservative voters. Precisely how far he went to the right has been a subject of dispute ever since.

His supporters describe his effort as a "populist" campaign. Carter portrayed himself as the candidate of Georgia's working class and Sanders as a tool of Atlanta

---

business interests. He charged that Sanders, who was a prosperous attorney in Augusta, had enriched himself while governor. Carter called Sanders "Cufflinks Carl" and challenged him to disclose his personal finances. Sanders declined to do so for most of the campaign, not relenting until the race was already lost.

Carter spoke out against federally imposed school desegregation plans and busing. He conceded the black vote to Sanders (who won an estimated 95 per cent of it) and concentrated instead on winning the votes of Maddox supporters.

Carter's critics assert that he constructed an artificial image for himself during the campaign which made him appear to be much further to Sanders' right than was actually the case. The critics say that once Carter was sworn into office, he promptly discarded his campaign image and sought to portray himself as a moderate, progressive, businesslike, "New South" governor.

In the primary, Carter received 48.6 per cent of the vote to 37.7 per cent for Sanders, almost enough to avoid a runoff. Carter won the runoff with 59.3 per cent of the vote to 40.7 for Sanders, and then went on to defeat Republican Hal Suit, an Atlanta broadcaster, 59.3 per cent to 40.6 per cent.

The Governorship

Carter's inaugural address Jan. 12, 1971, included this passage: "I say to you quite frankly, the time for racial discrimination is over. Our people have made this major and difficult decision, but we cannot underestimate the challenge of hundreds of minor decisions yet to be made. No poor, rural, weak or black person should ever have to bear the burden of being deprived of the opportunity of an education, a job or simple justice."

The statement made Carter the subject of a number of national news stories about "New South" political trends. It also marked the beginning of the end for Carter's detente with Lt. Gov. Maddox. The two nominally had run together, but Maddox rapidly became one of Carter's major foes in the state legislature.

Carter lists his executive reorganization program and his reform of budgeting techniques as his main achievements as governor. Under the reorganization plan, 300 state agencies, boards, commissions and departments were consolidated into 22 major agencies. Carter invested a great deal of political capital in the effort to push the measure through the legislature. In the end, he did get a large majority of his plans approved, although the legislature eventually repealed the governor's power to reorganize by executive order.

Carter claims that reorganization, budgeting reforms and other economy measures have saved Georgia $50-million a year. The figure is difficult to document, because it represents reductions in projected spending increases rather than actual budget declines. The size of the state budget increased during Carter's administration. A budget analysis done by the U.S. Census Bureau supports Carter's claim to have substantially changed Georgia's spending priorities, with increases in social services and corrections.

Spending on natural resources increased from $55-million annually to $70-million. Carter established a Heritage Trust Commission to preserve selected lands and historic sites. He pushed for greater water pollution cleanup efforts and was one of the most vocal protesters among the nation's governors when President Nixon impounded federal pollution control grants.

Significant budget increases also were recorded for education, highway construction, welfare and hospitals. A report by his office on his four years as governor—"A State In Action"—lists special education, vocational education, mental retardation, drug treatment and enforcement and economic development as areas in which his administration made gains.

On the other hand, some major Carter initiatives were unsuccessful. He was unable to get a consumer protection bill or a land use bill through the legislature. Carter's supporters say he lost the battles he did "for the right reasons"—because he did not bow to special-interest groups or the statehouse establishment. However, some observers note that Carter's propensity to be a political loner eventually eroded his effectiveness as governor.

There were no major scandals during his administration, but there were charges that he had not entirely followed through on his reorganization plans and had created some administrative nightmares. His Department of Human Resources (the umbrella health and welfare department) was a particular target for complaint.

1972 and 1974 Elections

Carter was a prominent figure in the 1972 pre-convention "ABM" (anybody but McGovern) movement. He said the South Dakota senator would be a disaster in the South if he were the Democratic nominee. Carter insists, however, that he worked for McGovern after the senator was nominated. Carter now has the support of a number of former McGovern backers in New Hampshire and other states.

Democratic National Chairman Robert S. Strauss named Carter the party's national campaign coordinator for the 1974 midterm election. The job gave Carter the opportunity to make appearances in about 30 states and to get acquainted with their Democratic leaders.

Another national involvement for Carter was his appointment to a citizens advisory committee to the U.S. delegation for the U.N. World Environmental Conference in 1972. He attracted some national attention in 1973 as a critic of the Nixon administration's revenue-sharing program, which he called a "hoax" intended to hide over-all cutbacks in federal aid to the states. He also attacked White House aide John D. Ehrlichman, then head of Nixon's Domestic Council, for failing to respond to Carter's request for an appointment to discuss the issue.

Positions on Issues

Hamilton Jordan concedes that Carter's policy statements in the 1976 campaign sometimes have been vague on details. The details, says the campaign manager, "can wait until we get into the White House.... Realistically, all a candidate can talk about now is his thoughts, ideas and attitudes." The campaign manager points out, however, that Carter has begun to release a series of major statements on issues.

Carter concentrates on selling himself rather than on issues. He has tried to place himself in the philosophical center of the Democratic candidates, running in effect as the most conservative of the liberals.

He has gone to joint candidate appearances sponsored by liberal organizations, but has been the dissenting voice among the candidates on some symbolic liberal-conservative issues. He opposes federal aid to New York City, for example, and recently said so in New York.

Efficiency, Integrity

Government efficiency and political integrity have been major themes of Carter's campaign. He has talked about applying to the federal government the reorganization and budgeting concepts he pushed in Georgia. He also has called for strict conflict-of-interest laws, an all-inclusive federal "sunshine" law, public financing of congressional campaigns and tougher lobbying laws.

Defense, Foreign Policy

Carter cites his trips abroad and his service under Admiral Rickover as having given him experience in foreign affairs and defense policy. He has said the United States must reduce its commitments abroad and be wary of future Vietnams and of being allied with repressive governments.

He also says that economic matters may become a dominant factor in international relationships, and has called for closer ties with our allies in Europe, Japan and Canada. Carter is against any U.S. military role in the Middle East and favors improved relations with Arab governments as well as Israel.

He has opposed the proliferation of nuclear weapons and has said the goal of the United States and the Soviet Union "should be the reduction of nuclear weapons in all nations to zero." He has said he believes substantial cuts can be made in the defense budget by eliminating waste.

Reform, Energy, Economics

In domestic policy, Carter advocates tax reform, welfare reform and regulatory agency reform. He has called unemployment "the number one problem facing this country today," and has been critical of the administration's economic and energy policies.

He favors oil import quotas, federal allocation, conservation and more use of coal to deal with the energy situation. He has not been especially specific about how he would implement his energy policy, however, and has talked about seeking voluntary cooperation before resorting to federal edict.

His economic policies have been similarly general. He has not committed himself one way or another on the question of running higher federal budget deficits in order to stimulate the economy, or on the issue of corporate tax cuts to promote capital formation.

—*By Al Gordon*

AN '80 PER CENT CERTAINTY' OF RUNNING

The prospective presidential candidacy of Idaho's Democratic Sen. Frank Church depended on the conclusion of his committee's investigation of the Central Intelligence Agency (CIA). Often mentioned by liberals as a potential nominee, Church was expected to make a final decision in late December or early January.

Church had told aides early in 1975 that he wanted to run, but suspended any plans after he was named in January to head the Select Committee on Governmental Intelligence Gathering Activities. "He didn't want to blow his biggest assignment yet in the Senate," press aide Bill Hall told Congressional Quarterly.

If Church announced, he would have a constituency of sorts waiting for him. A number of liberals who looked first to Massachusetts Sen. Edward M. Kennedy to lead the party and have since been hunting for a candidate have urged him strongly to run. They feel he can provide the moral fervor and inspiration the other candidates have lacked.

Church's approach to a final decision on entering the race, knowledgeable observers told CQ, would be cautious and pragmatic. One important factor he reportedly would consider would be whether any of the other liberal candidates had succeeded in pre-empting that wing of the party.

"He has the desire to run, but he also has such good judgment that if he thought it wouldn't work he wouldn't get into it," said Carl Burke, a Boise lawyer who probably would manage any Church presidential campaign. Burke ran Church's four Idaho Senate races.

Hall told CQ: "It's about 80 per cent certain he'll go."

If Church does contest the nomination, his major strengths will come from his legislative record in the Senate, where he is serving his fourth term. Only 51 years old, he is already one of that body's senior Democrats and occupies key seats on committees that influence national policy in a wide variety of fields. Besides chairing the CIA

probe, Church heads the Select Committee on Aging and cochairs (with Maryland Republican Charles McC. Mathias Jr.) the Special Committee on National Emergencies and Delegated Emergency Powers. Church is the third-ranking Democrat on Foreign Relations and second-ranking on Interior and Insular Affairs, which is important to his electoral security in Idaho.

But, as Majority Leader Lyndon B. Johnson's abortive quest for the nomination in 1960 demonstrated, influence in the Senate does not translate into primary votes and convention delegates without an active campaign and a well-tooled organization. And it is in precisely these areas that a late-blooming Church effort could have difficulty getting off the ground. He would have to begin fund-raising with the primaries just two months away and when other candidates would be receiving their first federal matching contributions.

Political Career

One of Church's earliest interests, which later proved useful in politics, was debating. He built up his skills in high school in his hometown of Boise, Idaho, where his father operated a sporting goods store. In his third year at Boise High, Frank won the American Legion national oratorical contest. He used the $4,000 prize to attend Stanford University.

In 1948, while studying law at Harvard, Church became seriously ill with what was later diagnosed as cancer. The prognosis was grave, but radical surgery and an intensive series of X-ray treatments resulted in a complete

Church's Background

Profession: Attorney.
Born: July 25, 1924, Boise, Idaho.
Home: Boise.
Religion: Presbyterian.
Education: Stanford University, A.B., 1947; LL.B., 1950.
Offices: Senate since 1957.
Military: Army, 1942-46; discharged as 1st lieutenant; Bronze Star.
Memberships: American Legion, VFW, Phi Beta Kappa, Mayflower Society, American Bar Association.
Family: Wife, Bethine Clark; two children.
Committees: Foreign Relations: chairman, Subcommittee on Multi-national Corporations; Interior: chairman, Subcommittee on Energy Research and Water Resources; chairman, Special Committee on Aging; chairman, Subcommittee on Consumer Interests of the Elderly; chairman, Select Committee on Governmental Intelligence Gathering Activities; cochairman, Special Committee on National Emergencies and Delegated Emergency Powers.

Congressional Quarterly Vote Study Scores...

	1974	1973	1972	1971	1970	1969	1968	1967	1966
Presidential									
support	27¹/25²	28	28	33	41	44	29	53	46
opposition	47¹/56²	59	63	50	41	44	29	31	17
Voting Participation	71	85	85	81	76	91	54	81	65
Party									
unity	58	81	76	81	65	79	32	58	54
opposition	13	7	7	7	5	11	21	28	13
Conservative Coalition									
support	14	11	13	12	14	14	24	16	20
opposition	55	82	72	71	58	77	24	64	57
Bipartisan									
support	59	74	74	56	67	75	47	64	51
opposition	11	9	12	19	12	17	8	15	12

1. During President Nixon's tenure in 1974.
2. During President Ford's tenure in 1974.

cure. He recovered in time to receive a law degree from Stanford in 1950.

Returning to Idaho, Church briefly taught public speaking before taking a job as legal counsel for the Idaho Office of Price Stabilization. From 1951 to 1956, he practiced law in Boise, taking time out for periodic forays into local politics. From 1952 to 1954, Church was state president of the Idaho Young Democratic Clubs. He keynoted the 1952 state Democratic convention. The same year, he sought elective office for the first time, running for the Idaho House of Representatives; he was defeated by about 12,000 votes.

Senate Victory

In 1956, Church set his sights on national office and took on Republican Sen. Herman Welker, who was seeking a second term. Welker had a conservative voting record and had been a strong defender of Sen. Joseph McCarthy (R Wis. 1947-57).

A political unknown outside Boise, Church began an extensive series of automobile trips to increase his visibility around the state. His travels paid off with a Democratic primary victory over former Sen. Glen H. Taylor (D 1945-51). Taylor was an entertainer, a former singer and one of the most colorful figures in Idaho politics. But his campaign for Vice President in 1948 on the ticket of Progressive Party nominee Henry Wallace made him anathema to Idaho Democrats, who dumped him in the 1950 primary. He became the party's Senate nominee again in 1954, but lost overwhelmingly.

The 1956 primary campaign was bitter, with Taylor accusing Church of being a "captive candidate of corporation politicians." In disputed returns, the political newcomer won the Democratic nomination by 200 votes. Taylor refused to accept the result and sought evidence of fraud or error in the tally, meanwhile preparing for an independent campaign for the seat.

In the general election, Church effectively attacked Welker's conservative voting record and opposition to the proposed Hells Canyon dam. Other major issues were development of industry in Idaho, reclamation projects for desert lands and aid to the aged. Welker had won only a minority of the vote in the Republican Senate primary, and his belated attempts to portray himself as a moderate Eisenhower Republican failed to convince party loyalists.

On election day, the voters split their tickets in record numbers as Church won with a 46,315-vote plurality, even though President Eisenhower was carrying Idaho. Church became, at 32, the Senate's youngest member.

Church's initial Senate committee assignments were modest ones—Post Office and Civil Service, Interior and Insular Affairs and Public Works. He gave up the Post Office and Public Works positions in 1959 in a move to the more prestigious Foreign Relations Committee, an honor for such a junior member.

But the post on the Interior Committee, which has jurisdiction over federal lands, mining, water policy and other issues vital to Idaho, was the forum Church used for strengthening himself politically during his early years in the Senate. His maiden speech, six months after taking office, was a detailed and impassioned plea for federal construction of the Hells Canyon dam.

In 1962, Church won favorable publicity back home for his defense of Bruces Eddy, a $186-million dam project on the Clearwater River in Idaho. He fought for it strongly in the Senate, only to see it threatened in conference as House conferees sought to delete funds from an appropriations bill. To discourage them, Church threatened to tie up the entire bill in a filibuster. "If they strike out Bruces Eddy," he warned, "I shall hold the Senate floor as long as God gives me the strength to stand."

Keynoter

Because of his speaking ability and the party's desire to show off a promising newcomer, Church was chosen as the keynoter of the 1960 Democratic national convention. It was his first national exposure, and he planned carefully for it. Before the convention, Church informed reporters

. . . Covering 18 of Church's years in Senate†

	1965	1964	1963	1962	1961	1960	1959	1958	1957
Presidential									
support	55	63	69	62	77	48	33	50	63
opposition	16	24	15	18	18	43	45	42	26
Voting Participation	69	91	85	78	94	90	79	92	88
Party									
unity	58	71	80	66	79	78	69	89	61
opposition	9	22	8	12	13	13	10	5	21
Conservative Coalition									
support	11	22	19	24	26	13	12	*	*
opposition	46	73	70	68	63	70	55	*	*
Bipartisan									
support	54	59	70	64	83	81	72	81	81
opposition	15	25	12	13	12	9	7	10	10

† Explanation of studies, p. 107.
* No ratings in those years.

that he would deliver "a fighting speech directed at the appalling failures of the Republican administration, at home and abroad."

The speech itself, however, demonstrated a potential weakness in Church's speaking skills—a capacity for verbal overkill and rhetorical flourishes at the expense of substance. It did not live up to advance expectations. Recalling it in a 1975 interview, Church said that "all I can say in my defense is—I didn't know any better."

Later Campaigns

In 1962, Church faced his most serious electoral threat in Idaho from Republican Jack Hawley, the same candidate who had beaten him in 1952 in the state house race. Hawley employed the themes Republicans were to use repeatedly and unsuccessfully against Church in future elections—that he did not care about local problems and was too involved in foreign affairs. But Church defeated Hawley with almost 55 per cent of the vote and became the first Democrat ever re-elected to the Senate from Idaho.

His races in 1968 and 1974 were easier, as his seniority grew more important to Idaho and Republicans had increasing difficulty finding strong candidates to run against him. In 1967, as he was preparing to run for a third term, Church faced a bizarre "recall" petition campaign supported by extreme conservatives incensed over his dovish views on the war. Even though members of the Senate cannot be voted out of office before the end of their terms, the organizers thought the effort would help mobilize opposition to Church for the benefit of a conservative candidate. But it had just the opposite effect, garnering sympathy for the senator and bringing in campaign funds and support from around the nation. The recall bid collapsed quickly after it was discovered that it was financed by a right-wing California millionaire.

In 1968, the Republican nominee was Rep. George V. Hansen (R Idaho 1965-69, 1975-), who based his campaign on accusations that Church was giving aid to the North Vietnamese through his votes in the Senate. The effort proved much too shrill for Idaho voters, who re-elected Church by 59,000 votes, the largest margin received by an Idaho senator except for Republican William E. Borah in 1924.

Church's fourth-term victory in 1974 was by a more modest 36,068 votes over Bob Smith, a former aide to Rep. Steven D. Symms (R Idaho), who campaigned on the general theme of opposition to "big government."

Senate Record

Idaho voters have allowed their senators to pursue a broad range of interests—so long as local problems receive prompt attention. Church has been able to take advantage of this freedom to exert influence in many policy areas.

Foreign Affairs

His best-known work in the Senate has been in foreign affairs, which had been the special interest of his old idol, Borah, one of the leading isolationists of the 1920s. A major reason for Church's influence is his seniority on the Foreign Relations Committee.

Church has been consistently skeptical about the effectiveness of the foreign aid program and has frequently offered amendments to reduce or restrict the scope of authorizations or appropriations. His activity in this area has caused him no problems in fiscally conservative Idaho.

Church's views on most foreign policy issues have been broadly internationalist. He was a strong supporter of the 1963 nuclear test ban treaty with the Soviet Union and advocated strengthening American ties with the North Atlantic Treaty Organization.

Church has favored use of American military power in specific instances in which he thought the national interest was clearly at stake, but he has argued for regular re-examination of foreign policy and against excessive commitments abroad. He voted for the 1964 Gulf of Tonkin Resolution authorizing President Johnson to take action against the North Vietnamese and made a speech in favor of the 1965 U.S. intervention in the Dominican Republic. He voted for funds for military operations in South Vietnam in 1965, but cautioned that his vote could not be construed as support for the use of American ground forces.

By 1966, Church had moved into a position of general opposition to Johnson administration policy in South Vietnam. He urged a bombing halt and cautioned the President against over-extending American commitment to the Saigon regime. "No nation—not even our own—possesses an arsenal so large, or a treasury so rich, as to damp down the fires of smoldering revolution throughout the whole of the awakening world," he said.

During the Nixon administration, Church was a cosponsor of the most significant anti-war amendments of the period.

In 1970, he and Sen. John Sherman Cooper (R Ky.) sponsored an amendment to prohibit the continued deployment of U.S. ground troops in Cambodia. Introduced in the wake of the invasion of Cambodia by U.S. troops, the amendment touched off a six-month debate over whether Congress could use its budget authority to limit the President's war-making powers. It finally became law in revised form late that year.

In 1972, an amendment by Church and Sen. Clifford P. Case (R N.J.) was the vehicle for an attempt to terminate American military activities throughout Southeast Asia. It was defeated after intensive debate. Both proposals, however, identified Church with the anti-war movement and gained him wide respect among liberals.

The Aged

As chairman of the Select Committee on Aging since 1971, Church has been active in the Senate on behalf of senior citizens. Although the committee does not have the authority to report legislation, it conducts investigations and makes recommendations. Church has played a significant role in pushing through legislation extending Social Security and Medicaid benefits and keeping them in step with increases in the cost of living.

Investigations

Church's principal efforts on Foreign Relations in the past three years have been as chairman of the Multinational Corporations Subcommittee, which was created in 1972. In 1973, Church conducted widely publicized hearings into the role of the CIA in its efforts to block the election of Marxist Salvador Allende as president of Chile. The subcommittee called for a more active oversight role by Congress in supervising the CIA. Church's performance in the hearings reportedly was a factor in his being considered for the chairmanship of the 1975 Senate CIA probe.

Church Staff, Advisers

Administrative assistant: Michael Wetherell.
Press secretary: Bill Hall.
Counsel, Foreign Relations Subcommittee on Multinational Corporations: Jerome I. Levinson.
Staff director, Special Committee on Aging: William E. Oriol.
Staff assistant, Interior Subcommittee on Energy Research and Water Resources: Ben Yamagata.
Political adviser: Carl Burke, Boise attorney and manager of Church's four Senate campaigns.

Church's Interest-Group Ratings

Americans for Democratic Action (ADA)—ADA ratings are based on the number of times a senator voted, was paired for or announced for the ADA position on selected issues.

National Farmers Union (NFU)—NFU ratings are based on the number of times a senator voted, was paired for or announced for the NFU position.

AFL-CIO Committee on Political Education (COPE)—COPE ratings reflect the percentage of the times a senator voted in accordance with or was paired in favor of the COPE position.

Americans for Constitutional Action (ACA)—ACA ratings record the percentage of the times a senator voted in accordance with the ACA position.

Following are Church's ratings since Congressional Quarterly began publishing them in 1960, plus a composite ACA score for 1957-59:

	ADA[1]	COPE[3]	NFU[3]	ACA
1974	71	56	88	23
1973	70	78	100	22
1972	70	80	88	17
1971	93	83	100	17
1970	75[4]	100	100	11
1969	78	90	75	29
1968	43	75	43	68
1967	92	70	100	20
1966	55	75[2]	79	22
1965	88	75[2]	77	22
1964	86	80[2]	68[2]	7
1963	83	80[2]	68[2]	0
1962	75	73[2]	75[2]	4[2]
1961	100	73[2]	75[2]	4[2]
1960	92	80[2]	100[2]	6[5]
1959	77	80[2]	100[2]	6[5]

1. Failure to vote lowers score.
2. Scores listed twice indicate rating compiled for entire Congress.
3. Percentages compiled by CQ from information provided by groups.
4. ADA score includes some votes from December 1969.
5. Score for votes on selected issues since 1957.

In 1974, Church took after the multi-national oil corporations and their Arab clients. He sponsored an amendment to the 1974 trade act requiring the government to gather more information on the foreign activities of the multi-nationals.

Church's conduct of the CIA inquiry has been cautious, an indication of his concern over future legislation that could come out of the probe rather than in using it as a launching pad for the presidency. He compromised with committee Republicans and strove to avoid confrontation with President Ford, but vehemently resisted White House attempts to draw a veil of secrecy around the committee's assassination probe. After Ford juggled personnel in the country's defense and intelligence agencies in November 1975, Church led the opposition to the confirmation of former Rep. George Bush (R Texas 1967-71) as director of the CIA.

—By Matt Pinkus

AGAIN, A THUNDERING 'NEW POPULISM'

The basic issue in 1976 is privilege...whether the government will begin to look after the interests of the average family, or whether it will continue to protect the interests of the super-rich and the giant corporations.

—Fred R. Harris

Fred Harris is not the nation's first populist, but the former senator from Oklahoma (D 1964-73) aims to be its first populist President. Other incarnations of the wealth-and-power redistribution movement have foundered despite the leadership of such inspirational candidates as William Jennings Bryan and Robert LaFollette. Yet Harris, at 45, is convinced that this time the American people are ready for the populist gospel.

The Campaign

For more than a year, he and his political partner, his wife LaDonna, have been patiently cultivating small groups of supporters through their low-budget "people's campaign." The style and substance of the campaign are intertwined in this standard message from Harris: "If you're going to be a citizen President, you ought to be a citizen candidate. That means living the way other people live, and traveling without any staff, or very little of it, to get between you and the people."

That approach reached its apex last summer. For the entire month of August, the Harrises and a skeleton staff traversed the country in a camper bearing the label, "On the Road to the White House." Kicked off by a modestly attended rally in Washington's Lafayette Park, at the door of the White House, the humble caravan logged 6,300 miles and 55 events in 13 states. It paid for itself by passing of the plate (total expense: under $9,000). Meals often were cooked over an open fire, and the staple of the trip was the small towns and small groups of citizens invariably skipped over by the moneyed and jet-borne candidates.

Harris' theory is that the crucial element in this campaign, far more than money or even media attention, is cells of committed supporters. With that in mind, he passes out little green sign-up cards at every kaffeeklatsch and after every speech. Those who sign up (2,500 more did so on the camper trip) are then mailed the campaign newsletter, urged to "reach out" to still other potential supporters and tapped to function as unpaid advance men upon Harris' next foray into their territory.

Such campaign visits are a full-time occupation for Harris. His national campaign coordinator, James Hightower, noted with satisfaction that "we can have Fred 'on the ground' all the time, attending five to seven events a day." The strategy into early 1976 calls for most of that time to be spent in the key primary states of New Hampshire, Massachusetts, New York and Wisconsin, with the early caucuses in Iowa and Mississippi also receiving the candidate's close attention. His rough-hewn technique always invites comparison with his smoother competitors.

The Populist Message

Wherever the campaign takes populist lawyer Harris, his earthy, hard-hitting rhetoric pounds home the same theme. The core of his populist appeal is the attack on aggregated, maldistributed wealth and power in a society that aspires to be democratic. He upbraids the individual rich, but his real fire is aimed at the giant corporations, with their intricate, pervasive economic advantages over the "little man." His stance on virtually all specific issues flows from that prime position. As Harris warned in his third and most recent book advocating his views, *The New Populism*, "Unless we are willing to deal with the underlying evils of concentrated economic power, everything else is a snare and a delusion."

Harris is hardly reluctant to spell out the specific implications of his attack on aggregated economic power. Among other things, it means:

● Tax reform—"getting the rich off welfare," as Harris calls it. This includes the elimination of such provisions as the accelerated depreciation of business capital investments and special treatment of capital gains, passage of a more steeply graduated income tax and enactment of a tougher minimum income tax to thwart those rich who pay little or no taxes under existing law.

● A Jeffersonian antitrust policy, coupling tough enforcement to break up monopolies and oligopolies (Harris calls them "shared monopolies") with legislation to aid small businesses.

• Guaranteed public employment where private work is unavailable, "a job as a personal, enforceable right." For those who cannot work, a negative income tax would provide income maintenance.

• Placement of the federal reserve system under public control through effective congressional oversight.

• The requirement of federal charters for, hence greater federal control over, corporations doing business in interstate commerce.

• Regulatory reform, including abolition of the Interstate Commerce Commission and the Civil Aeronautics Board, aimed at eliminating government-sanctioned, inflation-inducing monopolies.

• Elimination of complex subsidies to agribusiness corporations, and an explicit policy of support for the renascence of the small farmer.

Serving Self-interest

Harris' positions on complex economic issues sometimes defy categorization. Some, such as taxpayer-supported public service employment and regulatory reforms, have been endorsed by some conservatives. Yet the majority of the planks in Harris' economic platform are, in traditional terms, liberal or even radical.

His record on race relations appears unequivocal. His wife, LaDonna Crawford Harris, is a Comanche Indian who takes pride in recalling that Comanche was the primary language spoken in her home. Harris helped establish the Oklahoma Human Rights Commission. His work on the National Advisory Commission on Civil Disorders (the Kerner Commission) in 1967 was firm in its focus on white racism as the root cause of black urban riots. His Senate record on civil rights was one of solid support for minorities. As Democratic national chairman from January 1969 to March 1970, he led the way in opening up the party to women and racial minorities.

Despite these well-defined and long-held liberal positions, Harris is vocal in his desire to reach those voters inclined toward Alabama Gov. George C. Wallace. He has stated that "I believe I can appeal to the same people Wallace does, and I'm the only one with a serious chance to be nominated who can." That apparent, dramatic inconsistency is bluntly addressed by Harris. Both in his *The New Populism* and in his campaign talk he declares that "self-interest" has to be the basis of the populist coalition he envisions.

"You can't appeal to black people and poor people on the basis of their own self-interest and to everybody else on the basis of morality," he wrote. "That kind of appeal is the luxury of the intellectual elite.... The basis of the coalition must be self-interest. Those in the coalition don't have to love one another...all they have to do is recognize that they are commonly exploited, and that if they get themselves together they are a popular majority and can take back the government."

He is not the favorite of the Democratic Party's left wing standing alone. For some on the left, he is in fact too radical in his proposals; for others, he is too glib and simplistic in prescribing remedies for exasperatingly complex problems. Still others may be "closet Harris supporters," as one House aide terms it, but they fear that Harris' strident pitch could spell a second McGovern-style disaster for the party. Only if Harris adds to his share of the fractured left-wing vote by attracting support from the right can Harris emerge from the pack and capture the much-sought momentum needed to win the party nomination. Likewise, only by attracting those voters can Harris quell the fears of Democrats who fear another rejection of the party by its traditional labor supporters.

The New Law's Impact

Both in style and substance, the Harris campaign has to be marked as a renegade operation. It is in stark contrast to Harris' previous abortive run for the presidency in 1971. Despite his denigration then of "rich, manipulative advertising campaigns," his six-week campaign was largely just that. He spent over a quarter of a million dollars in that brief period, in what his 1976 campaign manager mocks, in a reference to one authority on presidential contests, as the "Teddy White" approach to presidential politicking: jet around, get media attention, get some big money and parlay all that into more media attention and primary victories.

This time is different, said National Coordinator Hightower, partly because Harris decided to return to a more congenial mode of campaigning. "Fred has run a populist campaign before," said Hightower. "His 1964 Senate race was like this. That time he went to every Oklahoma town with a zip code—and that's some small towns."

Vastly more important in allowing Harris to attempt his "people's campaign," however, is the new federal election campaign financing law and the Federal Election Com-

---

Harris' Interest-Group Ratings

Americans for Democratic Action (ADA)—ADA ratings are based on the number of times a senator voted, was paired for or announced for the ADA position on selected issues.

National Farmers Union (NFU)—NFU ratings are based on the number of times a senator voted, was paired for or announced for the NFU position.

AFL-CIO Committee on Political Education (COPE)—COPE ratings reflect the percentage of the times a senator voted in accordance with or was paired in favor of the COPE position.

Americans for Constitutional Action (ACA)—ACA ratings record the percentage of the times a senator voted in accordance with the ACA position.

Following are Harris' ratings during his years in the Senate:

	ADA[1]	COPE[3]	NFU[3]	ACA
1972	65	100	100	0
1971	63	78	100	17
1970	94[4]	100	100	0
1969	83	100	81	8
1968	57	67	90	0
1967	62	100	80	0
1966	60	75[2]	100	17
1965	76	75[2]	77	25

1. *Failure to vote lowers score.*
2. *Scores listed twice indicate rating compiled for entire Congress.*
3. *Percentages compiled by CQ from information provided by groups.*
4. *ADA score includes some votes from December 1969.*

mission that administers it. That law is the key to the existence of the 1976 Harris campaign. Should he achieve any ultimate success, it will be dramatic testimony to the impact of the new law on the American electoral process.

As Harris freely admitted in 1971, his campaign blitz self-destructed for lack of money. "I'm broke," he reckoned openly the day he folded. The next spring, in a *Harper's* article, Harris concisely laid out the problem which plagued him and other candidates who lacked well-heeled backers under the old campaign financing system: "It's a circle. The press doesn't take you seriously because you haven't got the money. You don't get the money because the press doesn't take you seriously. What's a poor candidate to do?"

Under the new law, poor candidate Harris is relying predominantly on small contributions garnered first through the bands of signed-up loyalists, next through sophisticated direct-mail solicitations. Once he accumulated the required minimum of at least $5,000 in each of 20 states in gifts of $250 or less—he announced on Oct. 8 that he had reached that goal—he qualified for the federal matching funds provided under the new law. No longer does he have to persuade the press to anoint him a "serious" candidate. The Federal Election Commission did that for him once he achieved the statutory threshold. At the start of the election year, he could look forward to having those small contributions matched by the commission, dollar for dollar.

Thus less money stretches farther. Since the Harris campaign is careful to spend only what it has actually taken in, accumulating no debt, the matching federal funds will be money in the bank. Those funds will ensure Harris' staying power through at least the early round of primaries and caucuses. "This time we'll get our shot at the primaries," said Hightower.

The second aspect of the law that Harris strategists view as favorable to their cause is the spending limitation. Their reliance on unpaid volunteers rather than on media blitzes makes them impervious to spending limitations, whereas they argue that the campaign strategies of other candidates, such as Senators Henry M. Jackson (D Wash.) and Lloyd Bentsen (D Texas) might be cramped by those restrictions.

Finally, should the Harris strategy actually work out and render him a serious contender for the Democratic nomination, the Harris theory is that the party need not balk at nominating him for fear of alienating moneyed supporters. The money to wage the general election campaign

Harris Staff, Advisers

National campaign coordinator: James Hightower, 32, previously a staff member for former Sen. Ralph W. Yarborough (D Texas 1957-71) and, for the past five years, director of the Agribusiness Accountability Project in Washington, D.C.

Media coordinator: Frank Greer, 29, on leave from the Public Media Center in San Francisco, a public-interest group advocating citizen access to the news media.

Issues coordinator: Gary Wasserman, 31, on leave from the political science department of Medgar Evers College of the City University of New York.

Field organization coordinator: Andy Schuman, 24, formerly on Harris' Senate staff.

Fund-raising and political troubleshooter: Ralph Collins, 32, a Texan who has been involved in statewide campaigns there.

Harris' Background

Profession: Attorney.
Born: Nov. 13, 1930, Walters, Okla.
Home: McLean, Va.
Religion: Baptist.
Education: University of Oklahoma, B.A., 1952; LL.B., 1954; Phi Beta Kappa.
Offices: Oklahoma State Senate, 1957-64; U.S. Senate, 1964-73.
Military: None.
Memberships: Phi Alpha Delta legal fraternity, Masons, Oklahoma and American Bar Associations.
Family: Wife, LaDonna Crawford; three children.

will, he reasons, come from the federal coffers rather than from the big spenders anyway. And that means, the theory continues, that Harris would not have to alter his anti-corporate pitch in order to placate Wall Street.

Background of Poverty

Populist politics sits naturally on Fred Harris. He was born poor and never has been rich. As a child, he worked in the fields alongside his family, not only in the Oklahoma fields but on cropland all the way through the Midwest to North Dakota, where the Harrises followed the wheat harvest as migrant laborers. Even in the past two years, as a Washington attorney and a former senator, Harris has made less than $45,000 a year. (Harris has filed copies of all his federal tax returns since 1971 with the Federal Election Commission.) That income hardly compares either with that of many senators or with that of most of the other presidential candidates.

Likewise, Harris does not have the veneer of an eastern education. All his formal schooling was in his home state. It was at the University of Oklahoma that his zest and aptitude for law and politics became apparent. He graduated at the head of his law class and established his own firm. In 1956 he was elected a state senator at age 26, the youngest in Oklahoma history.

Harris' ambition became equally apparent in 1962. By then a leader in the state senate, he made a premature bid for the governorship and placed fifth. Undaunted, he began in 1963 to prepare for a shot at the U.S. Senate. He was elected to a two-year term in 1964 and was re-elected to a full term in 1966.

Harris critics observe that his ambition has at times led Harris away from the stated idealism of the New Populism and back to the old expediency, and there are facts to support that view. Despite an over-all reform record in the Oklahoma Senate, he did sponsor a bill increasing the oil and gas depletion allowances. In his early years in the U.S. Senate, he meshed well with the entrenched party leadership, as proved by his cochairing of the 1968 Humphrey presidential campaign and then by his leadership of the party itself.

Yet by 1971, Harris had emerged as an independent voice. He had broken with the Johnson administration on the war in 1968; he had been vocal on urban affairs and race relations, despite the cost to his Oklahoma popularity, and his voting record had become demonstrably more liberal. *(Box, p. 38)*

Such behavior had earned him trouble in Oklahoma, where he would have had stiff opposition if he had decided to run again for the Senate in 1972. He ran instead for the

Harris' CQ Vote Study Scores*

	1972	1971	1970	1969	1968	1967	1966	1965
Presidential								
support	13	20	45	57	55	70	62	77
opposition	46	30	42	40	9	15	23	19
Voting Participation	39	51	76	86	65	85	82	95
Party								
unity	42	56	73	73	61	71	60	75
opposition	3	5	5	11	9	13	20	21
Conservative Coalition								
support	3	4	4	16	17	27	27	33
opposition	45	43	75	70	41	61	56	62
Bipartisan								
support	26	30	61	71	52	77	78	89
opposition	10	14	14	17	10	8	5	5

* Explanation of studies, p. 107.

presidency and began in that campaign to give full voice to the positions he advocates in the current campaign.

Positions on Issues

While Harris spends the bulk of his campaign time spreading the populist economic message, he is also vocal on a panoply of other issues. Often he sees these as being inextricably related to the basic demand for a fairer distribution of wealth and of access to power.

Foreign Policy

The keys to Harris' approach to crafting a foreign policy are these: Let the people know what is being done, stop conducting foreign affairs for the benefit of the big, multinational corporations, and place international behavior on a more moral footing. "Some people warn against an isolationist foreign policy," he said. "What we've had is an isolationist foreign policy—it has isolated us from peoples and governments all over the world. What we need is a foreign policy that aims at a vision of the world we would like to see.... There was a time at the end of World War II when nations everywhere wanted to pattern themselves after us. That can happen again."

Such an open, moral foreign policy would involve many specifics: Terminate U.S. support of such regimes as that of Brazil or the now-defunct junta in Greece, end such covert operations as the opposition to the Allende regime in Chile and cut the defense budget substantially. Harris has even called for outright abolition of the exposé-ridden Central Intelligence Agency.

Civil Rights, Civil Liberties

In keeping with his record on civil rights for minorities, Harris has favored school racial integration; while in the Senate, he introduced legislation aimed at facilitating it.

The major votes on the busing issue have occurred since his tenure in the Senate, but he has declared that where neighborhood control of schools amounts to racial discrimination, the right to equality before the law must take precedence over local control. Harris' major focus, however, is on working to end white prejudice rather than simply reducing the impact of discrimination.

On women's rights, Harris has been a constant supporter of the adoption of the Equal Rights Amendment, which he cosponsored in the Senate. He favors the appointment of women to cabinet posts and to the Supreme Court. In both government and private employment, he supports the affirmative action principle.

He also endorses the Supreme Court decision on abortion, viewing that as a question of the privacy of the individual woman. Privacy issues are of particular concern to Harris. He opposes governmental assertions of the right to wiretap and to conduct electronic surveillance on citizens, and he views the criminalization of marijuana and of sexual activities among consenting adults as additional examples of unacceptable governmental intrusion into private lives.

The Young and Old

The populist themes are easily adapted to the wants of both the young and the old of the society. For the old, Harris advocates greater control over their own lives through increased Social Security benefits that are indexed to inflation; more reliance on direct income support that allows the old to choose the services they prefer, and an end to compulsory retirement.

For the young, he supports greater control over the educational institutions in which they spend their formative years. In the Senate, Harris successfully offered an amendment to the omnibus education amendments of 1972 which declared it to be the sense of the Congress that there be student representation on the governing boards of colleges and universities.

Energy, Environment

Harris' opposition to the oil companies is inseparable from his positions on energy and the environment. He would begin by restructuring the oil industry through the antitrust laws. He would curb consumption of fuel by forcing the automobile companies to build more gas-efficient cars, by abolishing discounts for big-volume users of electricity and possibly by a fuel allocation program.

He would then promote the development of alternative energy sources by intensive funding of research into geothermal, solar and other sources. He emphatically would not support the continued development of nuclear power, however, favoring instead a moratorium on nuclear plants.

Other Issues

Harris demonstrated an interest in conservation while in the Senate by sponsoring one of the bills advocating ocean mammal protection. As passed, the Marine Mammal Protection Act of 1972 (PL 92-522) set a permanent moratorium on most killing of ocean mammals and on the importation of their products.

Familiar with the problems of cities through his work on the National Urban Coalition's Commission on the Cities in the 70s, Harris strongly criticizes the federal failure to bail out New York City from its fiscal distress. He advocates both emergency financial assistance for hard-hit cities and long-term aid through assumption of health and welfare burdens and through greater control of interest rates that increase the cities' debt maintenance problems.

As for health care, Harris' populist answer is a universal, federally funded system. The costs of the system should be reduced through greater emphasis on group medical practice and the use of paraprofessionals. More reliance on preventive care and improvement in the national record on infant mortality and the doctor-patient ratio are also urged by Harris.

—By Barry Hager

THE LAST LONG WAIT FOR LIGHTNING TO STRIKE

Hubert H. Humphrey, who has actively sought the Democratic presidential nomination in three of the past four elections—and won it once—is marking time in the 1976 race, on the slim chance that the top prize will be served up to him at a deadlocked national convention. The strategy of the Minnesota senator—if a professed non-candidate can be said to have a strategy—is based on the chance that the abundant crop of Democratic hopefuls will cancel each other out in the primaries and leave the party without a candidate who can claim the nomination.

If that or any other sequence of bizarre events results in a convention vacuum, Humphrey leaves no doubt that he would joyously fill it, given the opportunity. The "happy warrior" of yesteryear still hungers for the presidency, and his friends see 1976 as his last shot at it. He will be 65 next May 27.

On Nov. 2, 1975, Humphrey summed up his position on NBC's "Meet the Press": "I have said to you that I am not a candidate for the presidency; I will not seek that office; I will not be entering primaries. That is my judgment. That has been my statement. I have also said to you that if the convention perchance should turn to me—which I think is highly improbable—but if it should, that I will be ready to accept the challenge, and I will go out and conduct a campaign that will be worthy of the Democratic Party, and I would win."

The role of non-seeker is doubtless a difficult one for the energetic Minnesotan. And his watching from the wings was not made easier by certain enticements that were bombarding him in the autumn of 1975:

• As the campaign season approached, there was no generally recognized front-runner. The murky Democratic situation involved the unpredictable influences of George C. Wallace and a host of previously untested newcomers to national politics.

• An Oct. 25 Gallup Poll showed Humphrey beating Wallace 23 to 19 per cent for the first time as top choice of Democratic voters, with others far behind.

• *U.S. News & World Report* Nov. 9 wrote that 49 per cent of 162 Democratic National Committee members who responded to a survey thought Humphrey would get the nomination.

Such developments, called the "Humphrey phenomenon" in a *Washington Post* story Nov. 3, are bound to exert increasing pressure on the Minnesotan. Humphrey reported that some Democratic senators want him to enter the primaries—at least some of the late primaries—so that he will have a legitimate claim on the nomination if the other candidates knock each other out of contention.

"Humphrey's had it," said one union leader. "He can't possibly get the nomination if he doesn't run in the primaries."

But Humphrey, who has been down the primary route many times before—and not too successfully—believes that staying out of them in 1976 is his smartest tactic. He said, "It's my judgment that right now the person that has no ambition, no declared ambitions, is more creditable. He's

freer. You don't have to go around weighing every word as you inevitably do when you become a candidate.... I feel I have a role to play in the party of keeping everybody on the beam. Not just a referee or healer. Somebody that's just a little cut above the pack. The minute you get in it, you're just another one of them."

The Bruised Liberal Battler

If he were to campaign actively again for the nomination, Humphrey admits that a sizable segment of American voters would send up a chorus: "Oh, no, not Humphrey again!"

For many battling years, he was the liberal's liberal. Then, as President Johnson's Vice President, he found himself trapped in the pit of the administration's Vietnam policies. With that albatross around his neck, Humphrey won the presidential nomination in 1968 in Chicago, where the war was debated in the city's streets with fists and nightsticks.

Humphrey's Herculean task was to put the shattered Democratic Party back together for the fall campaign. But many of his old liberal comrades shunned him, including fellow Minnesotan Eugene J. McCarthy, a peace candidate whom Humphrey defeated for the presidential nomination. Even with these handicaps, Humphrey nearly beat Republican Richard M. Nixon. One of the ironies of the 1968 contest was that Nixon, perhaps more than any other politician, had long been the *bete noire* of the liberal intellectuals who turned their backs on a Humphrey fallen from grace.

The 1968 wounds carried over to the 1972 presidential race, in which Humphrey, after contesting in numerous primaries, ended up in sixth place on the first ballot at the national convention that nominated South Dakota Sen. George McGovern for President.

During the campaign, Humphrey had to bear the humiliation of the Americans for Democratic Action (ADA) narrowly rejecting a move to put him on a list of "unacceptable" presidential candidates. He had been an ADA founding father.

At another point, a political analyst said of Humphrey's 1972 bid: "He's absolutely anathema to the kids. He is a joke on the campuses. He's perilously close to being a comic figure in large segments of the party."

Humphrey went out of his way to renounce his earlier support of Johnson administration war policies. In California in May 1972, he said, "Not all of us can come with all clean hands. I know I can't...but now I am in the center, where I can call the shots as I see them. You hear a lot about liberation these days. Well, I am one emancipated senator."

Smoldering Fires

Humphrey returned to the Senate in 1971 after a six-year interlude, and he again wears the mantle of liberal causes, which includes keeping a skeptical eye on the military-industrial complex. Obviously, he believes he has made atonement for past trespasses. But some observers think Humphrey does not want to run the risk of reopening old wounds in a 1976 all-out fight for the nomination.

Whatever, the glib and garrulous senator is not idle, idleness being a deficiency alien to his character. Humphrey misses few chances to show that the old fires are smoldering and ready to be rekindled if the Democrats beckon to him. He addressed the fall 1975 AFL-CIO convention in San Francisco and, according to *The New York Times*, George Meany and other labor chieftains viewed it as one of the most remarkable speeches of Humphrey's long career. The Times reported that the senator "tore the house down...on the floor, delegate after delegate expressed hope that Mr. Humphrey would be the nominee."

Meany and company have long held Humphrey among their ideological own. The hard-hat unionists, who are traditional anti-Communists, have no quarrel with Humphrey's former defense of the Vietnam war. Meany has been credited with helping the surge toward Humphrey in the waning days of the 1968 race, when organized labor unleashed an "educational" campaign to pry blue-collar workers away from the independent presidential candidacy of George Wallace.

It is Humphrey's stated intention in 1976 to file disclaimers of candidacy in any states that might put his name, without his consent, on their primary ballots. Betty South, his senatorial press secretary, said that he has written letters to friends in a few states where there had been talk of a "draft Humphrey" movement to squelch any such drives before they gained momentum. South added that Humphrey has no organization in any state except Minnesota, where he seeks a new Senate term in 1976.

Deep-Dyed New Dealer

Minnesotans have elected Humphrey to the Senate at every chance offered to them since 1948, when he became the state's first Democrat elected to that office by popular

---

Interest-Group Ratings[1]

Americans for Democratic Action (ADA)—ADA ratings are based on the number of times a senator voted, was paired for or announced for the ADA position on selected issues.

National Farmers Union (NFU)—NFU ratings are based on the number of times a senator voted, was paired for or announced for the NFU position.

AFL-CIO Committee on Political Education (COPE)—COPE ratings reflect the percentage of the time a senator voted in accordance with or was paired in favor of the COPE position.

Americans for Constitutional Action (ACA)—ACA ratings record the percentage of the times a senator voted in accordance with the ACA position.

Following are Humphrey's ratings since Congressional Quarterly began publishing them in 1960, plus available scores for 1959:

	ADA[2]	COPE[3]	NFU[3]	ACA
1974	81	80	100	0
1973	85	90	100	0
1972	60	100	100	0
1971	89	91	100	5
1964	97	100[4]	85[4]	1
1963	94	100[4]	85[4]	1
1962	92	100[4]	100[4]	0
1961	100	100[4]	100[4]	0
1960	100	100[4]	100[4]	0
1959	100	100[4]	100[4]	4

1. Humphrey was Vice President 1965-69; in private life 1969-70.
2. Failure to vote lowers score.
3. Percentages compiled by CQ from information provided by groups.
4. Indicates score compiled for entire Congress.

---

vote. The home folks also delivered Minnesota's electoral votes to Johnson and Humphrey in 1964 and to Humphrey and Muskie in 1968.

Young Humphrey came into manhood with a political home (the Democratic Party), a political hero (Franklin D. Roosevelt) and a political credo (FDR's New Deal). As a 10-year-old boy, Humphrey had cut his political teeth on the writings of Thomas Jefferson and Thomas Paine, given to him by his father, Hubert H. Humphrey Sr. The elder Humphrey was a Wilsonian Democrat in a then Republican middle western fortress, South Dakota, where Hubert Jr. was born in 1911.

Two disasters crippled rural South Dakota in the 1930s—the Great Depression and the Dust Bowl. Huron, where the Humphrey drugstore is still located, nearly became a ghost town as hard-working Dakotans sank into poverty through no fault of their own. Farmers and merchants turned to the government in Washington for help. Young Humphrey saw New Deal relief checks save the town and the family business. He was to say later: "I learned more about economics from one South Dakota dust storm than I did in all my years in college."

The Depression had forced Humphrey to interrupt his college education for six years, but he was able to return to the University of Minnesota in 1937. The campus was full of New Deal talk, and Humphrey swallowed its ideology with gusto. He went on to get a master's degree in political science at Louisiana State University. He wrote his thesis on "The Philosophy of the New Deal." When he returned to Minnesota, he worked for a time as an adult education director in the Works Projects Administration, a landmark New Deal program.

Humphrey was elected a reform mayor of Minneapolis in 1945, the same year that President Roosevelt died. The young mayor pushed programs for improved public housing and increased social welfare services at the local level—the same type of social experiments that FDR had introduced on the national scene in the 1930s.

On to the Senate

When Humphrey entered the Senate four years later, he was to become a ubiquitous spokesman for and sponsor of New Deal-type legislation, although President Truman called it the Fair Deal and later Democratic Presidents would invent their own slogans.

During his long career, Humphrey always has clung to the belief that the government, acting benevolently, should intervene, sometimes necessarily at the expense of private interests, to promote the collective general welfare. His speeches are replete with pleas for that activist philosophy. At the 50th anniversary convention of the National Association for the Advancement of Colored People in 1959, Humphrey put it succinctly: "I am the first to grant that nothing would be as effective in achieving racial equality as a change of heart in the people who harbor racial prejudice. But it is a grievous error to assume that governmental action can do nothing to cause a change of heart."

It was civil rights that first put Humphrey in the national spotlight. At the 1948 Democratic national convention, he was in the liberal vanguard that fought successfully to incorporate a civil rights minority report into the party platform. From the podium he declared, "It is now time for the Democratic Party to get out of the shadows of states' rights and walk forthrightly in the bright sunshine of human rights." That victory caused angry southern delegates to walk out of the convention and form the Dixiecrat third party of that year. It also marked the first of many Humphrey confrontations with the conservative South.

President Johnson tapped Humphrey to lead the Senate fight for the monumental Civil Rights Act of 1964. Played against the background of marches and violence in Selma, Ala., and mass demonstrations in Washington, proponents overcame a filibuster that tied up the Senate for 57 days by voting to cut off debate on a civil rights issue for the first time in history. The final act included titles barring racial discrimination in public accommodations, enforcing the desegregation of public education and guaranteeing equal employment opportunity.

Humphrey's Senate Staff

Administrative assistant: David G. Gartner.
Director of legislation: Al Saunders.
Press secretary: Betty South.
Executive director, Joint Economic Committee: John R. Stark.

Humphrey's Background

Profession: Pharmacist, college professor.
Born: May 27, 1911, Wallace, S.D.
Home: Waverly, Minn.
Religion: Congregational.
Education: Denver College of Pharmacy, 1933; University of Minnesota, B.A. *magna cum laude*, 1939; Louisiana State University, M.A., 1940.
Offices: Mayor of Minneapolis, 1945-48; Senate, 1949-64, since 1971; Vice President, 1965-69.
Military: None.
Memberships: Phi Beta Kappa, American Political Science Association.
Family: Wife, Muriel Buck; four children.
Committees: Agriculture and Forestry: chairman, Subcommittee on Foreign Agricultural Policy; Foreign Relations: chairman, Subcommittee on Foreign Assistance and Economic Policy; chairman, Joint Economic Committee; Select Committee on Nutrition and Human Needs.

By the mid-1970s, the two-decades-long battle over civil rights had centered on enforced busing to achieve racial balance in public schools. Humphrey's position was that if busing is to be used to improve the quality of education as a temporary measure, then it has validity and should be used. He said, "I am opposed to massive forced school busing solely for the purpose of racial balance on a quota basis. No parent, black or white, wants his child to have an inferior education. It makes no sense to bus a child from a good school to a bad school. It makes sense to bus a child from a poor school to a better school. It makes better sense to improve schools in all neighborhoods." He said that this would be his position at the 1976 Democratic convention.

The Presidential Quest

When Humphrey launched his first presidential bid, in 1960, *Time* magazine called his 12-year record in the Senate a "phenomenal performance." The magazine said that the senator's fingerprints were on nearly every piece of major legislation that had passed through the chamber and that he had sponsored a total of 1,044 bills and joint resolutions. Among many items, he supported labor reform, opposed tight money policies as a deterrent to economic growth and backed minimum wage increases as an economic momentum-builder, and favored price supports for farmers, rural electrification programs and "sound" development of natural resources.

Armed with formidable liberal credentials, Humphrey ran up against the youthful appeal of John F. Kennedy in the early 1960 primaries. The Minnesotan, running what he described as a "poor man's" race, had to contest against the well-financed, smoothly operating campaign machine mounted by the Massachusetts senator.

Kennedy won an inconclusive victory over the Minnesotan in neighboring Wisconsin. But their next clash, in the West Virginia primary, loomed as a do-or-die affair for Kennedy. The big question was Kennedy's Catholicism in a state that was 96 per cent Protestant. After a hard, bitter campaign, Kennedy scored a major triumph, demonstrating that his religion was not an insurmountable barrier to his election by knocking Humphrey, a Protestant, out of the running.

Humphrey returned to the Senate, where he was elected assistant majority leader in 1961. Ever the loyalist

Humphrey's CQ Vote Study Scores[†]

	1974	1973	1972	1971	1964	1963	1962	1961	1960	1959	1958	1957	1956
Presidential													
support	36[1]/47[2]	34	24	37	84	88	81	85	21	36	43	65	52
opposition	54[1]/43[2]	59	46	44	6	2	6	10	40	46	55	23	48
Voting Participation	85	88	53	75	92	88	81	92	49	81	89	87	95
Party													
unity	74	82	47	67	87	91	79	92	58	69	86	55	86
opposition	15	7	6	13	4	0	2	1	3	8	7	29	14
Conservative Coalition													
support	13	10	5	11	2	2	6	0	0	2	*	*	*
opposition	76	83	51	69	82	90	71	94	63	80	*	*	*
Bipartisan													
support	76	82	47	57	74	78	75	91	35	69	66	75	69
opposition	8	6	7	16	13	8	6	2	8	16	19	13	21

† Explanation of studies, p. 107.
* No ratings in these years.
1. During President Nixon's tenure in 1974.
2. During President Ford's tenure in 1974.

Democrat, he took on the role of shepherding President Kennedy's program through the legislative labyrinth. His work helped produce such New Frontier achievements as the Peace Corps and Job Corps—programs adopted by Kennedy from ideas espoused by Humphrey in the 1950s.

Humphrey's devoted and productive service made him a natural choice as President Johnson's running mate in 1964. The Democratic ticket had no problem in registering a popular- and electoral-vote landslide over the Republican nominee, Sen. Barry Goldwater (Ariz.). When Johnson became deeply involved in Vietnam, and Humphrey became his loyal defender, Humphrey's liberal friends were to come to hold the vice presidency as the nadir of his career. More critical observers have pointed out that Humphrey, in his own right, was very much in that liberal school of Cold War warriors that emerged in the late 1940s and in the 1950s. Early in his career, he had fought successfully to eliminate Communist influence in the Democratic-Farmer-Labor Party of Minnesota.

He coupled his anti-communism with internationalism, supporting foreign aid for friends and third-world nations. In one speech, he called for a new deal for the whole world, defining it as a "massive dose of health, education and love and understanding" and "for better living for people everywhere." He continued, "Where we should be boasting of our efforts and desire to help other nations with economic and technical assistance, our government seems to apologize for these efforts.... We seem to be ashamed of being Christian in our behavior—of helping our fellow man because he is our brother and needs our help."

When the national rage over Vietnam forced Johnson out of the 1968 race, Humphrey made his second presidential try. In June, before the convention, a newspaper editor had said that Humphrey was on the verge of disavowing Johnson's Vietnam involvement. Reacting quickly, Humphrey denied that it was his intention to recant "this week or ever." He said that administration Vietnam policy was designed "to protect the right of self-determination, to promote representative government and to prevent the success of aggression...and I have supported this policy enthusiastically."

At the convention, Humphrey won the nomination easily on the first ballot, but he rejected the essentials of the McCarthy peace plank and made certain the Democratic platform did not repudiate Johnson policy. That sealed the alienation of the peace activists.

Although Humphrey inched away from the Johnson position during the fall campaign, it was obvious that neither he nor Nixon could fire up real enthusiasm among the voters. Nixon was elected as a minority president, winning 43.4 per cent of the popular vote to 42.7 for Humphrey and 13.5 for Wallace.

After the 1972 presidential effort, during which Humphrey posed only a minor threat to McGovern's march to the nomination, the Minnesotan, back in the Senate, cemented his 180-degree turn on the war. In the spring of 1975, as the Communists were overrunning the entire Indochinese peninsula, the Foreign Relations Committee voted out a military aid bill for Cambodia that was somewhat short of the amount asked by President Ford. Humphrey was one of four senators who issued a minority report, opposing any further military assistance whatsoever, saying it "will serve only to prolong a hopeless, bloody struggle."

Meanwhile, on the domestic front, Humphrey was pursuing the same federal interventionist course that has marked his political life. During hearings on the New York City crisis before the Joint Economic Committee, which he chairs, Humphrey lambasted Ford for not helping the metropolis, saying, "I'm an internationalist, but I'm damn sick and tired of thinking you can save everybody else in the world but the eight million people in New York City."

—*By Ed Johnson*

MARKETING A RECORD OF EFFECTIVE LEGISLATING

For his second try at the presidency, Sen. Henry M. Jackson (D Wash.) is presenting himself, on the basis of wide experience and long seniority, as the man with the best answers for a troubled time.

In 1972, Jackson ran as an ideological alternative to the Nixon administration and to the numerous liberals crowding the Democratic field. Three years later, issues that Jackson has dealt with for years have become the nation's major concerns, and he has suddenly become a key figure in national policy-making.

Not a charismatic figure, Jackson is counting on his reputation as an effective legislator to make up for what he may lack in style. Accordingly, he is trying to draw national attention to his performance as a senator. "As a declared candidate," he said the day after his Feb. 6, 1975, announcement, "I intend to spend the majority of my time not on the road but on the job."

Background

The son of working-class Norwegian immigrants, Jackson was raised in Everett, Wash., a small lumber mill town north of Seattle. He worked his way through Stanford University and the University of Washington Law School, then returned to Everett in 1936 to practice law.

Jackson immediately immersed himself in local Democratic politics, beginning his career as head of the area First Voters League for FDR. Two years later, he won his first political campaign by beating the incumbent, an alleged alcoholic, for Snohomish County prosecutor. In that job, he was known as "Soda Pop" Jackson for his crackdown on gambling, prostitution and bootlegging. But his boyhood nickname of "Scoop" has stuck.

In 1940, Jackson, at age 28, easily won election to Washington's vacant 2nd District House seat. He remained in the House until 1953, fending off five challenges to his seat. In 1946, he was the only Democrat sent to the House from Washington.

Senate

Jackson moved from the House to the Senate in 1953, after he unseated the one-term incumbent, conservative Republican Harry P. Cain (1946-53). Bucking a Republican tide that gave Dwight D. Eisenhower a margin of 106,262 votes over Adlai E. Stevenson and captured six of Washington's seven House seats, Jackson defeated Cain by 134,404 votes.

Jackson's subsequent Senate elections have been a cascade of increasing margins. He won 52 per cent of the vote in 1952, 67 per cent in 1958, 72 per cent in 1964 and a record 82 per cent in 1970. "I'll have to admit," said his 1970 opponent, Republican Charles W. Elicker, after the election, "Jackson's virtually unbeatable."

Although not an electrifying campaigner, Jackson has built a reputation for invulnerability through constituent service and legislative ability. Compounding the problem for potential opponents has been the reluctance of national Republicans to oppose Jackson. "Hell, there'll be no money

going to an opponent of Scoop in the state of Washington," Sen. John G. Tower of Texas, head of the Republican Senatorial Campaign Committee, was quoted as saying by *The Wall Street Journal* in 1970. "We aren't going to do anything to hurt Scoop."

The foundation of Jackson's presidential candidacy is his long tenure in Congress. He has spent more than half his 62 years in Congress—12 years in the House and 23 in the Senate. His seniority has enabled him to use his office as a power base in dealing with the administration, his colleagues and the public. With the staff and expertise that seniority brings, he has cast himself as an authority on issues of national concern.

Energy, Environment

While he was in the House, Jackson showed an early interest in two subjects, energy and the environment, that have buoyed him to national prominence. Among the committees and subcommittees on which he served were Appropriations, Indian Affairs, Flood Control, Rivers and Harbors and the Joint Committee on Atomic Energy. His Pacific Northwest constituency naturally led him to concentrate on environmental interests—forestry, roads, dams, soil conservation.

A member of the Joint Atomic Energy Committee since 1948, Jackson developed some expertise on atomic energy and became an advocate of its use for both peaceful and wartime purposes. He worked with the chairman, Sen. James O'Brien (Brien) McMahon (D Conn. 1945-52), to transfer control over atomic energy development from military to civilian authority. He sponsored in the House in 1951 a McMahon resolution to divert funds from the nuclear arms race to peaceful purposes. In his home state, one of his best-known accomplishments is his role in bringing a nuclear power station to Hanford, Wash., in 1965. The federal project was one of the nation's first peacetime reactors. "There we literally did beat swords into plowshares," Jackson said, "and provided jobs."

Jackson has been equally as interested in the wartime uses of atomic energy. As a member of the joint committee, he participated in the initial decision to proceed with development of the hydrogen bomb. He is a close ally of Adm. Hyman G. Rickover, for years the head of the Navy nuclear submarine program, and he has been a key figure in development of the Nautilus/Polaris and Trident submarines.

Jackson's Interest-Group Ratings

Americans for Democratic Action (ADA)—ADA ratings are based on the number of times a representative voted, was paired for or announced for the ADA position on selected issues.

National Farmers Union (NFU)—NFU ratings are based on the number of times a representative voted, was paired for or announced for the NFU position.

AFL-CIO Committee on Political Education (COPE)—COPE ratings reflect the percentage of the times a representative voted in accordance with or was paired in favor of the COPE position.

Americans for Constitutional Action (ACA)—ACA ratings record the percentage of the times a representative voted in accordance with the ACA position.

Following are Jackson's ratings since Congressional Quarterly began publishing them in 1960, plus a composite score for 1955-59:

	ADA[1]	COPE[3]	NFU[3]	ACA
1974	62	82	100	11
1973	55	100	100	21
1972	40	100	90	38
1971	56	100	82	27
1970	56[4]	100	100	24
1969	78	100	88	14
1968	57	100	77	12
1967	69	100	100	0
1966	80	100[2]	93	11
1965	71	100[2]	92	15
1964	68	73[2]	76[2]	24
1963	65	73[2]	76[2]	13
1962	83	100[2]	100[2]	3[2]
1961	100	100[2]	100[2]	3[2]
1960	100	100[2]	100[2]	1[5]
1959	92	100[2]	100[2]	1[5]

1. Failure to vote lowers score.
2. Scores listed twice indicate rating compiled for entire Congress.
3. Percentages compiled by CQ from information provided by groups.
4. ADA score includes some votes from December 1969.
5. Score for votes on selected issues since 1955.

Anti-McCarthy Cold Warrior

Despite his long-standing distrust of the Soviet Union, Jackson avoided the red-baiting politics of the McCarthy era. He voted against creation of the House Un-American Activities Committee in 1945 and declined an opportunity to be its chairman. When he went to the Senate, he stepped into the heat of Sen. Joseph R. McCarthy's (R Wis. 1947-57) anti-Communist campaign as a member of McCarthy's Permanent Investigations Subcommittee.

When McCarthy tried to assume the subcommittee's full hiring and firing power in 1953, Jackson and the two other Democratic members resigned in protest. He rejoined the subcommittee a year later during the Army-McCarthy hearings and nettled the chairman so much during the televised proceedings that McCarthy aide Roy Cohn promised to "get" Jackson for "stuff that he has written favorable to communism."

"The true test of a man is where he stands on national defense," Jackson declared in 1971. It is ironic that he won his first national attention for his stand against red-baiting, for Jackson's reputation in foreign affairs is largely based on his hard-line distrust of the Soviet Union and his insistence on military preparedness. "His whole gambit in foreign policy," observed Robert J. Keefe, his campaign director, "is: what do we get out of it?"

The same year as the Army-McCarthy hearings, 1954, military leaders testified secretly before a Jackson subcommittee that the United States was falling behind the Soviet Union in nuclear technology. Jackson expressed concern over the threat in a series of secret letters to the Defense Department and President Eisenhower in 1954 and 1955. In 1956, warning of "ballistic blackmail" by the Soviets, he called for a crash missile program and an increase of funds to bridge the so-called missile gap.

Since then, Jackson has carved out a role as the Senate watchdog of U.S.-Soviet relations. In 1962, he criticized as "unrealistic" the Kennedy-negotiated nuclear test ban treaty with Great Britain and the Soviet Union, and 10 years later, he attacked President Nixon's arms limitation agreement as political posturing. "The question is how much we're going to give up and give in for international cosmetics," Jackson said. "Summitry is dangerous business."

Jackson's hawkish image is hardened by his predilection for expensive weaponry. Breaking ranks with his liberal colleagues in the Senate, Jackson consistently has supported such costly weapons systems as the Sentinel anti-ballistic missile, the Trident submarine and the F-111 fighter-bomber. "You can never have enough security for Henry," complained Senator Eugene J. McCarthy (D Minn. 1959-71) in 1969. "If he had his way, the sky would be black with supersonic planes.... He was that way in the House. He is just one of those people who are always saying, 'If you only knew what I know.'"

Jackson's rigid national defense posture derives in part from his attitude toward the Soviet Union. "The only way you get the Soviets to the conference table," he has said, "is from a position of strength."

He resents being referred to as "the senator from Boeing," but the Boeing Company of Seattle is the largest corporation in his state, and its executives have contributed to his Senate and presidential campaigns. Jackson came under strong criticism for allowing a Boeing lobbyist to operate out of his office during the SST debate, and he was accused during the 1972 presidential campaign of accepting

Congressional Quarterly Vote Study Scores...

	1974	1973	1972	1971	1970	1969	1968	1967	1966
Presidential									
support	45¹/41²	47	61	40	51	61	77	75	78
opposition	55¹/56²	53	15	23	37	31	16	16	22
Voting Participation	99	99	74	65	85	87	92	93	98
Party									
unity	85	78	42	50	66	72	82	83	84
opposition	15	22	29	18	22	16	12	10	14
Conservative Coalition									
support	21	33	38	28	32	16	29	11	19
opposition	78	67	37	36	56	77	67	79	81
Bipartisan									
support	90	96	69	57	74	71	79	84	91
opposition	9	4	7	5	9	16	12	10	7

1. During President Nixon's tenure in 1974.
2. During President Ford's tenure in 1974.

illegal Boeing money. Jackson denied any wrongdoing, and no charges were ever filed.

Jackson's foreign policy views reportedly earned him an offer in 1968 to be Nixon's secretary of defense. Jackson is said to have declined because he felt he could be more effective in the Senate. Yet his incessant criticism of Republican foreign policy, especially of detente with Russia, has placed him squarely in confrontation with Secretary of State Henry A. Kissinger, and Jackson seems to relish the role. "Kissinger is afraid of me," he told one reporter. He has challenged Kissinger in hearings over strategic arms limitations talks, and he has used his Permanent Investigations Subcommittee to attack Kissinger and Secretary of Agriculture Earl L. Butz for their roles in what Jackson calls the "great grain robbery" of 1972—the sale of huge quantities of American wheat to the Russians.

Israel

An unswerving defender of Israeli independence, Jackson's position again has been shaped, in part, by his suspicion of the Soviets. He has portrayed conflict in the Middle East as part of a Soviet scheme of aggression and has blasted the Nixon and Ford administrations for abetting that scheme. "Without Soviet support and material encouragement, without Soviet training and equipment, without Soviet diplomatic and political backing, this war would not have been started," Jackson said at the outbreak of the 1973 Arab-Israeli war. "And yet Dr. Kissinger...comes before the American people to say that Soviet behavior has been moderate and not irresponsible. I cannot agree."

Jackson's attitudes toward Israel and the Soviet Union came together in a dramatic way in 1974, when he almost singlehandedly forced the Soviets to allow freer Jewish emigration in return for a loosening of American trade barriers. But the agreement broke down early in 1975, when the Soviets repudiated any *quid pro quo* and the administration indirectly laid blame for the breakdown, and any adverse effect on detente, at Jackson's feet.

Vietnam

Jackson's reputation as a hard-line anti-Communist in foreign affairs is due chiefly to his unyielding support of the Vietnam war. Early in the hostilities, he characterized the American presence in Vietnam as part of "our opposition to Communist expansion." In 1967, he sketched an elaborate scenario, along the lines of the "domino theory," by which the fall of Vietnam would lead to a Communist takeover of Southeast Asia, then all of Asia and ultimately Europe. "It would be only a matter of time," he asserted.

Jackson did support the U.S. withdrawal from Vietnam, and in the end he refused to give support to the Ford administration's request for emergency military aid for the collapsing Saigon government. But the outcome of the involvement apparently did not shake his support for the original American entry into the war. "The basic decision to go into Vietnam was right," he said in April 1975.

Domestic Policy

Jackson is normally in the mainstream of liberal Democrats on domestic issues, although his ratings from liberal groups have fallen in recent years. For his votes on issues selected by the liberal Americans for Democratic Action, Jackson received ratings of 100 per cent in 1960, 80 per cent in 1966, 56 per cent in 1970, 40 per cent in 1972 and 62 per cent in 1974. The drops in 1970 and 1972 can be attributed in part to Jackson's support of the Vietnam war. *(Ratings box, p. 47)*

In the 1960s, Jackson supported most of the Johnson administration's "Great Society" programs, although he is not strongly identified with any particular one. He has, through his chairmanship of the Senate Interior Committee, worked on legislation to improve the lives of Indians and other native Americans. He played a central role in passage of the Alaska Native Claims Act of 1971 (PL 92-203), which settled long-standing land claims against the United States by Eskimos and other native Alaskans, and the Indian Education Act of 1972 (PL 92-318), which

...Covering 19 of Jackson's Years in Senate †

	1965	1964	1963	1962	1961	1960	1959	1958	1957	1956
Presidential										
support	82	56	73	90	85	41	40	42	65	43
opposition	15	29	15	10	15	48	59	42	33	57
Voting Participation	98	84	90	98	100	99	98	87	98	100
Party										
unity	82	55	81	97	96	86	84	80	79	96
opposition	15	25	10	3	4	13	14	6	21	4
Conservative Coalition										
support	21	16	30	24	12	7	5	*	*	*
opposition	79	69	63	76	88	91	92	*	*	*
Bipartisan										
support	91	68	78	90	95	83	86	69	82	66
opposition	7	10	12	7	5	15	12	18	9	34

†Explanation of studies, p. 107.
*No ratings in these years.

provided for comprehensive upgrading of Indian school programs.

In domestic affairs, Jackson is best known for his interest in the environment. He cites as one of his greatest accomplishments passage of the National Environmental Policy Act of 1969 (PL 91-190), which articulated the nation's first real environmental goals. More recently, he has been identified with the battles in Congress over land use and strip mining. He managed land use legislation (S 268) through the 93rd Congress and strip mining legislation through the 93rd (S 425) and 94th (S 7) Congresses, only to see the land use bill die twice in the House and the strip mining bill be vetoed twice by the President. His efforts have won him support among environmentalists.

But Jackson himself has undermined that support by voting for some major programs opposed by environmentalists, including votes for the ABM, the supersonic transport, the Alaska pipeline and Amchitka Island nuclear tests. In those cases, Jackson's interest in the nation's military and economic strength apparently took precedent over environmental concerns. Jackson has made no claims to be an environmental purist. As adviser Ben Wattenberg has put it, "He's not an ecology freak who's about to write off industry as a villain."

Jackson has placed himself in the middle of the conflict between Congress and the Republican administration over energy policy. With his long experience and his large staff, he has been ready with instant responses to Ford energy proposals. In January 1975, for instance, after the President announced a comprehensive energy plan to the 94th Congress, Jackson was ready with his own plan. And the same day that Ford released his fiscal 1976 budget, Jackson presented his own economic and energy plan.

In 1975, Jackson has seen at least two of his energy bills, one providing standby energy powers (S 622) and the other opening military oil fields for commercial drilling (S 677), passed by the Senate. When Ford proposed increases in the oil import tariff, Jackson helped lead the Senate opposition that resulted in a compromise.

National Politics

Jackson first reached real prominence in national politics in 1960, when his friend and fellow senator, John F. Kennedy, won the party presidential nomination. Jackson had been lobbying most of the year for the vice presidential spot and, with the support of Kennedy's brother, Robert, was considered the top choice at convention time.

But Jackson was shoved aside at the last moment in favor of Senate Majority Leader Lyndon B. Johnson (D Texas 1949-61), and afterward he made no effort to hide his disappointment. "I will do whatever Senators Kennedy and Johnson want me to do," Jackson said at the time. "I will do whatever a good sport should do." Jackson was given the chairmanship of the national party as a consolation prize, but he quit in a few months and remained an outsider during the Kennedy administration.

In 1972, Jackson offered himself as a presidential candidate to fill what he saw as a void left by liberal and conservative candidates. "The great center of our party has been alienated," Jackson proclaimed. "And the Democrats are inviting real trouble if they depart from this centrist concept." He drew a particular contrast between himself and the eventual nominee, Sen. George McGovern (D S.D.), whom he derisively labeled the candidate of "amnesty, acid and abortion."

With solid financial support and the prospect of labor backing, Jackson skipped the liberal-dominated New Hampshire primary and started his campaign in Florida. The strongest contender there was Alabama Gov. George C. Wallace, who forced Jackson on the defensive for his record of support for civil rights. Bombarded by Wallace for his votes against busing curbs, Jackson finally retaliated by proposing a constitutional amendment against all forced busing. Wallace won the primary, however, and Jackson finished a weak third with 13 per cent of the vote.

After dismal showings in the Wisconsin and Ohio primaries, among others, he withdrew from the race for lack of funds. Although no longer an active candidate in the primaries, Jackson finished second behind McGovern in balloting at the Democratic convention, inheriting some moderate Humphrey and Muskie delegates who could not reconcile themselves to McGovern's candidacy.

1976 Campaign Strategy

Jackson entered the 1976 campaign as a front-runner, a label that four years previously had proved a burden and a jinx for Sen. Edmund S. Muskie (D Maine). Muskie quit the race in 1972 after failing to live up to expectations in the early primaries. When he announced his candidacy in February 1975, Jackson was the leading money-raiser among announced candidates, and he had a full-time campaign staff that had been operating since July 1974. By October 1975, he had raised $2.8-million, according to his financial reports.

Jackson aides downplay the early front-runner problem, noting that under new party delegate selection rules most of the important primaries will be proportional contests, yielding few clear-cut winners or dramatic victories.

Because he figures there will be no make-or-break primaries at the start of the campaign, as in the past, Jackson is devoting his resources to big primary states such as New York, California and Pennsylvania. Campaign Director Keefe feels the campaign will be an accretion process, one of methodically picking up delegates in the primaries to ensure a strong position by convention time. Accordingly, the campaign in 1975 was concentrating on fund-raising, in order to build a treasury to carry Jackson through the gauntlet of primaries. "We're trying to get the money in hand now so we can project it over the primaries," said Keefe. "We want to guarantee ourselves to be at the convention."

One of Jackson's primary assets, he hopes, is organized labor. He always has voted with labor in Congress, and he has enjoyed a close relationship with AFL-CIO President George Meany. Labor has contributed generously to his Senate campaigns.

But labor support may be difficult for Jackson to marshal in 1976. In the first place, Meany has expressed displeasure over Jackson's 1974 call for ties with China and his support of the 1974 trade bill, which removed protections dear to industry and unions. In addition, the labor federation has taken a neutral stand on the presidential election, releasing member unions to find their own candidates. Some of the unions may turn to candidates more liberal than Jackson.

Jackson is targeting his campaign at the broad band of mostly industrial states extending from the Northeast down through New Jersey and Pennsylvania and west to the Upper Midwest states. With his western background and environmental record, he assumes that he has a natural constituency in the Far West.

To attract votes in the first, largely urban target area, Jackson is striking a populist chord in hopes of appealing to the large working-class population that has been hard-hit by economic decline.

It was to these people that he directed himself when he announced his candidacy: "For the past six years, the Republican administration has been tilting in favor of big business, the large corporations, the people who can take care of themselves," Jackson said in a five-minute, $23,000 nationwide telecast in February. "And the little people—little business, the elderly, the young, across the board—have been the ones who have been taking the beating."

Jackson's Background

Profession: Attorney.
Born: May 31, 1912, Everett, Wash.
Home: Everett.
Religion: Presbyterian.
Education: University of Washington, LL.B., 1935.
Offices: Prosecuting attorney, Snohomish County, 1938-41; House, 1941-53; Senate since 1953.
Military: Army, 1943-44.
Memberships: Phi Delta Phi, American Legion, Elks, Eagles, Sons of Norway, Masons.
Family: Wife, Helen Hardin; two children.
Committees: Chairman, Interior and Insular Affairs; Government Operations: chairman, Subcommittee on Permanent Investigations; Armed Services: chairman, Subcommittee on Arms Control; Joint Committee on Atomic Energy: chairman, Subcommittee on ERDA, Nuclear Energy.

Image Problem

Jackson faces two image problems that could hold him back in 1976. First, he is still trying to shake the pro-military image that puts off liberals. He has been able to soften that image to some extent by his votes against emergency aid to South Vietnam before the fall of Saigon and for reductions in the Pentagon budget.

His charge, just before the Communist takeover of Saigon, that the Nixon administration had made secret pledges of aid to South Vietnam helped prevent congressional approval of emergency aid. Jackson attempted to placate the liberals by campaigning in 1974 for such Democratic congressional candidates as Allard K. Lowenstein (N.Y.), Abner J. Mikva (Ill.), Robert F. Drinan (Mass.) and Gary Hart (Colo.). Hart was McGovern's campaign manager in 1972.

Jackson's other image problem is that his campaign style has been, as one columnist put it, "stupefyingly dull." Aides indicate that Jackson is aware of the problem. "His demeanor on the stump has changed dramatically in the last six months," Keefe said in July.

Positions on Issues

Following is a summary of the positions taken by Jackson since he has been in Congress:

National Defense

Jackson has been a consistent proponent of a strong national defense and has regularly supported Pentagon requests for major weapons systems.

A member of the Armed Services and Joint Atomic Energy Committees, he has been a reliable source of support for Navy nuclear submarine programs. In 1957 and 1958, he led floor fights in the Senate to provide funding for the fledgling Polaris submarine system. In 1973, he managed a successful effort, opposed by Senate liberals, to fund an accelerated Trident missile-firing submarine program. The base for the 10-vessel fleet has been assigned to Jackson's home state.

Jackson's national security stance has its roots in the Cold War era. During the 1950s, he constantly warned of a growing "missile gap" between the United States and the Soviet Union. In 1962, he raised a conspicuous voice of opposition to the nuclear test ban treaty negotiated with the Soviets by President Kennedy. Jackson lobbied against the treaty in the Senate, then switched his position at the last moment and voted for ratification.

Similarly, after President Nixon's 1972 visit to the Soviet Union, Jackson questioned the interim strategic arms limitation talks (SALT) agreement that grew out of the trip. For several months he held up Senate approval of the agreement by his insistence on an amendment guaranteeing that any future treaty "not limit the United States to levels of intercontinental strategic forces inferior to" those of the Soviet Union. The Nixon administration feared that the amendment would bind its bargaining hand in future negotiations, but accepted it after attempts to weaken it were defeated.

Jackson has charged that the United States was frozen into a position of inferiority by the SALT I treaty, and he has been a ceaseless critic of the ongoing negotiations. In 1975, he criticized President Ford's Vladivostok agreement for setting too high a ceiling on the two countries' strategic weapon levels.

Anti-Ballistic Missiles

In 1969, Jackson was a leader of Senate Pentagon supporters who fended off an attack by liberals on the Safeguard anti-ballistic missile (ABM) program. With Jackson wielding charts on the Senate floor to illustrate what he claimed was a Soviet missile threat, the ABM supporters defeated by only two votes an amendment to limit the Safeguard system. He helped lead support for the ABM in a similarly bitter but less prolonged debate in 1970.

In recent years, Jackson has tempered his national security position. In 1974, for instance, he led opposition to a Pentagon plan to test its Minuteman intercontinental force over the western United States. In 1975, he joined other senators in cutting back the Pentagon's arms procurement request.

Foreign Policy

The keystones of Jackson's foreign policy position have been his unswerving support of Israel and his antipathy to the Soviet Union. The two became entwined in 1974, when Jackson managed to hold up Senate passage of the trade bill (HR 10710—PL 93-618) with an amendment requiring the Soviet Union, in order to qualify for trade benefits, to allow freer emigration of Russian Jews. The bill was passed after an "understanding" was reached with the Soviets in October 1974, but the Soviets repudiated the putative agreement in early 1975 and refused to cooperate on the Jewish emigration issue.

Jackson cites as a major accomplishment his role in 1970 of securing for Israel military aid that appeared to be in jeopardy. That year's foreign aid bill, which contained an Israel arms sales authorization, became stalled in the Senate Foreign Relations Committee, so Jackson pushed through the Armed Service Committee a military procurement amendment authorizing a $500-million sale of Phantom jet fighters and other military supplies to Israel.

In 1975, Jackson won Senate approval of a measure (S 920) extending that credit authority and authorizing unlimited loan credits to Israel to purchase U.S. aircraft and other military equipment.

As chairman of the Government Operations Permanent Investigations Subcommittee, Jackson conducted two sets of hearings into U.S. grain sales to the Soviet Union. The first was in 1973, after massive sales that critics said depleted the domestic stock and drove up prices in this country. The subcommittee in July 1974 issued a report criticizing details of the transaction, then launched a new investigation into a proposed sale that had been stymied at

the last moment by the intervention of President Ford. Jackson criticized the administration for its judgment and the Soviets for their intentions in the two deals.

Jackson was a defender of the U.S. role in Vietnam. He consistently voted for continued funding of the war and against congressional efforts to limit or end the American involvement. As late as 1974, he voted against a successful defense supplemental appropriations amendment (HR 125-65—PL 93-307) that barred further U.S. military aid commitments to Southeast Asia in fiscal 1974.

Jackson began softening his support of South Vietnam as the United States began to withdraw its troops. He opposed Nixon's May 1970 decision to send troops into Cambodia, because it conflicted with the policy of withdrawal. And in a Senate showdown with Nixon in 1970, Jackson voted for the Cooper-Church amendment (HR 15628) barring funds for U.S. troops in Cambodia after July 1, 1970.

In 1975, Jackson voted in the Armed Services Committee against the emergency military aid to South Vietnam sought by the Ford administration.

While remaining a critic of detente with the Soviet Union, Jackson has gone beyond administration policy in his attitude toward the People's Republic of China. Upon his return from a visit there in July 1974, Jackson called for full diplomatic relations with Peking and withdrawal of the U.S. embassy from Taiwan.

After the Turkish invasion of Cyprus in 1974, Jackson voted to cut off further arms sales to Turkey (H J Res 1131, H J Res 1163). In 1975, he voted against a bill to resume military aid to Turkey.

Environment

The most notable environmental legislation introduced by Jackson is the National Environmental Policy Act of 1969 (PL 91-190), which established the Council on Environmental Quality and articulated the nation's first environmental policies and goals. Jackson lists among his major environmental accomplishments his role in establishing the Redwood National Park in California (PL 90-545) and North Cascades National Park in Washington (PL 90-544). He managed both bills to Senate passage in 1968.

In 1975, Jackson remained frustrated in his efforts to win passage of legislation regarding two hotly disputed environmental issues, land use and strip mining. He led a successful Senate effort to pass a land use bill (S 268) in 1973, only to see it die the next year in the House Rules Committee. The House killed a similar bill (HR 3510) in 1975.

Jackson and Rep. Morris K. Udall (D Ariz.) pushed through the 93rd Congress major legislation to regulate strip mining, but the bill (S 425) was vetoed by President Ford. The two sponsors rushed out a similar measure (HR 25) in 1975; but Ford vetoed it again, and the House sustained the veto.

Jackson's environmental interests often have given way to his concern for defense and the economy. He led unsuccessful fights for development of the supersonic transport plane (SST) in 1970 and 1971, arguing that its benefit to the economy and American aviation outweighed possible threats to the environment.

Environmentalists have faulted Jackson for his stands on the Alaska pipeline and a proposal for nuclear testing in Alaska. Jackson steered through his Interior Committee a bill (S 1081—PL 93-153) permitting pipeline construction, then helped lead support for the bill on the Senate floor. On a key vote designed by environmentalists to delay the start of construction, Jackson voted against an amendment to allow consideration of an alternative pipeline route through Canada instead of Alaska. He sided with environmentalists, however, in voting against an amendment, which was approved by one vote, to bar judicial review of the environmental aspects of the project.

In 1971, Jackson declared opposition to two unsuccessful amendments that would have delayed a proposed underground nuclear test at Alaska's Amchitka Island. The test was opposed by environmentalists, some scientists and West Coast residents on the grounds that it could result in radioactive leakage and tidal waves.

Energy

As chairman of the Interior and Insular Affairs Committee since 1963, Jackson got an early start on his Senate colleagues in grappling with energy issues. He warned of possible oil shortages as early as 1971. When such shortages appeared imminent in 1973, Jackson pushed through Congress a bill (S 1570—PL 93-159) directing the President to draw up a fuel allocation plan.

Also in 1973, Jackson engineered Senate passage of a bill (S 1283) to promote long-term energy research and development, with emphasis on finding fuel alternatives to oil. The 10-year, $20-billion program became law late in 1974 (PL 93-438).

Jackson in 1973 and 1974 led Senate efforts to enact an omnibus emergency energy bill. The bill was stalled twice by Senate-House disagreements before the two chambers reached agreement on a version (S 2589) in February 1974 that included a rollback of oil prices. President Nixon vetoed the bill March 6, 1974.

A bill similar to the emergency energy bill was passed by the Senate in 1975. The Standby Energy Authorities Act

(S 622), introduced by Jackson, authorized emergency powers that had been requested by President Ford, but it reserved to Congress the right to review plans for their use.

In 1973, Jackson introduced and floor-managed legislation (S 2776), requested by the administration, creating a temporary Federal Energy Administration to manage federal programs dealing with short-term fuel shortages. The bill was enacted in May 1974 (PL 93-275).

A major Jackson bill before the 94th Congress would provide for development of the energy resources of the outer continental shelf. The bill (S 521) would require development of a federal leasing program and set up a coastal states fund to help states affected by the program. It was passed by the Senate in July 1975. A similar bill (S 3221) passed the Senate but died in the House in 1974.

Economy

Jackson professes a Keynesian approach to economic policy, advocating federal intervention in the marketplace to relieve specific problems. To counter inflation in 1973, Jackson proposed an across-the-board freeze for six months on all prices, rents, wages, salaries, interest rates and dividends. His amendment to the wage-price law extension (S 398) was rejected by the Senate.

In 1975, Jackson proposed standby wage and price control authority for the administration. To pump more money into the recession-struck economy, he has called for a national goal of 2.6 million housing starts a year, with two million federally subsidized units going to low- and middle-income families. He also proposed creating a temporary agency to provide emergency capital for cash-strapped businesses.

Civil Rights

Jackson has supported most major anti-discrimination legislation. He voted for the Civil Rights and Voting Rights Acts of 1964 and 1965, respectively, and for the Open Housing Act in 1968.

However, he has taken equivocating positions on busing, opposing it in his public statements but voting against statutory efforts to curtail forced busing. During the 1972 presidential campaign, he introduced a constitutional amendment to stop all forced busing. But in a key 1974 vote (S 1539), he voted to kill an amendment limiting busing to the school nearest a child's home and only as a final resort.

Other Issues

During the 1960s, Jackson supported most of the "Great Society" social programs. He voted for the initial Medicare, model cities and rent supplements programs and against a series of efforts to destroy the poverty program.

As chairman of the Senate Interior and Insular Affairs Subcommittee on Territories during the 1950s, Jackson sponsored and floor-managed the bills that granted statehood to Alaska (PL 85-508) in 1958 and Hawaii (PL 86-3) in 1959.

—By Ted Vaden

THE NON-CANDIDATE EVERYBODY TALKS ABOUT

Three times, Sen. Edward M. Kennedy of Massachusetts has said "no" to a campaign for the Democratic presidential nomination. But the widely held view that sooner or later he will say "yes" keeps his name alive in political speculation.

He withdrew from consideration in the 1976 presidential campaign Sept. 23, 1974, citing family obligations. He said that his decision was "firm, final and unconditional." He had made similar decisions in 1968 and 1972, and most political leaders take him at his word now. There are no indications that the 43-year-old senator has had a change of heart or that the Kennedy forces are organizing for any political activity other than his 1976 campaign in Massachusetts for a fourth term.

Nevertheless, public-opinion polls consistently have put Kennedy far out in front of other Democratic presidential possibilities. He has done the best of any Democrat in pollsters' nationwide "trial heats" against President Ford. Kennedy's assets include his personal attractiveness, his talents as a campaigner, his potentially strong political organization, his acceptability to a broad range of Democratic factions and the Kennedy name.

At the same time, the senator has a number of liabilities as a presidential candidate, among them the unsettled questions of Chappaquiddick, the strain of a national campaign on his family and the threat of assassination—a danger made all the more real by the recent attempts on Ford's life.

Still, as long as he continues to outshine the active Democratic candidates, speculation is likely to continue that circumstances could force him to reconsider his decision not to run. That speculation may not cease until the national convention nominates someone else.

Personal Background

The youngest of nine Kennedy children, Edward (Ted) spent many years in the shadow of his older brothers. In the 1950s, while John F. Kennedy and Robert F. Kennedy were becoming nationally known, Edward was finishing his education at Harvard and getting his law degree.

He had been forced to leave Harvard during his freshman year after it was discovered that he had asked a friend to take a Spanish exam for him. The first in a series of personal crises that have marked his career, the episode was an issue in Kennedy's first Senate campaign.

After two years in the Army, Kennedy returned to Harvard, graduating in 1956. He attended the International Law School in The Hague and, in 1959, received his law degree from the University of Virginia.

He managed John Kennedy's 1958 Senate re-election campaign in Massachusetts and was coordinator for a number of western states in his brother's successful 1960 presidential campaign.

First Senate Campaign

Returning to Massachusetts in 1961, Edward became a $1-a-year assistant district attorney in Suffolk County

(Boston) and prepared to launch his own political career. A Kennedy family friend, Benjamin A. Smith II (D 1960-62), had been appointed to John Kennedy's Senate seat. An election to fill the remaining two years of the unexpired term was to be held in 1962, and it was widely believed in Massachusetts that Smith was just holding the seat until Edward Kennedy was 30—the constitutionally required minimum age for a senator.

This proved to be the case as Kennedy entered the 1962 race and Smith made no attempt to stay on. Kennedy was challenged for the Democratic nomination by State Attorney General Edward J. McCormack Jr., the nephew of House Speaker John W. McCormack (D Mass. 1928-71).

In addition to the conflict between Edward Kennedy's and Edward McCormack's personal ambitions, the race represented a renewal of the continuing clash between the Kennedys and the McCormacks for dominance in Massachusetts politics. McCormack bitterly attacked Kennedy's qualifications and campaign tactics; the Kennedy forces were angered by McCormack's hard-line approach.

Despite the high emotions and deep divisions within the party, Kennedy emerged with the endorsement of the Democratic state convention and easily defeated McCormack in the primary by a margin of more than 2-to-1. Kennedy went on to defeat Republican George Cabot Lodge, son of Ambassador Henry Cabot Lodge Jr., and an independent peace candidate, Harvard Professor H. Stuart Hughes. Although this race, too, had symbolic meaning—in 1952, John Kennedy had taken the Senate seat away from the elder Lodge (R 1937-44, 1947-53) in another classic

Massachusetts campaign—it was mild by comparison with the Democratic primary. Kennedy emerged with a comfortable 290,000-vote plurality.

1964 Campaign

Just a year after Edward Kennedy's election triumph, President Kennedy was slain in Dallas Nov. 22, 1963. Ten months later, Edward narrowly escaped death himself.

Sen. Kennedy, his administrative assistant, Edward Moss, and Sen. and Mrs. Birch Bayh (D Ind.) were flying to the Massachusetts Democratic state convention in Springfield Sept. 19, 1964, when their private plane crashed. Moss and the pilot were killed, the Bayhs were injured and Kennedy was seriously hurt. Bayh pulled him from the wreckage. Kennedy was rushed to a hospital, where he was found to have suffered a severe spinal injury.

Kennedy was confined to a hospital bed for the rest of the 1964 campaign. His wife, Joan, made campaign appearances on his behalf. Public sympathy, a strong campaign organization and the nationwide Democratic landslide that year combined to give Kennedy victory over an obscure Republican opponent, Howard Whitmore Jr., by a record 1.1-million-vote margin. His 74.3 per cent of the vote was also a record, both marks eclipsing those set by John Kennedy in 1958.

Kennedy's Interest-Group Ratings

Americans for Democratic Action (ADA)—ADA ratings are based on the number of times a senator voted, was paired for or announced for the ADA position on selected issues.

National Farmers Union (NFU)—NFU ratings are based on the number of times a senator voted, was paired for or announced for the NFU position.

AFL-CIO Committee on Political Education (COPE)—COPE ratings reflect the percentage of the times a senator voted in accordance with or was paired in favor of the COPE position.

Americans for Constitutional Action (ACA)—ACA ratings record the percentage of the times a senator voted in accordance with the ACA position.

Following are Kennedy's ratings since he became a member of the Senate in 1962:

	ADA[1]	COPE[2]	NFU[2]	ACA
1974	81	70	100	0
1973	90	91	100	4
1972	90	89	90	5
1971	100	83	100	5
1970	84	100	100	5
1969	100	100	94	9
1968	71	100	88	0
1967	92	100	90	0
1966	100	100	100	8
1965	94	100	100	0
1964	89	100	100	0
1963[3]	94	100	100	0

1. Failure to vote lowers score.
2. Percentages compiled by CQ from information provided by groups.
3. Kennedy took office Nov. 7, 1962, after the adjournment of the 87th Congress. Thus he did not cast his first Senate vote until 1963.

1968 Presidential Campaign

After President Kennedy's death, Attorney General Robert F. Kennedy was looked upon as the family's leader, especially after he was elected to the Senate from New York (1965-68). Several Democrats opposed to the Vietnam war pressed Robert Kennedy in 1967 to challenge President Lyndon B. Johnson for the Democratic nomination in 1968. He resisted the pressures for many months, but finally gave in and entered the race on March 16, 1968. Edward Kennedy had advised against running but later was active in the campaign.

In the early hours of June 5, 1968, Robert Kennedy was murdered in the Ambassador Hotel in Los Angeles, moments after he had claimed victory in the California presidential primary. The sole surviving Kennedy brother, Edward, was shoved into the spotlight that previously had focused on his brothers. He delivered the eulogy at his brother's funeral in New York June 8 and then went into seclusion.

There had been speculation that spring that Edward Kennedy might be the vice presidential candidate on a "unity" ticket with Vice President Humphrey if Robert Kennedy's campaign failed. The vice presidential speculation was revived by the assassination, but on July 26, Edward issued a statement that it would be "impossible" for him to run.

He ended his seclusion on the eve of the 1968 Democratic national convention with a speech at Holy Cross College, Worcester, Mass., on Aug. 21. The address primarily was an attack on Johnson administration Vietnam policies, but Kennedy also used the occasion to reject suggestions that he retire from public life. "There is no safety in hiding," he said, adding: "Like my three brothers before me [the oldest, Joseph P. Kennedy Jr., had died in World War II], I pick up a fallen standard. Sustained by the memory of our priceless years together, I shall try to carry forward that special commitment to justice, to excellence, to courage that distinguished their lives."

As the Democratic convention opened in Chicago Aug. 26, 1968, rumors began circulating that Edward Kennedy might accept a draft for the presidential nomination. A "draft Kennedy" operation was set up, largely by former Robert Kennedy supporters in the California delegation. In part a tactical move to increase the chances of including a strong anti-war plank in the Democratic platform, the draft movement reached a peak with convention floor demonstrations by the New York and California delegations. Kennedy brought the effort to a halt with a statement asking his supporters "to cease all activity in my behalf."

Chappaquiddick

After the Democrats' defeat in the 1968 presidential election, Kennedy was widely regarded as the party's probable presidential nominee for 1972. But the seeming inevitability of that nomination was abruptly ended July 19, 1969, when the automobile he was driving plunged off a bridge on Chappaquiddick Island, Mass. A woman riding in the car—Mary Jo Kopechne, a former campaign worker for Robert Kennedy—was drowned.

Kennedy pleaded guilty July 25 to charges of leaving the scene of an accident. In a television address that night, he described his actions following the accident as "indefensible." But he denounced "the innuendo, the whispers" of immoral conduct on the part of himself and Kopechne, and he denied rumors that he had been driving under the influence of alcohol.

At the conclusion of his remarks, Kennedy asked the voters of Massachusetts to advise him whether he should remain in office. Notwithstanding substantial editorial criticism of the television speech, the senator's office announced July 30 that the public response had been "overwhelmingly favorable" and that he was returning to the Senate.

Questions about Kennedy's account of the incident have continued, in the press and elsewhere. Shortly before the senator made his final non-candidacy statement in 1974, several articles on Chappaquiddick had appeared in national publications. Chappaquiddick remains a large obstacle for Kennedy to surmount in any national campaign.

1970 and 1972 Campaigns

In 1970, Kennedy ran an intense, tightly organized and expensive re-election campaign in Massachusetts. He was returned to a third Senate term by a 487,000-vote margin over Republican Josiah A. Spaulding. Kennedy received 62.1 per cent of the vote, well behind his 1964 margin but ahead of Republican Sen. Edward W. Brooke's winning percentage in 1966.

Thereafter, Kennedy's name ebbed and flowed in discussion of the 1972 presidential nomination. He never made an absolute statement taking himself out of the race. But he consistently said he was not a candidate and took his name off the ballot in the primary states where it had been listed.

At one or two points in 1972, Kennedy seemed to be leaving the door open to accepting the vice presidential nomination. But when the Democratic nominee, South Dakota Sen. George McGovern, asked Kennedy to be his running mate, he declined.

Pre-1976 Problems

McGovern's defeat once again turned Democratic eyes toward Kennedy, this time as a candidate for the 1976 nomination. And this time, Kennedy made some of his most tangible moves yet toward an actual presidential campaign.

He reportedly spoke with supporters in several states about a possible campaign and informed close family associates that he planned to run. He maintained an extensive schedule of national and international appearances. Among them was a highly publicized joint appearance with Alabama Gov. George C. Wallace (D) in Decatur, Ala., July 4, 1973.

Again, personal and family crises intervened. In 1973, a rare form of bone cancer forced the amputation of one leg of his son, Edward Jr., then 12. The youth required a long series of hospital treatments that had harsh side effects. The regular treatments, apparently successful, were not discontinued until 1975.

Meanwhile, Joan Kennedy was hospitalized several times for treatment of psychiatric problems, including alcoholism. Sen. Kennedy also had obligations as a substitute father for his brothers' children, and the Kennedy family was reported to be against his running.

"My primary responsibilities are at home," he said in his 1974 statement of non-candidacy. "There is absolutely no circumstance or event that will alter the decision. I will not accept the nomination. I will not accept a draft. I will oppose any effort to place my name in nomination in any

---

Kennedy's Background

Profession: Attorney.
Born: Feb. 22, 1932, Boston, Mass.
Home: Hyannisport, Mass.
Religion: Roman Catholic.
Education: Harvard University, A.B. 1956; International Law School, The Hague, The Netherlands, 1958; University of Virginia Law School, LL.B., 1959.
Offices: Assistant district attorney, Suffolk County, Massachusetts, 1961-62; Senate since 1962.
Military: Army, 1951-53.
Memberships: Trustee, Children's Hospital Medical Center, Boston; Lahey Clinic, Boston; Boston Museum of Science; Boston Symphony Orchestra; John F. Kennedy Center for the Performing Arts; John F. Kennedy Library, and the Robert F. Kennedy Memorial Foundation; president, Joseph P. Kennedy Jr. Foundation.
Family: Wife, Joan Bennett; three children.
Committees: Judiciary: chairman, Subcommittee on Administrative Practice and Procedure; chairman, Subcommittee on Refugees and Escapees; Labor and Public Welfare: chairman, Subcommittee on Health; chairman, Subcommittee on the National Science Foundation; Joint Economic Committee: chairman, Subcommittee on Energy; Special Committee on Aging: chairman, Subcommittee on Federal, State, and Community Services; Select Committee on Nutrition and Human Needs; Democratic Steering Committee.

---

state or at the national convention, and I will oppose any effort to promote my candidacy in any other way."

Senate Record

During his first seven years in the Senate, Kennedy typically was described as a hard-working, fairly effective member who found legislative routines less confining than his brothers had and who was on reasonably good terms with most of his colleagues.

After the national publicity given his election in 1962, his first years in the Senate were quiet. His low profile was credited with containing resentment from some of his Senate colleagues. Sworn in on Nov. 7, 1962, Kennedy, then 30, had come to Washington as the youngest member of the Senate.

Kennedy's first two major committee assignments were Judiciary and Labor and Public Welfare, and he has stayed on these committees. His first subcommittee chairmanship came in 1965—the Judiciary Subcommittee on Refugees and Escapees. In 1969, he became chairman of the Judiciary Subcommittee on Administrative Practice and Procedure. In 1971, he became chairman of the Labor and Public Welfare Subcommittee on Health. He is also chairman of the National Science Foundation Subcommittee. To give himself an additional forum to express his views on economic policy, Kennedy joined the Joint Economic Committee in 1975 and acquired the chairmanship of a newly created Energy Subcommittee.

He now ranks 22nd in seniority among Democrats and 23rd over-all in the Senate. Moreover, he is fourth in seniority on the Judiciary Committee and probably will be the committee's next chairman if he stays in the Senate. Of those ahead of him in seniority on the committee, Chairman James O. Eastland (D Miss.) must face re-election in 1978 at age 74. Sen. Philip A. Hart (D Mich.) is retiring. And Sen. John L. McClellan (D Ark.) has said that he will retire after 1978.

Kennedy's CQ Vote Study Scores*

	1974	1973	1972	1971	1970	1969	1968	1967	1966	1965	1964	1963
Presidential												
support	31[1]/38[2]	30	22	30	33	44	39	68	66	75	31	75
opposition	61[1]/49[2]	58	52	50	40	44	5	18	16	11	5	4
Voting Participation	84	86	80	83	70	83	39	86	83	86	49	83
Party												
unity	78	80	80	78	73	78	26	69	67	81	37	84
opposition	8	5	8	10	4	5	4	15	9	10	6	3
Conservative Coalition												
support	4	4	4	13	3	3	4	0	1	11	2	5
opposition	80	85	82	76	74	85	34	89	86	80	41	86
Bipartisan												
support	66	73	58	54	51	60	30	66	69	73	23	66
opposition	17	14	18	25	14	23	14	22	21	9	5	13

Explanation of Studies, p. 107.
1. During President Nixon's tenure in 1974.
2. During President Ford's tenure in 1974.

Kennedy's visibility in the Senate abruptly shifted from low to high in 1969, after his brother Robert's assassination. He upset Democratic Whip Russell B. Long of Louisiana by a 31-26 secret vote of the Senate Democratic caucus Jan. 3.

The triumph was short-lived. In 1971, Kennedy was beaten 31-24 by Sen. Robert C. Byrd of West Virginia in a similar caucus vote Jan. 21. Kennedy's long absences from the Senate during his 1970 re-election campaign, and Byrd's attentiveness to his colleagues' needs as secretary of the Senate Democratic Conference, were factors in the upset. The damage to Kennedy's political stature caused by Chappaquiddick was another factor.

But by 1975, there was general agreement about Kennedy's performance as a senator:

● The same flair for public speaking he displays on the campaign trail also serves him well in Senate debate. He can handle himself well in committee and on the floor.

● His ability to attract attention from the press has been an invaluable tool for mobilizing public support for his positions. It has caused his critics to call him a publicity hound, but it also is one reason why other senators have allied themselves with him. Further, White House consciousness of Kennedy as a potential rival has sometimes led to administration support for new programs to keep Kennedy from pre-empting potential campaign issues.

● His staff is generally well-rated if not universally beloved. The senator's aides give him good support and often play leading roles in dealings among offices.

Positions on Issues

In general outlook, Kennedy has been a liberal in the traditional sense of supporting an expanded role for the federal government and high levels of government spending. For example, he backs increases in the federal budget to fight the recession and to create jobs. Many of his issues positions are related directly to his committee work, but his interests are far more diverse than that.

Defense, Foreign Policy

On foreign policy, Kennedy is an internationalist, a point he underscores with numerous trips abroad. He shares his brothers' interest in Latin America and Africa. He has supported U.S. aid to Israel and close ties with Europe.

At the same time he has been a critic of many U.S. commitments abroad, such as those to Turkey and Korea. He also is a critic of the size of the defense budget. He is opposed to a number of new weapons systems, including the anti-ballistic missile, multiple, independently targeted re-entry vehicle (MIRV) warheads and the B-1 bomber. He favors better relations with the Communist world and arms limitation agreements.

The Refugees Subcommittee has been one of Kennedy's main foreign policy forums. He has used it to advance his proposals for international humanitarian aid, including assistance to Biafra, Bangladesh, India and Africa. He has also used the subcommittee as a forum for attacks on U.S. policies on Vietnam, Chile and Cuba.

Civil Rights, Civil Liberties

On the Judiciary Committee, Kennedy has been interested in civil rights and civil liberties issues. He sponsored legislation extending the vote to 18-year-olds in federal elections and to abolish poll taxes, and he has advanced amendments to liberalize committee bills in the area of criminal justice.

Kennedy's strong civil rights stand and his advocacy of minority interests has included opposition to congressional attempts to block school busing orders. This has not been a popular position in Massachusetts, where controversy and some violence have accompanied a court-ordered desegregation plan in Boston.

Notwithstanding the family's great wealth—Kennedy's annual income, according to tax returns he released in 1974, is about $450,000, most of it from family trust funds—blue-collar and middle-class voters have been a core of the Kennedys' political base. There now is talk in Massachusetts that Kennedy's stance on busing and his general advocacy of poor and minority-group interests has weakened that base.

Kennedy was Senate floor manager for a revision of immigration laws. During Senate debate on the 1965 Voting Rights Act, he led a floor fight for an amendment to ban the poll tax. The amendment failed, but the tax was outlawed by the courts the next year.

He sponsored gun-control legislation, proposed a number of successful amendments to President Johnson's anti-poverty bills and fought provisions of anti-crime and anti-riot statutes advanced in 1967 and 1968 which he thought infringed on civil liberties.

Health, Science, Education

He has been involved in the drafting of important health legislation, including such programs as the National Cancer Act, peer review for doctors, various research programs, manpower and nurse training bills, malpractice insurance and a series of health services bills. He has involved himself in the battles over appropriations for these programs, generally pushing for higher budgets.

In 1975, while floor manager of the health services bill (S 66), Kennedy successfully blocked an attempt to attach an anti-abortion amendment. This was a new role for Kennedy, who previously had not been active in debate on the issue.

Kennedy has become the main Senate proponent of a comprehensive national health insurance program. Although his efforts in that direction so far have been stalled, renewed interest in the issue is expected in 1976. He has pushed successfully for the restoration of the post of White House science adviser, which was abolished by President Nixon, and for the creation of an Office of Technology Assessment to assist Congress. Kennedy was the first chairman of that agency's board of directors.

A proposal he made with Sen. Gaylord Nelson (D Wis.) in 1965 for the establishment of a Teachers Corps to aid in poor areas was adopted by President Johnson as part of his anti-poverty program. Similarly, a 1966 Kennedy proposal for a system of neighborhood health centers became part of the Model Cities program.

Vietnam and the Draft

In contrast to Robert Kennedy's outspoken attacks on President Johnson's Vietnam policy, Edward, as chairman of the Refugees Subcommittee, concentrated on the effect of the Vietnam war on that country's civilian population. The subcommittee held extensive hearings on the subject in 1967 and issued a report in 1968 that focused national attention on the plight of the Vietnamese people.

As early as 1966, Kennedy was calling for changes in the nation's draft laws and was urging a switch to a lottery system. Kennedy's position was that the existing draft system was unfair to the poor and to minorities. He later had the same view of President Nixon's all-volunteer Army and was one of the few prominent liberals to oppose ending the draft.

Kennedy's first nationally publicized attack on administration war policy was his 1968 Holy Cross speech. Thereafter, he was a constant critic of the war. He criticized the Nixon administration on numerous occasions for prolonging the war. And most recently, he attacked the Ford administration's requests for aid to Vietnam and Cambodia.

Other Issues

His Administrative Practice Subcommittee has investigated the Civil Aeronautics Board's supervision of the airline industry. Kennedy has been pressing for airline deregulation.

He joined with Senate Minority Leader Hugh Scott (R Pa.) in 1973 and 1974 to advance new campaign finance legislation.

In 1975, he joined with Sen. Alan Cranston (D Calif.) and Sen. Dick Clark (D Iowa) in pushing new reform rules through the Senate Democratic caucus. Kennedy and Sen. Ernest F. Hollings (D S.C.) led the Senate fight for repeal of the oil depletion allowance.

Kennedy combined with Sen. Henry M. Jackson (D Wash.) to oppose President Ford's increased duties on imported oil, and with Jackson, Hollings and Cranston to oppose the President's efforts to decontrol domestic oil prices.

Again joining with Cranston, Kennedy participated in efforts to cut the Defense Department's arms procurement authorization bill.

Kennedy has participated in a number of efforts to push tax reform legislation through the Senate, often working with Sen. Walter F. Mondale (D Minn.). And Kennedy is cosponsoring with Sen. Robert T. Stafford (R Vt.) major revisions of federal lobby registration laws.

—By Al Gordon

FOUR YEARS AFTER DEFEAT, A LINGERING INTEREST

It has been nearly eight years since Sen. Edmund S. Muskie of Maine came onto the national scene as the Democratic nominee for Vice President. His calm rhetoric, asking for national unity and reconciliation at a time of disunity and dissent, made him appear to many observers as the most impressive figure in the tumultuous 1968 campaign.

It has been nearly four years since Muskie's presidential candidacy was halted in mid-course. After disappointing showings in the early primaries, he withdrew from the 1972 race, appearing to many observers as indecisive, inept and temperamental.

In his two tries for national office, Muskie projected well the first time but poorly the second. He examined the difference in a newspaper interview in January 1975: "In 1968 and again on election eve in 1970, I struck a chord with the American people that was lacking in 1972, either because I had changed or what the country thought it needed then was different. So I'm not going to assume lightly that what I have to offer by way of leadership or personal qualities is what the country wants in 1976."

Although Muskie's Senate spokesman stated in November 1975 that the 61-year-old Maine senator has "no plans to mount a presidential campaign in 1976," Muskie was embarrassed by his experience in 1972 and has admitted that he would be interested in another try for the White House. He has indicated, though, that he would run for the presidency only if he felt there was a demand for his style of leadership. He doubts that there is.

1976 Prospects

His presidential ambitions are further clouded by the fact that he is up for election to a fourth Senate term in 1976. Muskie has been chairman of the powerful new **Senate Budget Committee** only since 1974, and his first priority is to retain his Senate seat. The 1972 debacle cost him the aura of invincibility that he had built up in two decades of Maine politics. His need to campaign hard for re-election precludes any concerted effort for the presidential nomination.

Muskie is considered vulnerable to a Republican Senate challenge. His status as a national politician reportedly has caused wide segments of the Maine electorate to feel their senator has neglected them in recent years. One Maine source noted that the 1972 campaign "took off six of his seven veils."

Muskie's chances for re-election to the Senate depend largely upon whether Republican Rep. William S. Cohen decides to offer a challenge. Cohen, a two-term House member from Bangor, has indicated that he might seek Muskie's Senate seat. A member of Cohen's staff told Congressional Quarterly that a final decision would not be announced until January and that a Senate challenge is a "50-50 proposition at this time."

Maine observers see no chance of Muskie's having serious opposition in the June 8 Democratic senatorial primary, but polls taken in summer 1975 indicated that a Muskie-Cohen race would be close. Aware of the loss of prestige he suffered in his first presidential try, Muskie, in his frequent trips to Maine, has emphasized that he has no intention of making another bid for the presidency. During his fence-mending jaunts, he has stressed his desire to remain a senator.

But he told an interviewer in February 1975, "I've still got the itch. I wish I didn't—it gets you in trouble—but I do."

"Muskie is stubborn," said a source who follows his career closely. "He hates like hell to lose. He feels he was rudely treated in the last campaign. Something inside him wants to try again, but he'd never say it."

If he did say it, he would already have the advantage of being well known nationally and of having run comparatively well in presidential trial heats conducted by public-opinion pollsters. While he does not have the committed support of any constituency in the party, neither does he have many enemies. He could make an acceptable compromise candidate at a factionalized, stalemated convention. But Muskie is just one of several compromise possibilities if a stalemate should develop.

1972 Campaign

Muskie's 1972 campaign for the presidency suffered one of the most spectacular collapses in American political history. Considered a front-runner for the nomination in early March, Muskie withdrew as an active candidate six weeks later. His candidacy was designed to appeal to virtually all elements in the Democratic Party. But his campaign was more suited to a general election race, and his efforts to gain wide support were unworkable against a multi-candidate field of contestants for the nomination. He had the backing of no large, identifiable constituency in the party, and his lack of committed supporters soon became evident.

Muskie's road to front-runner status began with his well-received vice presidential campaign in 1968. Massachusetts Sen. Edward M. Kennedy's Chappaquidick accident the next year bolstered Muskie's presidential stock, and an effective nationwide telecast on behalf of Democratic candidates on the eve of the 1970 congressional elections solidified his position atop the party's presidential preference polls.

Throughout 1971, Muskie had the look of a winner. His poll ratings remained high, he benefited from favorable media attention and his strategy of gaining endorsements from leading Democratic politicians across the country made his nomination, to many observers, seem all but in-

Muskie's Interest-Group Ratings

Americans for Democratic Action (ADA)—ADA ratings are based on the number of times a senator voted, was paired for or announced for the ADA position on selected issues.

National Farmers Union (NFU)—NFU ratings are based on the number of times a senator voted, was paired for or announced for the NFU position.

AFL-CIO Committee on Political Education (COPE)—COPE ratings reflect the percentage of the time a senator voted in accordance with or was paired in favor of the COPE position.

Americans for Constitutional Action (ACA)—ACA ratings record the percentage of the time a senator voted in accordance with the ACA position.

Following are Muskie's ratings since he entered the Senate in 1959:

	ADA[1]	COPE[3]	NFU[3]	ACA
1974	100	73	100	0
1973	95	82	100	0
1972	70	86	80	0
1971	85	83	100	7
1970	91[4]	100	100	10
1969	94	100	86	0
1968	79	67	77	5
1967	62	91	100	4
1966	85	92[2]	83	4
1965	82	92[2]	92	9
1964	95	100[2]	76[2]	0
1963	88	100[2]	76[2]	9
1962	75	91[2]	100[2]	0
1961	100	91[2]	100[2]	9
1960	83	100[2]	89[2]	15
1959	92	100[2]	89[2]	12[5]

1. Failure to vote lowers score.
2. Scores listed twice indicate rating compiled for entire Congress.
3. Percentages compiled by CQ from information provided by groups.
4. ADA score includes some votes from December 1969.
5. Score for votes on selected issues since 1955.

evitable. But his vague theme of "trust Muskie" and his middle-of-the-road approach to issues was not winning many dedicated supporters, the ones who would work in grass-roots organizations and elect delegates to the national convention.

Muskie decided to compete for delegates in almost every state, and the thinness of his support was exposed in the early caucuses and primaries. He won pluralities in the Iowa and Arizona caucuses and the New Hampshire primary, but his showings fell below reported expectations. When it became apparent that the Muskie campaign was not as strong as first believed, slippage began. Poll ratings dropped, organizing and fund-raising became more difficult—and news coverage emphasized the problems.

Cracks in the Muskie campaign were evident after the March 7 New Hampshire primary, and the decline accelerated drastically after a fourth-place showing in Florida the next week. A series of losses in the Wisconsin, Massachusetts and Pennsylvania primaries led to Muskie's decision on April 27 to stop actively campaigning. Although he remained a candidate until July 11, the day before national convention balloting, his viability as a contender had been destroyed by the string of primary losses, and he was unable to regain it.

Testimony before the Senate Watergate Committee in 1973 disclosed that the Muskie campaign had been the victim of sabotage activities executed by operatives of President Nixon's re-election campaign. One of the most damaging incidents was the "Canuck" letter, written in February 1972 to *The Manchester (N.H.) Union Leader*, a powerful opponent of Muskie. The letter allegedly was written by a Florida man, who claimed that while Muskie was campaigning in Florida, he had made reference to "Canucks," a disparaging term for French-Americans, who make up a substantial minority of the New Hampshire population. Without checking the authenticity of the letter, the Union Leader published it on Feb. 24, less than two weeks before the state presidential primary.

Stung by the paper's use of the letter, as well as its earlier reprint of an unflattering *Newsweek* magazine article about his wife, Jane, Muskie reacted angrily. Standing in front of the newspaper's offices on Feb. 26, he denied the charge in the "Canuck" letter and bitterly denounced the Union Leader's editor, William Loeb. "This man doesn't walk, he crawls.... It's fortunate for him he's not on this platform beside me," he said. Although Muskie denied it, several reporters on the scene reported that he lost emotional control at the end of his remarks and cried.

The emotional display was disillusioning to many voters across the nation and was a factor in the rapid collapse of the Muskie campaign. Reflecting on the event in September 1973, Muskie agreed that it had a negative impact on his candidacy: "I don't know whether that particular episode was responsible for my disappointing showing in New Hampshire. But I suspect it cast a pall over the remainder of our effort. We could never quite get over it...."

Although agreeing that illegal campaign activities hurt his candidacy, Muskie, in an April 1974 newspaper interview, stated that his own centrist strategy was more responsible for his ultimate defeat. He noted that primary voters were making only a preliminary decision on the presidency and, as a result, were willing to vote for non-centrist candidates who had little chance to win the general election. In 1972, Muskie observed, the primary voters wanted someone who would "spit in the eye of the establishment. I think we read it wrong."

Political Background

Throughout his political career in Maine, Muskie has been a Democrat among Republicans, a Catholic among Protestants and a Polish-American among Yankees.

He was born in Rumford, Maine, the son of an immigrant Polish tailor. He was graduated from Bates College in 1936 and from Cornell University Law School in 1939. After four years as a Navy officer during World War II, he returned to law practice in Waterville, Maine.

Muskie entered politics in 1946, when he was elected to the Maine House of Representatives. The next year he ran for mayor of Waterville, but lost—his only defeat until he ran for the vice presidency in 1968. Muskie remained in the legislature after this loss and in 1949 was made house minority leader. Two years later, he resigned from the legislature to become Maine director of the federal Office of Price Stabilization.

In 1952, he declined an invitation to be the Democratic gubernatorial candidate, but accepted two years later and defeated the Republican incumbent, Burton M. Cross (1952-55), 54.5 per cent to 45.5 per cent. Muskie's victory was a breakthrough for Maine's Democratic Party, which had not won a gubernatorial or senatorial election since the early 1930s. Muskie was the state's first Catholic governor.

His personal qualities that have made him appealing to Maine's traditionally Republican voters have been described by one former administrative assistant, Donald E. Nicoll, this way: "...He sees himself as a first-generation American—not abused, not discriminated against, but a little separate. But he also feels very much a part of Maine, very much at home with the WASPs of Maine.... He has their reticence, a low-key quality, a kind of flinty insistence on facts and precision in getting answers to problems. A kind of deliberate approach to life...."

Muskie won re-election as governor in 1965 with 59.2 per cent of the vote. During his four years as Maine's chief executive, he stressed programs to rehabilitate the state's economy, winning considerable Republican as well as Democratic support for his efforts.

Muskie became Maine's first popularly elected Democratic senator in 1958, when he unseated incumbent Frederick G. Payne (R 1953-59) with 60.8 per cent of the vote. Muskie twice has won re-election to the Senate, easily defeating Rep. Clifford McIntire (R 1951-65) in 1964 with 66.6 per cent of the vote and Republican Neil S. Bishop in 1970 with 61.7 per cent.

Senate Career

If Muskie was indecisive in his 1972 campaign, as critics have charged, this indecision has not been evident in his Senate activities, according to another former administrative assistant, John T. McEvoy, now chief counsel

Muskie's Background

Profession: Attorney.
Born: March 28, 1914, Rumford, Maine.
Home: Waterville, Maine.
Religion: Roman Catholic.
Education: Bates College, Lewiston, Maine, A.B., 1936; Cornell University, LL.B., 1939.
Offices: Maine House of Representatives, 1947-53; governor, 1955-59; Senate since 1959.
Military: Navy, 1942-45; discharged as lieutenant.
Memberships: Waterville, Kennebec County, Maine and Massachusetts Bar Associations; Commercial Law League; Lions; AMVETS.
Family: Wife, Jane Gray; five children.
Committees: Chairman, Budget; Government Operations: chairman, Subcommittee on Intergovernmental Relations; Public Works: chairman, Subcommittee on Environmental Pollution; Special Aging: chairman, Subcommittee on Health of the Elderly.

to the Senate Budget Committee. McEvoy observed: "The kind of cerebration involved in policy issues is what he thrives on.... His decision-making process was notorious during the campaign, but in areas he knows he's very sure of himself.... There's no trace of indecision in his performance in Congress."

Two of Muskie's chief legislative interests have stemmed from the committee assignments he has held since he entered the Senate in 1959. Muskie has dealt with environmental problems as chairman of the Public Works Subcommittee on Environmental Pollution. And his chairmanship of the Government Operations Subcommittee on Intergovernmental Relations has led to a concern with improving communications between the states and the federal government.

Muskie is the author of the Clean Air Act of 1963 (PL 88-206) and the Water Quality Act of 1965 (PL 89-234), both of which expanded federal standards and participation in pollution control. Muskie's Clean Air Act amendments of 1970 (PL 91-604), which passed over the strenuous opposition of the automobile industry, set a 1975 deadline for the production of a virtually pollution-free car. But, influenced largely by difficulties created by the energy crisis, Muskie was floor manager of legislation enacted in 1974 (PL 93-319) which temporarily delayed certain clean air standards established under the 1970 act. He has proposed that final auto emission standards go into effect in 1978, except for cars that get more than 20 miles per gallon in city driving, which would be given a two-year reprieve.

Muskie has promoted legislation to curtail noise pollution and to establish federal standards for solid waste management. On the related environmental issue of mass transit, he cosponsored legislation in 1972 and 1973 that authorized, for the first time, use of money from the highway trust fund for urban mass transit needs. The Muskie proposal passed the Senate each year, but was killed in conference in 1972 and was modified in the bill enacted in 1973 (PL 93-87).

Muskie is a recognized expert in the Senate on intergovernmental affairs and was an important early supporter of former President Nixon's revenue-sharing plan. But Muskie objected to revenue sharing once it became law, claiming that it failed to deliver adequately to the state and local governments in most need.

Muskie Senate Staff

Administrative assistant: Charles J. Micoleau.
Legislative assistant: Richard Bayard.
Press secretary: Robert Rose.
Budget Committee staff director: Douglas J. Bennet.
Budget Committee chief counsel: John T. McEvoy.

Muskie's CQ Vote Study Scores*

	1974	1973	1972	1971	1970	1969	1968	1967	1966	1965	1964	1963	1962	1961	1960	1959
Presidential																
support	35¹/43²	26	15	21	40	51	60	76	68	71	78	88	83	75	44	41
opposition	61¹/54²	54	46	40	44	42	12	9	13	7	6	6	9	15	35	44
Voting																
Participation	93	84	48	59	74	89	65	82	76	77	90	88	88	90	87	87
Party																
unity	84	82	45	63	71	79	52	81	71	77	86	75	90	85	62	71
opposition	10	8	3	5	5	11	11	4	3	5	4	5	1	6	20	15
Conservative																
Coalition																
support	7	7	1	8	4	9	16	9	1	15	2	16	18	8	15	10
opposition	87	83	58	62	78	81	49	75	74	72	90	74	68	80	61	75
Bipartisan																
support	81	69	39	40	61	69	54	72	62	69	72	88	71	84	79	80
opposition	11	11	10	14	13	20	12	9	15	5	9	5	14	5	11	9

*Explanation of studies, p. 107.
1. During President Nixon's tenure in 1974.
2. During President Ford's tenure in 1974.

Similarly, Muskie objected to Nixon's concept of "new federalism," designed to slash programs at the national level while increasing responsibility at the state and local levels. Muskie argued that the "new federalism" would merely increase state and local taxes, because these governments would be forced to assume the financing of services the national government was trimming.

To provide hard-pressed state and local governments with anti-recession help, Muskie worked successfully for Senate passage in July 1975 of a measure that provided federal aid on the basis of local unemployment and tax rates (S 1587). The legislation was consistent with his belief that federal legislation should take into account the different needs of each state and locality and should impose responsibilities on states and localities that wished to qualify for federal aid.

In 1971, Muskie gained a seat on the Foreign Relations Committee, a coveted assignment for a presidential aspirant. As chairman of the Subcommittee on Surveillance, Muskie became a frequent critic of illegal intelligence-gathering. Terming the Nixon administration's concept of government secrecy "a nightmare for a democracy," Muskie in 1973 proposed congressional control over the classification of government documents. The next year, on the related issue of personal privacy, he cosponsored legislation to provide safeguards and standards for information-gathering and to create a federal privacy board (PL 93-579).

In 1975, Muskie gave up his seat on Foreign Relations after he had been chosen chairman of the Budget Committee. He had been active in Senate passage of the budget reform bill (PL 93-344). His selection as chairman of the new committee in July 1974 increased his power in the Senate. The new post gave Muskie and his fellow committee members the authority to analyze budget options and prepare budget resolutions that would set target figures for appropriations bills.

Muskie has taken his new job seriously, becoming a steady presence on the floor of the Senate whenever bills affecting spending have come up. For each such bill, he has presented an analysis of how the measure fits into the targets and how passage might affect other bills in the same category that remain to be voted on. Although he has rarely opposed one of these bills, he has made plain their impact on the over-all budget.

In 1975, Muskie's efforts brought spending cuts in the school lunch, military procurement and federal pay raise bills. His slicing of funds from programs that are cherished by both liberals and conservatives has brought protests from both sides.

But Muskie has drawn high marks from Senate colleagues. Sen. Henry Bellmon (R Okla.), a Budget Committee member, commented in September 1975: "I think he has been fair and courageous, because he's taken some positions that are plainly not popular in the circles in which he normally moves. I have nothing but praise for him at this point."

Muskie's ultimate power in the Senate will be determined in part by future confrontations with the Appropriations and Finance Committees, the two committees that formerly had the greatest impact on budget review. But regardless of the outcome, Muskie is enjoying his new role. A Democratic colleague told *The Washington Star* in an October 1975 interview: "It's almost like he came back to life after losing everything in 1972. He really enjoys the action, the leadership role this Budget Committee has given him. He's helped to spawn a major new institution, and he's done a tremendous job of it."

—By Rhodes Cook

MAKING AN ASSET OF DISTANCE FROM WASHINGTON

James Terry Sanford, a 58-year-old university president who has not held public office in 11 years, is making a long-shot stab at the presidency by offering himself as a fresh face in a crowd of well-known Democrats mostly nurtured in Congress.

Factors that his rivals portray as liabilities—his absence from politics, his isolation in academia, his anonymity—Sanford claims as assets. "I bring experience not born of Washington and not tainted by Washington," he proclaimed in his announcement address. "We need freshness. We need change."

But to establish his claim on the White House, Sanford has set himself the task of knocking off George C. Wallace, another southern Democrat and Washington outsider whom most of the other candidates are treating very gingerly. Sanford eschews the giant-killer billing for fear that it will cast him into too narrow a role, but he says the confrontation is inevitable, a responsibility. "My mission in life is not to eliminate the George Wallaces from the political scene," he said. "However, I came up at the same time in similar climate, region and crucial times, and it is my responsibility to challenge him."

Personal Background

Terry Sanford "came up" in Laurinburg, a small farming town in conservative eastern North Carolina. His father was a hardware merchant; his mother, a public school teacher for more than 40 years. Terry attended the public schools in Laurinburg, went to a local junior college for two years and then transferred to the University of North Carolina, where he obtained his B.A. in 1939. He returned there after World War II to earn his law degree.

Sanford served briefly as a special agent in the FBI in 1941-42 before joining the Army as a private. As a paratrooper in Europe, he fought in five campaigns, won a Purple Heart and emerged from the war as a 1st lieutenant.

After the war and law school, Sanford taught at the University of North Carolina for two years, then opened a law office in Fayetteville, N.C. Except for his term as governor, Sanford practiced law in Fayetteville and Raleigh until he became president of Duke University in 1970.

Early Politics

Sanford established a reputation early as an energetic worker in the liberal wing of the state Democratic Party. In 1949, he was elected president of the state Young Democrats. The next year, he worked in the unsuccessful Senate re-election campaign of Frank P. Graham (D 1949-50), a former president of the state university who was regarded as a progressive. Graham was defeated in a bitter primary runoff by Willis Smith (D 1950-53), who painted Graham as a left-leaning friend of Communists and blacks.

Four years later, in a campaign similarly fought on the grounds of racism and red-baiting, Sanford ran the Senate race of Democrat W. Kerr Scott, a progressive former

governor (1949-53) who had appointed the first black to the state school board and the first woman to the state superior court. Stealing the offensive from incumbent Alton A. Lennon (D 1953-54) on controversial issues, Scott and Sanford accused Lennon of "McCarthyism" and called for criminal prosecution of candidates raising the race issue in political campaigns.

"What I learned from the campaign against Dr. Frank [Graham]," Sanford later recalled, "kept me from letting them get away with the same thing against Kerr Scott four years later." Scott won the highest vote ever received in a North Carolina primary until that time, and then was elected to the Senate, where he served until his death in 1958.

Sanford himself won a seat in the state senate in 1952. He served one term, then returned full-time to his law practice. In 1956, he was a member of the North Carolina delegation that gave almost all its Democratic national convention votes to Adlai E. Stevenson.

In 1960, Sanford ran for governor on a platform of improving education and attracting new industry to the state. When pressed, he acknowledged that his program would involve tax increases; but his platform, his progressive background and his strong party roots won him wide backing from labor, teachers and blacks, as well as from party regulars. After finishing with a comfortable plurality in the four-man primary, he went on to beat segregationist I. Beverly Lake in a runoff by a 56-44 margin.

Although a Democratic primary victory in North Carolina traditionally had meant easy election in November, Sanford came close to being the first Democrat in 50 years to lose the governorship to a Republican. Splitting from a solid southern bloc for Lyndon B. Johnson, he had seconded the presidential nomination of John F. Kennedy at that summer's Democratic convention, and there was speculation before the election that his speech would cost him the governor's office. Sanford defeated Republican Robert L. Gavin by a 55-45 margin, but Gavin had the largest vote ever received by a Republican until that time.

Record as Governor

In recalling his four years in the governorship, Sanford stresses his accomplishments in education; his campaign literature touts him as "the education governor." But in North Carolina, Sanford is remembered still as "High Tax Terry," a title hung on him by his enemies. The two labels are related.

Shortly after taking office, Sanford pushed through the state legislature a sales tax on food and medicine to finance a general increase in teacher pay. Salaries for teachers rose dramatically during his administration—22 per cent in the first year—but the sales tax remains a highly visible and, especially to lower-income groups, painful reminder of the Sanford administration. Sanford says now that the tax should be removed.

Sanford used his office to initiate several social and educational programs that in some cases served as models for other states and the federal government. His North Carolina Fund, for example, built on the gifts of the Ford and other foundations and implemented through neighborhood action councils, is said to have been studied by the Office of Economic Opportunity as a basis for the federal antipoverty program. Other Sanford projects provided special aid for gifted as well as deprived students, vocational and career training for adults and special attention to the arts.

Sanford drew national attention as governor for his moderate racial stand. He entered office calling for "massive intelligence, not massive resistance" in school desegregation, and he enrolled his own children in Raleigh's only integrated school. He undertook a campaign to open up public and private jobs for blacks, and he appointed a number of blacks and women to state jobs. He helped push

---

Sanford Staff, Advisers

Campaign director: Jean M. Westwood, a longtime party activist from Utah, national cochairman of George McGovern's presidential campaign committee in 1972 and, in 1972, the first woman Democratic national chairman.

Campaign manager: Dennis W. Shaul, formerly an Akron, Ohio, city councilman and director of the Ohio Department of Commerce under Gov. John J. Gilligan (D 1970-75).

Campaign chairman: Hulett C. Smith, former governor of West Virginia (D 1965-69).

Financial director: Vicki L. Bagley, a North Carolinian and former Rand Corporation employee.

Treasurer: Barbara Morgan, Democratic national committeewoman from the District of Columbia.

---

through the state legislature the repeal of a law requiring segregated rest rooms in public restaurants, and he ordered removal of all signs designating separate facilities in state-owned buildings.

But Sanford's record as governor was subject to criticism, on racial issues and others. In 1961, he oversaw a Democratic gerrymander of congressional districts which created some of the greatest population disparities of any districts in the nation. When segregation opponents staged peaceful sit-ins during the gubernatorial campaign to choose his successor, the governor attacked the protestors for extremism, comparing their tactics to those of the Ku Klux Klan. Sanford was the last North Carolina governor to allow a prisoner to die in the gas chamber, although he now opposes capital punishment.

Record at Duke

After his departure from the governor's office, Sanford led a research project at Duke to study the role of states in the federal system. One result was his book, *Storm Over the States*, calling for a rejuvenated federalism with more power residing in the states. Another result was a strong tie with Duke, which led to a bid in 1969 for Sanford to become the sixth president of the respected private university in Durham, N.C.

Sanford was regarded warily at first by students and faculty, who were skeptical about his political ambitions and his credentials, as a lawyer with no other advanced degree, to lead a major university. But Sanford since has won a reputation as an innovative administrator, initiating a range of new programs and attracting money and respected names in the academic field.

He has reneged on an early promise to students not to seek further office. But he has assured the Duke community that his ambitions are limited to the presidency and that he is not interested in the vice presidency or a cabinet post. As part of his contract with Duke, he will take a one-year sabbatical in 1976.

National Politics

Because of his election as a moderate in a southern state and especially because of his ties to the Kennedy administration, Sanford won national attention when he became governor. His support for Kennedy at the 1960 convention, although a risk at the time, paid off well in terms of entree into the White House and federal aid to his state. Sanford was mentioned as a possible vice presidential candidate for Kennedy's planned re-election effort in 1964. When Johnson ran as an incumbent that year, Sanford again drew attention (and antagonized conservatives) by stumping against Republican nominee Barry Goldwater in the South.

Sanford made no secret of his interest in further political office after he left the statehouse in 1965, but the opportunities were not there. He considered running for the Senate seat of Sam J. Ervin Jr. (D N.C. 1954-74) in 1968, but dropped the idea after soundings taken around the state proved discouraging.

That same year, he had been preparing for a major role in the Johnson re-election campaign. When Johnson resigned, he jumped into the Hubert H. Humphrey campaign of 1968 as national chairman of Citizens for Humphrey-Muskie. They remain close friends.

Because of his party service and his image as a moderate southerner, Sanford has figured regularly among those "mentioned prominently" before presidential conventions as possible ticket-balancers. He was an undeclared candidate for Vice President in 1968 and 1972, and he was considered for national party chairman in 1969.

In 1974, Sanford was chairman of a Democratic commission that drafted the first charter ever adopted by a major party. He played a decisive role in engineering party agreement on a compromise charter that encouraged minority participation in party affairs without offending Democratic regulars who feared permanent capture of the party by "New Left" elements. Sanford was praised for his fairness and coolness in running the commission.

1972 Campaign

In 1972, the week after a New Hampshire Democratic presidential primary that produced no clear-cut winner, Sanford announced his candidacy as an alternative to Sen. Edmund S. Muskie of Maine and as a progressive southern alternative to Wallace. "If the front-runner falters," he declared in his announcement, "and in fairness, he has not caught the imagination of the people in a degree that can carry him to success in the fall election, the delegates will make the choice, most likely a fresh face."

By the May 6 North Carolina primary, Muskie was no longer a candidate, and the race had narrowed to "a Dixie classic," as a Raleigh newspaper called it, between Wallace and Sanford. Black Rep. Shirley Chisholm (D N.Y.) was also an active campaigner.

Sanford faced several problems from the start. The biggest was that few people in his own state took him seriously as a national contender. His candidacy was dismissed as a stop-Wallace effort, a front for other candidates or a maneuver by Sanford for the vice presidential nomination or a cabinet appointment.

"It's clear that he is nothing but a stalking horse for Hubert Humphrey," argued a Wallace aide just before the election. "He is running strictly as an anti-Wallace candidate with no chance of ever being nominated for the presidency. His only hope is to stop George Wallace in the South for Hubert Humphrey."

Another problem was Chisholm, who threatened to take North Carolina's 10 to 12 per cent black vote but whom Sanford could not attack without offending his own constituency.

Sanford's organization, which he started late, consisted primarily of students (the state party machinery had been committed to Muskie until late in the campaign), and his funding came from a few wealthy backers. Wallace mounted a strong effort, with numerous appearances in the state and some of the highest spending of his national campaign. He put Sanford on the defensive on the busing issue, especially in a vituperative election-eve challenge, in a state that had just undergone a convulsive busing struggle.

Sanford's showing was poor. He won 37 per cent to Wallace's 50 per cent, with scattered votes going to Chisholm, Muskie and others. After the election, Sanford did not disguise his feeling that he had lost votes on the busing issue. "To win, I would have to take positions I would be unwilling to take," he said. But he also blamed his defeat on his late start, weak organization and the siphoning of liberal votes by other candidates.

Sanford remained a candidate at the Democratic convention in Miami Beach, making himself available as a consensus choice if the convention deadlocked. He won 77.5 delegate votes.

> ## Sanford's Background
>
> **Profession:** Attorney, educator; president of Duke University.
> **Born:** Aug. 20, 1917, Laurinburg, N.C.
> **Home:** Durham, N.C.
> **Religion:** Methodist.
> **Education:** University of North Carolina, A.B., 1939, J.D., 1946.
> **Offices:** North Carolina Ports Authority, 1950-53; state senator, 1953-54; governor of North Carolina, 1961-65.
> **Military:** Army, 1942-45.
> **Memberships:** American Bar Association, American Academy of Political and Social Sciences, American Judicature Society, American Arbitration Association, National Municipal League.
> **Family:** Wife, Margaret Rose Knight; two children.

1976 Race

Sanford's campaign for the 1976 nomination is in many ways a rerun of his 1972 bid. Again he is stressing his Washington-outsider identity. Again he is a long shot, and again he is keying his chances on a showdown with Wallace in North Carolina. "We might as well shoot it out at high noon," Sanford said after his announcement, "and if we can't cut it there, get out." The North Carolina primary will be March 23.

Wallace and North Carolina have been accommodating. When the North Carolina Legislature was considering a 1975 bill to abolish the primary, Wallace appeared personally before a state senate committee to urge that the primary be retained. The legislature complied—and added new provisions to the primary law that almost assures a Sanford-Wallace duel. To be on the 1976 ballot, candidates must request that their names be listed, promise to "wage an active and highly visible campaign in North Carolina" and either have qualified for federal matching campaign funds or collected 10,000 signatures on a petition.

Indications in North Carolina are that Sanford's chances are better than in 1972, but he still has an uphill battle. Ferrell Guillory, a political reporter for *The Raleigh News and Observer,* has taken informal voter samples in the North Carolina hinterlands, especially the conservative eastern counties. His conclusion: support for Wallace is slipping, largely because of the Alabama governor's health, but that may not work to Sanford's advantage. "There were an awful lot of people who said they wished they had a third candidate," Guillory told Congressional Quarterly.

One of Sanford's biggest hurdles is to convince home-state voters that he is more than just a local boy out to stop Wallace. As one experienced North Carolina political observer put it, "His credibility problem as a presidential candidate starts here."

With that problem in mind, Sanford is concentrating his limited financial resources on earlier primaries in New Hampshire and especially in Massachusetts. "His strategy," observed Guillory, "seems to be to run in New Hampshire and Massachusetts at least in part to convince North Carolina people that he is a national figure, that it's not just Terry on an ego trip." A respectable showing in Massachusetts—not necessarily a win—would bolster Sanford's legitimacy as a candidate in North Carolina, his staff feels.

Two other problems, related to some extent, are image and money. It is an anomaly of Sanford's campaign that, as an old party war horse often mentioned for high jobs, he is a shopworn candidate but an unknown name.

For that reason, among others, he is having trouble raising money. In 1972, a 1975 campaign report showed, he received $700,000 from one source, an heiress of North Carolina's R. J. Reynolds tobacco family. The loan, which has since been forgiven, is likely to be an issue itself. But under the 1974 Federal Election Campaign Act amendments, such individual contributions are limited to $1,000, and Sanford already has exhausted his supply of wealthy backers. In October 1975, he announced that he had collected the required minimum of $100,000 in small contributions to qualify him for federal matching funds.

Sanford's third-quarter campaign finance report, filed Oct. 10 with the Federal Election Commission, showed the former governor to be in the worst shape of any 1976 contender. The campaign had an operating deficit of $10,000 for the quarter and was more than $78,000 in debt, with less than $7,000 cash on hand, according to the report. A Sanford staff member said the report did not reflect $30,000 raised by Sanford since the figures had been compiled.

At a February 1974 "coming-out party" in New York City, Sanford was asked if he were there to test his strength. "I'm not testing the water," the North Carolinian said. "I already know it's just as cold as can be."

Jean Westwood, a 1972 McGovern supporter, former Democratic national chairman and now Sanford's campaign manager, concedes as much. But, given the glut of candidates, she said, Sanford's chance is as good as any. "I don't think there's anybody whose campaign isn't a long shot. I don't feel bad about that at all."

Positions on Issues

Following is a summary of some positions, besides those already mentioned, taken by Sanford as governor and in campaign statements:

Economy

Sanford has made economic issues the centerpiece of his campaign. He has proposed creation of a national economic council, similar to the President's National Security Council, to provide over-all direction for the nation's spending. He has called for bringing the Federal Reserve Bank, a quasi-independent agency that shapes monetary policy, under the control of the President. To gain greater control over fiscal policy, he would have Congress grant the President limited authority to apply surtaxes or tax rebates through administrative action.

Much of Sanford's emphasis has been on jobs. He has called for full employment, meaning "everyone who wanted to work could get a job." That could be accomplished, at least in part, he says, by an executive with authority to raise or lower interest rates. In addition, he espouses the plan of corporation lawyer Louis Kelso to allow businesses to increase their tax investment credit by providing stock to employees. Such an employee stock ownership plan, he argues, would bring employees into the corporate structure while providing corporations with a major new source of financing, thus smoothing out "boom or bust" cycles that affect jobs.

To fight inflation, Sanford has called for standby wage and price controls that would be triggered by predeter-

mined levels of inflation and would provide automatic price rollbacks.

Sanford has said he would support federal aid to bail New York City out of its financial crisis, but on the condition that the city reduce expenditures and show that it had solved its problems on a permanent basis.

Civil Rights

Sanford claims to have been the first southern governor to pledge an end to job discrimination. To that end, he established as governor a North Carolina Good Neighbor Council to boost employment of blacks in government and private industry.

Expressing personal dislike for busing, Sanford nevertheless says he supports court-ordered busing. He has proposed a search for alternatives, particularly through "enrichment" of schools in deprived areas.

Sanford appointed a number of women to state jobs while governor, including the first woman member of the North Carolina Supreme Court. He supports the Equal Rights Amendment.

Education

During his governorship, Sanford initiated or lent his support to several programs to meet special education needs. Included were a North Carolina School of the Arts; a two-week summer "Governor's School" for gifted high school seniors; the Learning Institute of North Carolina, for education research, and the start of a community college system that has become the second largest in the country.

After leaving the governor's office, Sanford helped organize the Education Commission of the States, a 40-state compact that provides technical and advisory assistance to state and local school systems.

In his 1976 campaign, Sanford has called for decentralization of education spending and decision-making, with greater reliance on local school boards. He has proposed increased federal funding of public education, with more attention to post-high-school vocational education and career training.

Defense, Foreign Affairs

Early in his campaign, Sanford announced that as President he would cut the defense budget by 15 per cent.

Warning against isolationism in the wake of Vietnam, Sanford has said that he would insist on a continuing U.S. commitment to European allies. In his announcement speech, he called for support of the United Nations and for greater cooperation with that body's "third and fourth world" members. Such cooperation would include extending trade benefits to the poor nations, he said.

Sanford has visited both the Soviet Union and the People's Republic of China, and he has said that neither country has "designs" on the United States. While in the Soviet Union in 1975, he said that he sensed from talks with Premier Alexei Kosygin that the United States might obtain an accounting of its citizens missing in Vietnam by approving membership of both Vietnams in the United Nations. The United States vetoed such a proposal in the U.N. Security Council in August.

Sanford is a supporter of Israeli independence and says the United States has a responsibility to supply the country with defensive weapons.

—By Ted Vaden

PERSISTENTLY WORKING AT BEING TAKEN SERIOUSLY

Milton J. Shapp is an unusual politician. He plays the violin, writes poetry and songs and is the author of several unproduced Broadway musicals. He is also the governor of the nation's third largest state, Pennsylvania.

And soon, he expects to be the front-runner for the Democratic presidential nomination, although a nationwide survey indicated that he was known by only one-sixth of the country's Democratic voters in mid-1975. With little visible support outside Pennsylvania, and with an aura of corruption surrounding his administration, the 63-year-old Shapp is regarded as one of the longest of the long shots in the crowded Democratic field.

A millionaire electronics manufacturer elected governor as an opponent of political bosses, Shapp is presenting himself as an economic expert who can get the nation's stagnant economy moving. He discerns an anti-Washington sentiment—a growing dissatisfaction by voters across the country with the federal government, especially Congress. As a governor, Shapp is counting on his ability to tap such a mood in competition with his challengers for the nomination, many of whom are members of Congress.

The Campaign

"I think in four to six months I'll be looked at as the strongest contender in the race," Shapp declared Sept. 25 when he made his official announcement of a presidential candidacy that had been known for months. It was a brash statement for a man whose candidacy is considered by most observers as, at best, a favorite-son effort—and not a very strong one at that. Even among some Pennsylvania Democrats, the response to Shapp's candidacy has not been encouraging. One Democratic legislator has called for Shapp's resignation as governor, and public comments from members of the state Democratic congressional delegation have been noncommittal.

To this widespread skepticism, Shapp has responded: "That's the story of my life. People haven't taken me seriously." But if there is one personal trait that both Shapp's friends and critics acknowledge that he possesses, it is persistence.

Why he is running for President is a matter of speculation. Some political observers believe his candidacy is an attempt to become a political power at the national level, to gain either the vice presidential nomination or a cabinet spot in a Democratic administration, or to set himself up for a run for the Senate in 1976. Shapp denies all this, claiming his only interest is in the presidency.

His bid for the White House, one Harrisburg reporter observed, is consistent with Shapp's background. For the past decade he has been interested in national issues, frequently going to Washington to attend conferences and to testify before congressional committees. His experience as governor has indicated to him that some problems at the state level can only be solved by federal action.

Shapp is offering a businesslike approach to the nation's economic problems as his chief qualification for

the presidency. "I don't think others [Democratic candidates] have studied or understand the economy as deeply as I have," he said.

Shapp alluded to his low-key rhetorical style and lackluster appearance in his announcement speech: "The last thing the American people need is another smiling politician or spellbinding orator spewing political rhetoric." He hopes to portray himself as the skillful administrator, and his campaign manager, Norval D. Reece, although recognizing his candidate's limitations, feels he can be successful. "Shapp is creative, innovative and highly personable," said Reece. "He's the best one-on-one guy I've ever seen. He's more persuasive in a small group or one-on-one situation than in mass meetings."

But before he can go anywhere, Shapp must become better known. A June 1975 Gallup Poll ranked him 27th on a list of 34 possible Democratic candidates. In a similar Harris Survey the next month, his name was not even on a list of 23 Democratic possibilities. But, because of the long list of Democratic candidates and the large number of undecided voters, he does not view his lack of recognition as insurmountable.

While Shapp is undertaking a national campaign, his efforts are focusing on a few key primary states where he hopes strong showings will ignite his campaign. He is planning to enter the early New England primaries, New Hampshire on Feb. 24 and Massachusetts on March 2, as well as the New York and Wisconsin primaries on April 6 and the Pennsylvania primary three weeks later. Reece also indicated that Shapp is looking at the Oregon, California, New Jersey and Ohio primaries (the last three on June 8), but that the Pennsylvania primary April 27 is viewed as the "watershed."

Pennsylvania's 178 votes will make it the third-largest delegation at the 1976 convention. While Shapp may not win the unbinding popularity vote in his home state, many observers believe that he should win a plurality of the delegates on the basis of his strong statewide organization. An impressive showing in the Pennsylvania primary would at least allow Shapp to go to the convention as a favorite son.

But the heart of any effective campaign is money, and this is an enormous problem for Shapp. In his campaigns for governor, he was able to contribute millions from his personal fortune. But under the new federal campaign finance law, a candidate and his family can contribute a total of only $50,000, a small fraction of the amount needed to run an effective presidential campaign. As of Sept. 30, 1975, the Shapp campaign had reported receiving a total of $121,742. More than 80 per cent of the money came from Pennsylvania, including a $15,000 contribution from his wife, Muriel.

Much of the money came from Jewish and black voters and liberal groups, which, along with labor and women's organizations, are expected to provide Shapp with his strongest support. Reece foresees his candidate as running as an "independent Democrat," pulling some liberal voters from Arizona Rep. Morris K. Udall, some labor support from Indiana Sen. Birch Bayh and some Jewish support from Washington Sen. Henry M. Jackson. Shapp is Jewish.

Business Career

Shapp was born in Cleveland, Ohio, in 1912, the son of Aaron Shapiro, a hardware wholesaler and traveling salesman. Shapp graduated from the Case Institute of Technology with a degree in electrical engineering. As a result of religious bigotry, in his mid-20s he legally changed his name from Shapiro to Shapp.

During World War II, Shapp served as an officer in the Army Signal Corps in Europe. After the war, he moved to the Philadelphia area, and, with his background in engineering, became an entrepreneur in the fledgling cable

---

Shapp Staff, Advisers

Campaign manager: Norval D. Reece, former special assistant to the governor for intergovernmental relations; candidate for the Democratic senatorial nomination in 1970.

Cochairman: Henry A. Satterwhite of Bradford, Pa., board chairman of Allegheny Airlines.

Finance director: Bronson P. Clark Jr., of Vinal Haven, Maine, and Washington, D.C., former executive vice president of Gilford Instrument Laboratories Inc. of Oberlin, Ohio, and former executive secretary of the American Friends Service Committee.

Treasurer: G. Thomas Miller, a Harrisburg attorney and former judge of the state court of common pleas.

Governor's executive assistant: Richard A. Doran, a former assistant to Rep. William J. Green (D Pa.).

---

television industry. In 1948, he established the Jerrold Electronics Corporation (titled after his middle name) with a $500 investment. The company initially employed two workers, but it expanded quickly and became profitable.

In 1966, when Shapp made his first run for the governorship of Pennsylvania, he resigned as president and chairman of the board of Jerrold and sold his 25 per cent share. Jerrold then employed 2,100 workers in six plants in the Philadelphia area, and Shapp's share sold for nearly $10-million.

In 1971, during his first year as governor, Shapp listed his personal worth at nearly $4-million. At a press conference in October 1975, Shapp revealed that his net worth had been $7.5-million in 1966 when he first ran for governor but had shrunk to $2.8-million by 1975.

He first became involved in politics in 1960, when he was statewide chairman of business and professional men for Kennedy and Johnson. After President Kennedy's election, Shapp became a consultant to the U.S. Commerce Department, concerned primarily with setting up the area redevelopment program. He also served as a consultant to the Peace Corps.

1966 Campaign

Shapp showed an increasing interest in state government. In 1965, he undertook a detailed study of major state issues, publishing reports on the Pennsylvania economy, transportation and organization of the state government.

He made his first run for office the next year, when he sought the Democratic gubernatorial nomination. Although party leaders appreciated Shapp's financial support, they did not take his candidacy seriously. They ignored him and endorsed State Sen. Robert P. Casey.

Little-known statewide, Shapp made his campaign a fight against the party bosses. His slogan: "Man against the Machine."

Shapp's extensive media campaign dramatically increased his voter recognition, and his reform candidacy attracted support from liberals, minority groups and large segments of the state's powerful organized labor movement. He gained the endorsement of the Pennsylvania AFL-CIO Executive Council.

Nearly all of Shapp's campaign money came out of his own pocket, and he reported spending $1.4-million. It was money well spent. In an upset, Shapp defeated Casey in the primary. He lost the November election to Republican Raymond P. Shafer, despite spending another $2.4-million of his fortune.

1970 Election

Shapp remained highly visible after his defeat, testifying on several occasions at congressional hearings. He remained active in Pennsylvania politics, creating and becoming chairman of the Pennsylvania Democratic Study Group, an organization that analyzed and proposed solutions to state problems. But he remained an adversary of the state party establishment, attending the 1968 Democratic convention as an anti-war delegate.

In 1970, Shapp again ran for the Democratic gubernatorial nomination, with Casey as his primary opponent. In a rematch of their 1966 race, Casey received the formal endorsement of party leaders, while Shapp stressed his independence of the state party organization. Organized labor, which had been with Shapp four years earlier, was officially neutral in the 1970 primary. In spite of the neutrality of the state labor leadership, many locals still supported Shapp.

Spending about $1-million of his own fortune, Shapp again launched a media blitz in the final days of the primary. It helped produce another narrow victory over Casey.

He ran his general election campaign completely independent of the party organization. Shapp's election drive was assisted by the general unpopularity of the incumbent administration. The state's faltering economy and expanded budget had brought an increased sales tax, and the necessity of a state income tax loomed. With the help of another $1-million of his own money, he won in a landslide over Republican Lt. Gov. Raymond J. Broderick.

It was a memorable victory. He became the first Jewish governor in Pennsylvania history. His margin of victory, more than 500,000 votes, was the largest ever achieved by any Democratic candidate for governor of Pennsylvania.

The Governorship

"Shapp was elected as an independent Democrat, and he's viewed with some suspicion by the legislature. He's not a club member. His interests are not the same as a majority of the legislature." So said Norval Reece in an interview with Congressional Quarterly. Shapp's relations with the state legislature have been cool throughout his administration.

Except for one term of the general assembly (1973-74), the Democrats have controlled both houses of the legislature during the Shapp administration. But the Democratic majorities have frequently been narrow, with the deciding votes cast by a group of conservative, rural Democrats. "He's a loner," said one statehouse reporter, "who runs the state government close to his vest."

Shapp's greatest problems have been with the state senate, which frequently has blocked confirmation of Shapp appointees. Only four hours after Shapp was sworn in as governor in 1971, the senate rejected his 10 choices for cabinet positions, in a protest over Shapp's failure to consult with them. Shapp's choices were subsequently confirmed, but the incident set the tone for the chilliness that has existed between the governor and the legislature.

Confirmations have not been the only source of friction between the governor and the legislature. Shapp has vetoed four major bills approved by the legislature in the past two years. In 1974, he vetoed bills banning pornography, limiting abortions and restoring the death penalty. In 1975, he vetoed an anti-busing bill. The abortion and death penalty bills were overridden by the legislature, and an attempt to override the anti-busing veto fell short by only three votes in the Senate.

The major achievement of the Shapp administration, mentioned by virtually all observers, has been restoration of fiscal stability in the state government. Pennsylvania was on the verge of bankruptcy when Shapp took office in 1971, with a state debt of about $500-million.

By March of that year, the legislature had passed a $1.5-billion revenue bill supported by Shapp; at the heart of the measure was the state's first income tax. Although Shapp pushed for a graduated tax, he had to settle for a flat-rate tax after the Pennsylvania Supreme Court declared the graduated tax was unconstitutional.

In conjunction with the revenue bill, Shapp commissioned 85 business and professional experts to under-

Shapp's Background

Profession: Electronics manufacturer.
Born: June 25, 1912, Cleveland, Ohio.
Home: Merion, Pa.
Religion: Jewish.
Education: Case Institute of Technology, B.S., 1933.
Offices: Governor of Pennsylvania since 1971.
Military: Army, 1942-46; discharged as captain.
Memberships: Jewish Community Relations Council, American Jewish Council, United World Federalists, National Council on Aging, Philadelphia Association for Retarded Children Inc., VFW, Jewish War Veterans, B'nai B'rith, American Legion.
Family: Wife, Muriel Matzkin; three children.

take an independent management review of the state's fiscal policy. The result was cutbacks in state spending and a tax cut of $360-million in 1974.

Although he dealt decisively with the economic chaos that engulfed the state government early in his administration, Shapp was faced with a budget deficit in 1975—a significant problem, because he promised in his 1974 re-election campaign that he would not raise taxes. While ruling out hikes in the income or sales taxes, the Shapp administration was studying increases in selected taxes, such as those on cigarettes, gasoline and auto registration fees.

Expanded programs for the elderly rank with economic reform as the greatest achievements claimed by the Shapp administration. All money raised in the state lottery goes into programs for the elderly. The state subsidizes free mass transportation for the aged, the first statewide program of its type in the nation. A tax break for elderly property owners and renters is also provided by the state.

But one statehouse correspondent noted that Shapp has "almost no record at all in the passage of major bills. He has put in very little." Rather than initiating many administration bills, Shapp has tended to support bills that have been introduced by legislators. As a consequence, many of the most innovative aspects of his administration have been made by executive decree rather than by work with the legislature. Notable are a financial disclosure requirement for cabinet members, the establishment of a bank delivery system to curtail welfare fraud, and the use of independent management review commissions to analyze the efficiency of various parts of the state government.

Reece describes his candidate as one who "goes where the action is." This penchant for involvement brought Shapp his first national exposure in February 1974, when he mediated negotiations between independent truckers and the White House over fuel prices and allocation.

While Shapp has not made a further impact nationally, he has consolidated his political base in Pennsylvania. Although he was an anti-organization candidate in 1966 and 1970, through his use of patronage and deals with individual leaders, he now is the dominant figure in the state's diverse Democratic Party. One reporter in Harrisburg described Shapp as a shrewd politician who "used the white knight image as long as he needed."

His political power was enhanced by a change in the state constitution in the late 1960s, allowing him to run for re-election in 1974—the first Pennsylvania governor in the

20th century permitted to do so. Shapp's re-election effort was aided by the decisions of leading Democratic adversaries, such as Philadelphia Mayor Frank Rizzo, not to run against him. With minimal opposition, Shapp easily won the primary. In the general election, he defeated Republican Andrew L. Lewis Jr. by a margin of 53.8 per cent to 45.2 per cent.

The Corruption Issue

In spite of its reform rhetoric, the Shapp administration has been labeled by some observers as the most corrupt in Pennsylvania history. By early October 1975, 23 state officials had been convicted since Shapp took office, and 29 others were under indictment. Among those convicted was Frank Hilton, Shapp's 1970 campaign manager and later the state secretary of property and supplies, and Democratic State Treasurer William Casper—both convicted of extortion. Among those under investigation for allegedly soliciting kickbacks were the Democratic state chairman, the secretary of revenue and officials in the Revenue Department, the Liquor Control Board and the State Bureau of Professional and Occupational Affairs.

While there were signs of corruption in various parts of the state government, Shapp himself was not implicated until August, when Michael Baker Jr., head of a large engineering firm that does business with the state, testified before a Pittsburgh grand jury. He said that twice during the 1970 campaign he personally had given Shapp $10,000 in cash—money that did not show up in the financial records of the campaign. Shapp appeared voluntarily before the grand jury on Oct. 9 and, while he admitted receiving the money from Baker, he denied any wrongdoing.

Positions on Issues

Following is a summary of Shapp's positions on various issues:

Economy

"No other issues will really be solved unless we have a healthy economic base," Shapp declared in his presidential announcement speech. "Unless we stimulate the economy, you'll have a crisis in this country of such proportions that you'll have an unstable government."

Shapp's plan to revive the nation's economy involves revamping the federal budgetary system and establishing a national investment policy. "The United States doesn't have a true budget in the business sense," Shapp stated, "but a cash flow sheet." He advocates creation of a budget system that would separate government operating costs from long-term capital investment funds. The latter would be freed for investment in private sectors of the economy, according to Shapp, increasing jobs and stimulating about $2.50 of private investment for each dollar invested by the government.

Energy

Shapp has opposed President Ford's fee on imported oil. In January 1975, he termed it a "blueprint for economic disaster" that would create "a shock wave of inflation through the country greater than the one we had when the Arabs lifted their embargo." He joined seven other northeastern governors, 10 utilities and Rep. Robert F. Drinan (D Mass.) in bringing suit against the Ford plan.

On Aug. 11, the plaintiffs received a favorable verdict from the U.S. Court of Appeals in the District of Columbia, which ruled that Ford had exceeded his legal authority in imposing the $2-a-barrel oil import fee. The White House appealed the decision to the Supreme Court.

Shapp has opposed increasing the gasoline tax as a method of fuel conservation, arguing that it is unnecessary and penalizes people who need to drive. But in September, Shapp indicated his support for an increased gasoline tax in Pennsylvania as a revenue-raising measure.

In remarks Sept. 11, Shapp attacked natural gas companies for claiming there was a gas shortage and urged Ford to conduct an investigation. Shapp contended that the American public would "be ripped off to the tune of $36-billion" in 1975 by the natural gas companies.

Transportation

Shapp has advocated a national rail trust fund as a specific part of his national investment policy. Under this proposal, the nation's railroads would receive $13-billion in federal money over a six-year period. The money would be spent for needed improvements such as track construction and repairs, electrification and new cars. Shapp estimates that this program would create about 120,000 new jobs in railroad construction and about twice as many in the steel industry. The federal government would apply a 4 per cent surcharge on rail shipping bills, paying off the entire $13-billion in 20 to 25 years.

Education

Another facet of Shapp's national investment policy is the education trust fund. It would remove the financing of education from local property taxes and place it in a national trust fund. The trust would be established with an initial federal investment of several billion dollars and subsequently be financed by an income tax surcharge based on personal income and years of schooling.

Although Shapp opposes busing in large cities, he would not support a constitutional amendment prohibiting forced busing.

Health

One of the primary areas of consumer activism in the Shapp administration has been health costs. In 1973, the Shapp administration sponsored a bill giving the state control over the budgets and rates charged by private health institutions and placing consumers on the boards of directors of all hospitals. The proposal was rejected by the legislature.

Shapp has proposed tighter government restraints on hospital construction in order to avoid building unnecessary facilities that ultimately increase hospital costs.

Other Issues

Shapp has said little about foreign policy. He said Sept. 25, "The U.S. needs a foreign policy. I don't think we have one...." Shapp has advocated more attention for Africa and Latin America and an end to American support for dictatorial governments.

Shapp favors implementation of Pennsylvania's strip-mining law at the national level. The Pennsylvania law permits strip mining, but with rigid restrictions.

Shapp favors legislation to limit the availability of handguns, especially "Saturday night specials."

—By Rhodes Cook

IN ENERGETIC PURSUIT OF THE 'KENNEDY LEGACY'

Sargent Shriver is the only 1976 presidential candidate whose in-laws are an issue. He is a brother-in-law of Massachusetts Sen. Edward M. Kennedy and the late President Kennedy. His wife, Eunice, was a Kennedy.

And so it is understandable that Shriver was surrounded by Kennedys on Sept. 20, 1975, when he announced his candidacy for the Democratic nomination. In his announcement speech, he laid claim to the "Kennedy legacy."

But there are paradoxes in Shriver's ties to the Kennedys. They are a curious mixture of blessing and curse. On the blessing side, they have contributed directly to Shriver's successes in business and government and have given him broad recognition among American voters. On the curse side, they have pushed him into the background of the famous family and have prompted allegations throughout his career that he has ridden the Kennedy coattails to suit his own ambitions.

Questioned after the announcement about his claim to the legacy, Shriver explained, "I meant, really, the tradition which his [John's] life and work exemplifies." That represents, he said, a search for peace and an appeal to youth and volunteers—"his desire to bring the ideals of America to the world in an acceptable way, not by military means...he was a practical man, a tough, hard-working, practical man, with a philosophy and with ideals."

But Shriver realizes that the only way he can succeed as a candidate in 1976 is on his own, not as a relative of the Kennedys. "I have to come before the American people as my own man, with my own ideas, with my own principles, with my own convictions—and I've got them—and I'm very happy to stand on my own two feet," he said.

Fairly overflowing with optimism, Shriver gives every appearance of being able to do just that. Energy and exuberance have become almost cliché words in describing him. He is handsome, exquisitely tailored and trim at age 60, and he looks many years younger. One writer observed, in a reference to his excellence as a tennis player, that he "enters a room as if he had just jumped over the net."

Even his enemies acknowledge the vitality that he exudes. They are also quick to point out his reputation as a super-salesman, a perennial booster for the causes he espouses. An unfriendly columnist wrote in 1972, when Shriver was George McGovern's vice presidential running mate, that Shriver was "a fast-talking salesman...but one who doesn't always stick around to back his product.... McGovern might have trouble capping the Shriver volcano at times."

A *New York Times* assessment that year said: "Mr. Shriver's style on the stump seems to be more an amalgam of Governor Rockefeller (gravel-throated, shouted delivery), Vice President Agnew (slashing personal attacks) and Senator Humphrey (perpetual motion and occasional hyperbole) than a resurrection of Kennedy charisma."

Executive Achievements

In 1976, for the first time, Shriver is running on his own for a major office. His main accomplishments so far

have been chiefly in private or appointive jobs. He managed the Chicago Merchandise Mart, one of the world's largest buildings, for the late Joseph P. Kennedy, patriarch of the clan. He was president of the Chicago School Board, which administered a budget of nearly $1-billion a year. He was the first director of the Peace Corps for President Kennedy and the first director of the Office of Economic Opportunity for President Johnson. He was ambassador to France for Presidents Johnson and Nixon.

"So I've had the kind of experience in government which a President has to have, that is executive experience," Shriver replies to critics who question his lack of experience in elective office. In reference to other Democratic presidential aspirants, he told an interviewer in November 1975: "Jimmy Carter was a governor. Lloyd Bentsen was successful in private business. But I'm the only one who's been successful in private business, in local government and in national government in the executive."

After a brief stint as an assistant editor of *Newsweek* magazine after World War II, Shriver was hired by the senior Kennedy to edit the letters of his oldest son, Joseph P. Kennedy Jr., who had died in the war. Shriver moved to Chicago in 1948 as assistant manager of Kennedy's Merchandise Mart. "Some people in Boston believe I was born the day I married my wife," he once said. But he points out, somewhat defensively, that he was a business success before he married the boss' daughter in 1953.

Elective Ambitions

Although he never has made it, Shriver long has nourished ambitions to be elected to something. In 1970, he resigned as ambassador to France and returned to Maryland with the intention of running for governor. The support simply was not there. Incumbent Democrat Marvin Mandel was popular at that time. Some resentful Marylanders regarded Shriver as a carpetbagger. He failed to make much of a showing in public-opinion polls. So he dropped it.

"I'm very disappointed that I'm not running myself," he said as the election approached. "But something comes up every time to mess me up. Ten years ago I wanted to run for governor of Illinois, but Jack was running for President, so I didn't. This year I wanted to run for governor of Maryland, but we didn't prepare for it far enough in advance."

Perhaps in part as a face-saving move after his gubernatorial plans had fizzled, Shriver in June 1970, at the urging of some Capitol Hill Democrats, headed an independent campaign operation called Congressional Leadership for the Future. Explaining that he had found a lack of faith in their institutions among Americans when he returned from Paris, he said: "They are looking for a new leadership, new motivations, new ideas—a new vision for America."

His enthusiastic leadership of the organization brought forth accusations that his committee was tailored for him to test a prospective presidential candidacy in 1972. He denied the charge. But, with the tireless campaign style that would later typify his vice presidential candidacy, Shriver traveled to nearly 40 states and spoke for more than 60 candidates for the House and Senate as well as for several Democratic gubernatorial candidates.

The 1972 Campaign

Shriver's 1970 travels strengthened his position in 1972, when he accepted the vice presidential nomination at a special Democratic National Committee meeting in August. The original nominee, Missouri Sen. Thomas F. Eagleton, had withdrawn under pressure after disclosures of his history of mental illness.

It was a strained situation that had got the Democrats "off to a bad start," as Montana Sen. Mike Mansfield ad-

---

Shriver Staff, Advisers

Campaign manager: Richard Murphy, a Washington, D.C., business consultant and Democratic Party professional; he managed the 1972 national convention and served as assistant postmaster general under Presidents Kennedy and Johnson.

Finance director: William Kelly, associate director of the Kennedy Institute for the Study of Human Reproduction and Bioethics at Georgetown University and a former official of the Peace Corps and the Office of Economic Opportunity under Shriver.

Political adviser: Richard Drayne, former press secretary to Sen. Edward M. Kennedy (D Mass.).

Press secretary: Don Pride, a former Florida newspaper reporter who served for four years as Florida Gov. Reubin Askew's press secretary.

Campaign consultants: Matt Reese and Al Nellum of Washington, D.C.

Polling consultant: Patrick Caddell, president of Cambridge (Mass.) Survey Research and George McGovern's pollster in the 1972 presidential campaign;

Ethnic affairs consultant: Michael Novak of Washington, D.C., author of *The Rise of the Unmeltable Ethnics* and a speechwriter for Shriver in 1972.

---

mitted in his nominating speech for Shriver. But McGovern and Shriver tried to put the best possible face on it.

Shriver's life, said McGovern, "has been marked by a special dedication to the needs of the poor and to those who suffer from racial injustice." Shriver's acceptance speech followed the same theme—with a Kennedy echo. "We will build again the coalition Robert Kennedy dreamed of," he said, "—of Poles, Italians, Irish, of blacks and Latinos, of farmers and workers." The Democrats, he said, must become "the party of the streets, of the neighborhoods."

Coming from the mouth of a man born to wealth and physical comfort in a landed Maryland family dating back to the 18th century, such words might have earned jeers. But no one jeered. Shriver had established his commitment to these goals, both in Chicago and in Washington. In the 1960 Kennedy campaign, he had headed a civil rights task force.

Even so, the glib and fashionably groomed Shriver stood out in stark relief as he campaigned for the votes of minorities and workingmen. He was, according to one of his staff members, almost "like an invading force."

But that in no way deterred him or even slowed him down. Much of his pitch was directed at the working class, the blue-collar force that had been so alienated by McGovern and what was widely perceived as his army of shaggy-haired, left-wing followers.

In an appeal directed at middle America, one of Shriver's lines was, "You can't even watch a football game with pretzels and a six-pack without paying a Nixon tax." And in language that was sometimes compared with that of Vice President Agnew at its most stinging, Shriver once called Nixon "the number one warmaker of the world at this time."

Shriver covered more than 75,000 miles during his three-month campaign. He made 173 stops and gave more than 500 speeches. And he was part of one of the most devastating defeats in presidential history.

His reaction was characteristically upbeat. "There's nothing in your life that goes wasted in an experience like this," he said three days before the election, long after the outcome had become predictable. "It's a test of everything you've ever done, everything you've ever thought. It's like a great big comprehensive exam at the end of four years of college. The nation examines you. I've said a lot of things I've wanted to talk about, even if—I think—I haven't got adequate consideration."

The 1976 Campaign

Since his 1972 loss, Shriver has been a partner in a Washington law firm. He has maintained his interest in party matters, and by the summer of 1975, reports were circulating that he would be a presidential candidate in 1976.

Heralding his candidacy in a speech at the Young Democrats' national convention in August, he said: "The Democratic Party must articulate a genuine alternative to Republican stagnation. Our party will deserve victory and serve the nation only if we stand for things worth doing and voting for. In 1976, there will be neither safety nor success in calculated noncommitment."

At a news conference after his formal announcement in September, Shriver was asked the inevitable question about his being a stalking horse for his brother-in-law, Sen. Kennedy, who by then had declared his non-candidacy so many times that most Democrats believed him. "I'm not a stalking horse," Shriver answered. "He doesn't need a stalking horse. All the candidates agree that if Sen. Kennedy wanted the nomination, he could get it."

Shriver was, at the time of his announcement, the only Democratic candidate who had already raised the required minimum of $100,000 in small contributions from 20 states in order to qualify for federal matching funds at the start of 1976. His report to the Federal Election Commission in October 1975 showed him far down the list of candidates, with total receipts of nearly $190,000 during the first nine months of the year.

A Shriver fund-raising letter listed four leadership qualities that a President must have: convictions, competence, control and concern. At a Sept. 29 breakfast with reporters, the candidate said, "A tremendous amount of spirit has gone out of this country. The most important task of any President at this time [is] to unite the country."

In offering himself as the best man to meet that test, Shriver is directing his attention to the old Roosevelt coalition of blacks, other minorities and ethnic groups. He demonstrated his appeal to those groups in 1972, and he earned the support of liberals for his enthusiastic campaigning on the doomed McGovern ticket. He has long-standing ties to many party regulars, not the least of whom is Chicago Mayor Richard J. Daley, whose first campaign Shriver supported in 1955.

One of Shriver's qualities is his ability to attract top-flight talent and to inspire long-lasting loyalties from those who work for him—despite his reputation as a hard taskmaster with a low boiling point. His campaign staff, many of them repeaters, is considered one of the most skilled and professional of any among this season's bumper crop of candidates.

But the campaigning skills of candidate and staff alike may be taxed severely because of Shriver's late entry in the race (he was the seventh Democrat to announce). "We recognize that we're starting eight months behind and have to run twice as fast," said Richard Murphy, the former assistant postmaster general who is Shriver's campaign manager.

Even so, Shriver's wide name recognition paid off in an October Gallup Poll surveying the popularity of prospective Democratic nominees. Shriver ran sixth, with 8 per cent (Minnesota Sen. Hubert H. Humphrey led, with 23). But he could take some satisfaction from the poor showing of several others—notably Rep. Morris K. Udall of Arizona—who had announced earlier but could not muster more than 3 per cent.

Murphy described the early elections in New Hampshire and Massachusetts as "make or break" primaries for Shriver, who will be competing with a large field of competitors who have had far longer than he to get their organizations in shape. Shriver will concentrate on the belt of industrial states in the Northeast and Midwest, and a few congressional districts in the South. "Sarge's basic strength is close to the pattern of Kennedy in 1960," said Murphy.

"I don't think the press is going to take him seriously until he starts winning some primaries," admitted Don Pride, Shriver's press secretary.

In an interview published by *The Baltimore Sun* Nov. 3, Shriver himself offered this evaluation: "In looking at a person to be President, I think it is time we looked at the total person, their character, their vision, their track record, because the problems that the President is going to face in the next four years or eight years are not the problems that are current. So it is a good idea to look at the

---

Shriver's Background

Profession: Attorney.
Born: Nov. 9, 1915, Westminster, Md.
Home: Rockville, Md.
Religion: Roman Catholic.
Education: Yale University, B.A., 1938; Yale Law School, LL.B., 1941.
Offices: Chicago Catholic Interracial Council, 1953-70 (president, 1955-60); Chicago School Board, 1955-60 (president, 1956-60); director of the Peace Corps, 1961-66; director of the Office of Economic Opportunity, 1964-68; ambassador to France, 1968-70; unsuccessful Democratic candidate for Vice President, 1972.
Military: Navy, 1941-45; returned to inactive duty as lieutenant commander.
Memberships: National Council of the Boy Scouts; director, National Catholic Conference for Interracial Justice; Navy League; VFW; Children's Lobby; Bankers' Club of America; chairman, International Patrons of the Israel Museum.
Family: Wife, Eunice Kennedy; five children.

---

total guy and to determine after such a look whether this fellow has got the...competence, the experience, the...gifts of a chief executive, or a President of this country. Now if you compare my record on these counts with the other people, I think I compare very favorably."

Positions on Issues

In the 1960s style of John F. Kennedy, Shriver's speeches are full of the sort of ringing pleas to "get this country moving again" that Kennedy used so effectively. The Shriver rhetoric glitters with generalities. It is often less than overflowing with specific proposals, although in the 1972 campaign Shriver demonstrated a capacity for spouting statistics. "Mr. Shriver's political philosophy is uncomplicated: eschew evil, do good, begin before breakfast," wrote columnist George F. Will.

Shriver said in his announcement statement that the nation was in the midst of the worst domestic crisis since the Great Depression, a "crisis of confidence" that demanded a leader capable of restoring the faith and confidence of the American people. "There is no conservative or liberal remedy for the sickness of the national spirit," he said. "The cure will come from honest, truthful leadership that summons the best in us—as we remember John Kennedy once did."

Shriver's tub-thumping ebullience may sometimes leave the impression that his salesmanship surpasses his thoughtfulness. But some people who know him well describe him as an intellectual Catholic liberal with a deep knowledge of philosophy, ethics and moral theology. His Catholicism colors his moral fervor; he carries a rosary in his pocket, and reporters traveling with him in 1972 noted that his speeches were better on the mornings he went to mass—which were frequent. Religious themes lace his speeches. He answered Richard Nixon's "work ethic" talk with references to the "Judaeo-Christian humanist ethic." In a 1968 speech, he said, "We must get down on our knees with the poor before we can get down on our knees to God."

Moving to shore up his occasional weakness on issues, Shriver at the start of his campaign put six task forces to work, under the direction of a Harvard law professor, drafting policy statements and proposals.

But he remains capable of occasionally fumbling. On the school busing issue, for example, he has come out squarely for the principle: "Busing is an absolutely essential tool in the educator's tool box for achieving quality education and for achieving integration, eliminating segregation, which is required by the Constitution.... Therefore, I am in favor of busing. I'm in favor of busing, but not in all situations."

Pinned down on NBC's "Meet the Press" on what some of those situations might be, Shriver answered: "I live in Rockville, Md. I am not an expert on the details of the Boston situation."

When a reporter asked Shriver if he had an energy policy, the candidate's only reply was that he had John C. Sawhill, former federal energy administrator (fired by President Ford) at the head of his energy policy committee.

Press reports Nov. 3 said that Shriver had stunned labor leaders at a Democratic conference in Atlanta the day before, when he showed a clear lack of knowledge of right-to-work laws, an issue dear to the heart of organized labor.

These are Shriver's positions on some issues:

Economy

Shriver says inflation is caused largely by unemployment and idle factories. He proposes to stabilize fuel prices, continue existing tax cuts and expand the money supply. Shriver believes the government should actively intervene to roll back "unjustified" price increases and to break up concentrated economic power. He advocates national and international stockpiles of basic commodities to protect against shortages and price fluctuations.

Bureaucracy

"Government and corporate bureaucracy are no substitute for self-reliant individual effort," Shriver said in his announcement statement. He says that people's frustration with red tape and layers of government are endangering domestic social programs. He urges a return to the philosophy of the war on poverty, which emphasized local action on local problems.

Shriver proposed reorganizing the Department of Justice in 1972 to create a new division under a second deputy attorney general to combat "official injustice." A major task of the new office, he said, would be to protect and represent citizens against arbitrary action by government agencies. "We have all seen such injustices—agencies summarily evicting families from housing, cutting off Medicare, denying claims, barring citizens from voting, refusing children free lunches, removing children from school," he said.

Social Programs

At the 1975 Young Democrats' convention, Shriver repeated his support for a national service program "whereby all citizens from 16 to 22 years of age could serve in private as well as public enterprises, locally as well as nationally, aimed at helping the elderly, the sick, the mentally retarded—working with the poor, working on the public lands, helping the police."

Shriver is highly critical of government welfare programs such as Aid to Families with Dependent Children, which, he feels, encourage families to break up. One of his frequently repeated themes is that government must find ways of helping families to stay together. He favors reviewing all federal policies for their impact on families. "Family impact statements should become as routine as those on environmental impact," he has said.

Abortion

As a religious Roman Catholic, Shriver said on a 1975 television interview that he always had been against abortion. "But," he continued, "the Supreme Court has laid down the law of the land on that, and as chief executive of the United States, I would be supporting that law. I have no intention to plug for a constitutional amendment to overturn the Supreme Court decision." As an alternative to abortion, Shriver supports "life support centers" to provide prenatal care for women all over the country.

Gun Control

Shriver is a strong supporter of firearms control. In 1970, he said that in areas of high urban density there should be "not only registration but confiscation" of weapons.

—By Rochelle Jones

A HOUSE REFORMER PRESSING FOR PRESIDENCY

Morris K. Udall of Arizona would like to perform a feat accomplished by James A. Garfield in 1880—and by nobody else before or since. He wants to go straight from the House of Representatives to the presidency.

Udall, 52, has spent the past 15 years in the House. During those years he has developed a reputation as one of the chamber's most thoughtful liberal Democrats, a serious legislator free with suggestions for change but ready to revise them when compromise is politically necessary. Udall's career in the House is more than incidental to his campaign for President; his political life and growth have been grounded in the complexities of the legislative process.

Despite the admiration Udall has won from colleagues in both parties, his House career has been marked as much by failure as by success. He sought to become majority leader in 1971—and was beaten decisively. He has spent more than five years working for strip mine control and land use planning legislation—and neither has become law. He was instrumental in the passage of a 1971 bill creating a Postal Service Corporation—but concedes now that the plan has not worked.

The Campaign

When Udall announced for the presidency in 1974, skeptics said that, too, was certain to end in disappointment. Udall entered the campaign without a national reputation, a middle-level member of a legislative body that provides few big names and less presidential speculation.

A year after the announcement, Udall's campaign still stood somewhere between success and failure. The Arizona Democrat was still the choice of only a small fraction of his party's voters, and money was short, but there was at least an element of hope that one early primary would give Udall the momentum that would carry him to the nomination.

Udall often has focused his self-deprecating style of wit on the long-shot image of his candidacy. He has told audiences of the time he entered a New Hampshire barbershop, announced who he was and what he was running for, and was told by a customer, "Yep, we were just laughing about that yesterday."

But much of Udall's campaign is dead serious. He has approached outright anger when it comes to the subject of George C. Wallace, Alabama governor and competing candidate for the Democratic nomination.

In June 1975, Udall devoted an entire speech before a union audience to his denunciations of Wallace. Calling him the "politician of negativism," Udall said he would not serve on any ticket with Wallace, would not support a ticket with Wallace on it and would not deal with Wallace to win the nomination for himself. In October, Udall went to Birmingham, in Wallace's home state, to repeat many of the same attacks.

Udall's anti-Wallace views brought him some badly needed national attention in 1975. But the Udall campaign was concentrating most of its effort on a quieter job,

organizing for the first primaries. In New Hampshire, site of the first primary Feb. 24, Udall's organization "is unquestionably the best and is in place," boasted Jack Quinn, the candidate's political director. The campaign also has targeted primaries in Massachusetts, Wisconsin, New York and Ohio.

Udall has three offices in Iowa, where delegates will be selected at party caucuses starting in January. He expects to do well there, although he fared poorly in a straw poll taken at an Iowa Democratic fund-raiser Oct. 27. Jimmy Carter, former governor of Georgia (D 1971-75), came in first in that survey, with 23 per cent of the vote. Udall finished a distant fifth. His aides disputed the significance of the non-scientific sampling.

During the early delegate-selection process, Udall does not plan a major effort in the South. He is almost certain to stay out of the Florida primary, said Quinn, because he feels that Carter should be given a chance to show his strength against Wallace there.

Udall has a paid staff of 32, half of them in his national headquarters in Washington, with the rest in offices in New Hampshire, New York, Massachusetts, Wisconsin and Iowa. He is operating on a monthly campaign budget of $50,000. At the start of the election year, he will count on matching funds made available by the campaign finance reform act of 1974 to keep him going. In October 1975, he was running a deficit of $80,000, but aides explained that these were obligations not due for payment until after the matching funds were awarded in January. Meanwhile, they said that he had raised about $600,000 since the inception of the campaign and that between 85 and 90 per cent of the dollars would be eligible for matching funds.

There is irony to the idea of the campaign finance act bailing Udall out, because Udall played a key role in its passage. He helped originally to draft the Federal Election Campaign Act of 1971 (PL 92-225), the first substantial revision of campaign finance laws since 1925.

That law required candidates for federal office to file detailed reports on the money they raised and spent, and limited amounts that could be used for political advertising. Its disclosure provisions helped expose the Watergate scandal in 1973.

After Watergate broke, Udall joined in the chorus of complaints that the 1971 law was not enough. He and Republican Rep. John B. Anderson of Illinois drafted a

proposal to use public funds to help pay election expenses for both Congress and the presidency. "Surely today," Udall argued, "the American people are ready to put up a dollar or two a year to have a clean, decent, brand-new system of House and Senate [publicly funded] elections in this country."

The proposal to use federal money for congressional elections did not survive on the House floor, but the Udall idea of "matching grants" was implemented for presidential candidates during the pre-nomination period.

The Leadership Challenges

Udall's role in the campaign finance debate reflected a style that his supporters see as one of his strongest assets—a willingness to go beyond protest and criticism and into the patient search for constructive legislative solutions. But he has also been willing, on occasion, to buck the entrenched ways of doing House business.

Udall was an early advocate of a stronger House Democratic caucus and a consistent opponent of the seniority system. On both fronts, he won a victory in 1967 as the House Democrat who introduced the caucus resolution that stripped Rep. Adam Clayton Powell (D N.Y. 1945-71) of his chairmanship of the Education and Labor Committee. But Udall opposed the successful House vote to deny Powell his seat.

In a far more brash challenge of the House Democratic leadership, Udall defied custom and ran for the speakership at the start of the 91st Congress in 1969 against John W. McCormack (D Mass. 1928-71). McCormack, then age 77, had been speaker for seven years, nearly as long as Udall had been in Congress.

In a letter to his House colleagues before the vote, Udall offered himself as a replacement for the aged McCormack, a symbol of the old guard, because of "an overriding need for new directions and new leadership."

He also said that if he beat McCormack on the first ballot, he would move to reopen nominations for speaker "so that other candidates can be considered with me on the final balloting."

That strategy failed. In the Democratic caucus, McCormack defeated Udall 178-58 on a secret ballot. But the challenge was not without impact. After his easy victory, McCormack endorsed a proposal for monthly caucus meetings at which all Democratic members could speak freely on party procedures and public issues, a pet proposition of the liberal Democratic Study Group (DSG), of which Udall was a leader.

Six years later, Terry Bracy, Udall's legislative aide, told Congressional Quarterly that Udall had made the challenge "because nobody else would take on John McCormack and because young Democrats had no influence in the House, and yet they had to go home and campaign as Democrats." The aide further described the challenge as "symbolic" and another attack on the House's "system of feudal fiefdoms" that precluded a representative from making his mark "unless he was 70 years old and had 30 years of service."

When McCormack retired from Congress in 1971, Rep. Carl Albert (D Okla.), the House majority leader, offered himself for speaker and drew no opposition. Rep. Hale Boggs (D La. 1941-43, 1947-72), who had served nine years as majority whip by appointment of McCormack and Albert, announced for Albert's job. Udall and three others entered the lists against Boggs.

Udall's Interest-Group Ratings

Americans for Democratic Action (ADA)—ADA ratings are based on the number of times a representative voted, was paired for or announced for the ADA position on selected issues.

National Farmers Union (NFU)—NFU ratings are based on the number of times a representative voted, was paired for or announced for the NFU position.

AFL-CIO Committee on Political Education (COPE)—COPE ratings reflect the percentage of the times a representative voted in accordance with or was paired in favor of the COPE position.

Americans for Constitutional Action (ACA)—ACA ratings record the percentage of times a representative voted in accordance with the ACA position.

Following are Udall's ratings since he entered the House in 1961:

	ADA[1]	COPE[3]	NFU[3]	ACA
1974	65	100	100	8
1973	84	82	90	8
1972	100	100	86	0
1971	81	82	100	4
1970	76[4]	83	100	0
1969	67	80	93	0
1968	92	100	93	0
1967	93	100	85	4
1966	82	85[2]	90	8
1965	74	85[2]	88	12
1964	100	82[2]	100	0
1963	75	82[2]	94	6
1962	62	88[2]	93	18
1961[5]	100	88[2]	50	0

1. Failure to vote lowers ADA score.
2. Scores listed twice indicate rating compiled for entire Congress.
3. Percentages compiled by CQ from information provided by groups.
4. ADA score includes some votes from December 1969.
5. Udall did not serve the full year, taking office May 17, 1961.

Despite his reformist reputation, Udall courted votes by playing down the idea that he would radically alter the House seniority system if he gained power, saying rather that he would support "significant but not drastic reforms." His hard core of support was again in the DSG.

Boggs' candidacy, based on House business as usual, was appreciated by the more conservative southerners and old-line Democrats. Although no Dixiecrat himself (he had supported the national Democratic Party on most major issues in recent years), Boggs made no commitment to reforming the procedures and the distribution of power in the House.

On the second ballot in the caucus, the traditionalists won, giving Boggs 140 votes to 88 for Udall and 17 for Rep. B. F. Sisk (Calif.). The other two Democrats had dropped out after the first round.

Udall analyzed the collapse of his drive as resulting from a combination of defecting freshmen, pro-labor members and liberals with 10 to 15 years of service in the House—in effect, those moving into senior seats on committees. He also ran into lingering bitterness over his challenge to McCormack two years earlier, especially among New England representatives. A magazine article quoted Udall as saying, "The leadership ladder bit—tradition, promotion, seniority—was stronger medicine than I originally thought. This House apparently just insists on people getting in line, serving time."

Personal Background

Until the 1976 campaign, Udall's search for votes had been limited to his 2nd Congressional District in southern Arizona. But his political experience in his home state dates back to the 1950s, and the Udalls are one of Arizona's best-known political families.

Udall was born June 15, 1922, in St. Johns, Ariz., a remote county seat located between the Petrified Forest and the Fort Apache Indian Reservation. His father, Levi S. Udall, the son of Mormon pioneers who founded St. Johns, was a farmer and lawyer, a believer in the frontier ethic of hard work. The father became a justice of the Arizona State Supreme Court, serving on the tribunal for 16 years until his death in 1960. Morris' mother, Louise, a civic affairs activist, became interested in Indian life and culture. In 1970, she published a book, *Mine and Me*, the story of a Hopi woman's life.

When he was 6, Morris Udall lost his right eye in an accident, and it was replaced with a glass eye. He was salutatorian of his St. Johns High School class and entered the University of Arizona in 1940. World War II interrupted his studies. He entered the Army Air Corps in 1942 as a private and was separated as a captain in 1946 after serving as an intelligence and personnel officer in the Pacific.

Back at the university, Udall was president of Associated Students, captain of the Arizona basketball team and an all-Border Conference forward. He played one season of professional basketball with the Denver Nuggets. He passed the state bar exams with the highest grade scored in January 1949 and entered private practice with his older brother, Stewart.

Morris served as chief deputy attorney of Pima County, Arizona, for two years, then was elected county attorney for another two. Brother Stewart was elected to the U.S. House in 1954, resigning from the post in 1961 when President Kennedy appointed him secretary of the interior, a post he held for eight years.

Udall's Background

Profession: Attorney.
Born: June 15, 1922, St. Johns, Ariz.
Home: Tucson, Ariz.
Religion: Church of the Latter Day Saints (Mormon).
Education: University of Arizona, LL.B., 1949.
Offices: Chief deputy Pima County (Arizona) attorney, 1950-52; Pima County attorney, 1952-54; U.S. House since May 17, 1961.
Military: Army Air Corps, 1942-46; discharged as captain.
Memberships: Arizona State Bar Association, American Bar Association, American Judicature Society, American Legion.
Family: Married Ella Royston Ward, 1968; six children by his first marriage, which ended in divorce in 1966.
Committees: Interior and Insular Affairs: chairman, Subcommittee on Energy and the Environment; Post Office and Civil Service; Democratic Steering and Policy Committee.

Morris ran for Stewart's House seat in a special election which drew national attention. Some interpreted the race as a test of Kennedy's first 100 days in the White House, with Udall campaigning for such Kennedy programs as federal aid to education, medical care for the aged and an increased minimum wage.

Udall won with only 51 per cent of the vote. At the time, he said a statement by Stewart nearly cost him the election—that farmers squatting on federal lands along the Colorado River would have to be evacuated. The statement was less than popular in Arizona's Yuma Valley.

Since that close contest, Morris Udall has been returned to the House seven times by solid majorities. His victories over Republican opponents have ranged from 58 per cent to nearly 71 per cent in a state that has swung sharply rightward since the 1950s. In response to skepticism among some urban Democrats about whether Udall would be tough enough to win the presidency, one of his aides said: "Udall has won consistently in a state as conservative as any in the country, and that is tough." He has been helped, however, by having the University of Arizona in his district.

Positions on Issues

Udall's campaign has emphasized the "three E's"—energy, environment and economy—as the issues of greatest importance.

Udall has been a member of the House Interior and Insular Affairs Committee since 1963, and this has shaped much of his legislative concern. It is an assignment well suited to his district, the desert country of southwestern Arizona, in which politics is largely a matter of land and water. Udall is chairman of the Interior Committee's Energy and Environment Subcommittee, and he has been at the center of nearly all recent House debate on these issues. Often, however, the final decision has not gone his way.

Energy

Udall's advisers describe strip-mining legislation as the centerpiece of his energy proposals. The Arizonan was in the forefront of that effort in the House for four years, only to see President Ford pocket-veto one bill (S 245) in 1974 and veto another (HR 25) in May 1975.

Udall's CQ Vote Study Scores*

	1974	1973	1972	1971	1970	1969	1968	1967	1966	1965	1964	1963	1962	1961[3]
Presidential														
support	42[1]/46[2]	38	43	23	62	64	83	76	81	80	88	96	90	89
opposition	45[1]/39[2]	57	41	63	26	34	6	9	6	9	2	3	7	7
Voting Participation	85	91	85	85	89	92	87	82	84	90	88	98	96	94
Party														
unity	78	82	85	85	75	85	79	82	90	85	90	93	84	90
opposition	7	12	7	3	14	13	5	4	1	7	5	5	14	7
Conservative Coalition														
support	9	19	5	5	11	11	8	7	3	10	8	13	25	12
opposition	70	74	88	82	77	82	78	81	84	86	92	87	75	82
Bipartisan														
support	77	82	70	69	84	80	84	69	74	81	76	85	88	84
opposition	8	7	12	13	6	8	4	12	5	6	4	13	5	5

* Explanation of studies, p. 107.
1. During President Nixon's tenure in 1974.
2. During President Ford's tenure in 1974.
3. Includes only part of the 1961 session; Udall was seated May 17 after special election.

"The history of this thing is that nothing satisfies him [Ford] unless the coal industry writes it," said Udall during debate on the 1975 bill.

In an address to the National Press Club in Washington April 22, 1975, he detailed a six-point proposal for restructuring the energy industry. Posing the "naked question of who will determine America's energy future," he made it clear that a President Udall would challenge energy decisions in the corporate boardrooms of New York, Pittsburgh and Houston.

"By any reasonable criteria of what constitutes a concentrated industry—high prices, inefficiency, lack of innovation and exploration, bloated profits and the power to control and direct the economy—the energy industry qualifies and is in clear violation of the intent of antitrust laws," he said.

Asserting that conventional antitrust proceedings are too slow with so much at stake, he called for legislation that would break up the energy conglomerates so that separate companies would explore, produce, transport, refine and market oil.

Environment

The strip-mining bills dealt primarily with preventing waste and repairing damage to the land caused by landslides, erosion and water pollution. Another energy-environment battle on which Udall was on the losing side was over the trans-Alaska oil pipeline. "The issue here," he said during floor debate in August 1973, "is whether we are going to cave in on the demands of the big oil companies or whether we are going to give due process to the environment." The final bill granting the pipeline construction permit did not incorporate Udall's environmental concerns.

Land-use planning has been another favored Udall legislative target. He has introduced bills that would make federal grants to states that establish land planning agencies to guide the use of lands, with special attention given to areas of critical environmental concern. Udall broadly defines those lands as ones where uncontrolled or incompatible development could harm long-range water conservation, food and fiber production, wildlife habitats, scenic values or scientific, historical and educational values. Also included are needs for housing, highways, airports and recreational and industrial development that is related to energy resources.

In 1974, Udall's land-use bill (HR 10294) lost by seven votes on a procedural step on the House floor. He fared no better in 1975, after the Ford administration stated that overriding economic and budget problems had forced a reconsideration of earlier support. Udall commented, "The administration evidently believes it is too costly to do something about the cost of sprawl, urban blight and the increasing misuse of our urban lands." The 1975 land-use bill (HR 3510) died in the House Interior Committee. Udall blamed intense lobbying by groups such as the U.S. Chamber of Commerce.

For his militant support of environmental protection and various national parks bills, Udall was named legislator of the year in 1973 by the National Wildlife Federation. In a friendly-warning address to the federation in Denver March 30, 1974, Udall said environmentalists must rid themselves of "elitism" and learn the art of "hard-headed compromise."

On occasion, Udall has broken with the environmentalists. One such occasion was the fight over the Lower Colorado River project, vital to Arizona. The Sierra Club, an influential conservation organization, waged an intensive campaign against the building of two hydroelectric dams near the Grand Canyon, claiming they would back up water 130 miles into the canyon gorge. In a House floor speech, Udall accused the Sierra Club of a "flagrant hatchet job." The dams were dropped from the legislation (PL 90-537).

Economy

Udall's positions on energy and the environment are inextricably linked with his economic proposals. As early as 1963, he cosponsored a major tax-reform bill calling for adjustment in taxes and exemptions. He has supported Internal Revenue Service amendments to double the "inadequate" personal exemptions allowed each taxpayer.

As a member of the special House task force to produce a Democratic alternative energy-economy program, Udall, in addition to restructuring the energy industry, would urge strong domestic energy conservation measures. He would seek a mechanism to limit oil imports in order to break cartel prices and stem the "petrodollar" drain; make a commitment to a 2 per cent energy growth rate, compared with the 4.5 per cent figure of recent years, and levy special taxes on "inefficient" automobiles.

Postal Legislation

Assigned to the Post Office and Civil Service Committee after his first election to the House in 1961, Udall chafed under the chairmanship of Tom Murray (D Tenn. 1943-66), who called meetings infrequently and ruled without rules. Udall and other younger liberals fought for and won regular meetings and orderly procedures on the committee.

After a few years, Udall began to use the seemingly innocuous committee as a vehicle for advancing his own ideas about subjects as important as postal service, congressional pay and the use of the frank.

A Udall-sponsored bill to reform the congressional franking (free mailing) privilege became law (PL 93-191) in 1973 after he had introduced it in three sessions of Congress. The law was the first modification of the mailing privilege in the 20th century. One provision prohibited mailings of more than 500 pieces of identical franked mail during the 28-day period before an election by incumbents seeking another term.

Through the Post Office Committee, Udall has been involved in the perennial debate over salaries and pensions. He has generally backed efforts to take the congressional pay raise issue out of the hands of the members, giving it to a federal commission that could deal with the issue outside the political pressures that members face.

Udall has also been involved in the issue of the pensions under which members retire. Critics have argued that Udall always has made his pension proposals excessively generous in order to extract retirements from members he considers to be deadwood littering the House. Udall allies never have denied this.

In 1970, Udall wrote the bill that created a new Postal Service Corporation in place of the financially ailing Post Office Department. In the bitter battle over the measure in Congress, he was allied with the Nixon administration, which wanted an independent postal service, supposedly free from congressional and other political influence.

Soon after the new system went into being in 1971, Udall broke with the administration's implementation of the bill. The Postal Service marketed a $250-million bond issue, hiring Nixon's former New York law firm, which specializes in bonds counseling, to handle the issue. Five underwriting firms were given the bond business. Udall, chairman of the Postal Service Subcommittee, made public

---

Udall Staff, Advisers

Campaign manager: Stewart L. Udall, Washington attorney and former secretary of the interior and Morris Udall's brother.

Financial director and treasurer: Stanley Kurz, a New York City lawyer and certified public accountant.

Legislative assistant: Terry Bracy, eight years on Udall congressional staff, and his major speechwriter.

Political director: Jack Quinn, a former staff member for Sen. Eugene J. McCarthy (D Minn. 1959-71) and for the Democratic National Committee.

Campaign administrative director: Ed Coyle, who worked in the 1972 presidential campaign of Sen. Edmund S. Muskie (D Maine) and later in the vice presidential campaign of Sargent Shriver.

Fund-raising coordinator: Marcie Kripke, who served as an aide in the successful Senate campaigns of Colorado Democrats Floyd K. Haskell in 1972 and Gary Hart in 1974.

Press secretary: Bob Neuman, former press and legislative aide to Rep. Jerome R. Waldie (D Calif. 1966-75).

Issues coordinator: Jessica Tuchman, who worked on Udall's Energy and Environment Subcommittee.

Director of scheduling and advance: Ron Pettine, who worked for the national Humphrey-Muskie staff in 1968 and for Gov. Milton J. Shapp of Pennsylvania.

Primary states field coordinator: Ken Bode, who worked for the delegate-selection commission of the Democratic National Committee, headed by Sen. George McGovern, and in the South Dakotan's 1972 presidential campaign.

---

an investigative report Sept. 21, 1971, which questioned the qualifications of two of the bond underwriters and the propriety of engaging the President's onetime law partners.

By the fall of 1975, the Postal Service had lost $2.9-billion over the preceding three years. There was a strong movement in Congress, highly critical of the service, which sought to revoke its financial independence and require it to go before Congress each year for appropriations—a partial reversal of the clock.

An aide said Udall now favors another restructuring, because he feels that the corporation has become part of the White House patronage system. "Udall believes the whole thing was fouled up by the Nixon White House," the aide said.

Labor

Organized labor has not always bestowed its unqualified blessing on Udall. In 1965, he voted against repeal of the Taft-Hartley Act section that permits state right-to-work laws. Repeal of those laws has long been a cherished labor objective.

His vote was cast on the grounds of political survival. Udall explained his 1965 position to two dozen labor leaders at a luncheon in Cleveland April 12, 1975. He said he had fought in Arizona to repeal its right-to-work act, but that after repeal failed twice, he and Arizona labor leaders agreed that he would not be bound to vote for repeal of the Taft-Hartley proviso while in Congress.

In 1965, Udall explained, he was seeking to consolidate his congressional constituency in a state that was becoming increasingly conservative. "But if I'm President, I'll be leading the fight with labor to repeal it," he told the Ohio leaders.

Civil Rights

Udall's Mormon religion has raised questions in the presidential campaign, as it did for Republican George Romney, also a Mormon, in 1968. The church prohibits blacks from entering its priesthood.

Udall has issued a brief position paper on the subject.

He says that since World War II he has not been active in the Mormon church. "For more than 25 years I have held and expressed a deep-seated and conscientious disagreement with the church doctrine on the role of blacks... I continue to hope that in its own way in good time the Mormon church will find a way out of the dilemma which distresses me and many other Americans both in and out of the church."

Defense, Foreign Policy

In 1967, in the midst of the Vietnam war controversy, Udall went home to hawkish Arizona and declared that U.S. involvement was wrong and should be ended. In April 1975, as South Vietnam crumbled, Udall said, "There is no time for recrimination and bitterness about who lost Indochina. It wasn't ours to lose in the first place."

In a July 1975 position paper on the Middle East, Udall stated "that there is no more powerful imperative in American foreign policy than the need to do everything in our power to help build a stable framework for peace in the Middle East." He would base that policy on a firm commitment to the right of the Israeli people to live in peace in their homeland and to the right of the Palestinians to lead a "normal life" in the region, and to recognize "the understandable concern and self-interest" on the part of the Soviet Union in having some say in future crucial events in the Middle East.

Udall has sought to check chemical and biological warfare and has voted against "exotic" weapons systems and in favor of defense cutbacks.

—By Ed Johnson

A FOURTH STRAIGHT DRIVE FOR THE WHITE HOUSE

George Corley Wallace entered the 1976 presidential race Nov. 12, 1975, with a call for a "political resolution" that would take control of the Democratic Party away from the "ultra-liberal, exotic left-wing few."

His announcement was one of the year's biggest political anticlimaxes. He has, in fact, been running since 1964, and there never has been serious doubt that he would try again, for the fourth consecutive time. The only questions this time relate to the strategy of Wallace, who, at age 56, is serving an unprecedented third term as governor of Alabama.

It is doubtful that Wallace, no matter how well he does in the primaries, will go on to capture the Democratic nomination. Opposition to him within the national party organization is deep and intense, and it is probable that some means will be found to deny the prize to the Alabamian at next summer's national convention.

Wallace knows this and is prepared for it. He has run at the head of a third-party ticket before, and he has given every indication that he is willing to do so again.

In any event, that contingency will not take shape—if it does—until after the July Democratic convention. Wallace heads into the election year with the fullest treasury of any Democrat. He has one of the best nationwide organizations. He has the demonstrated support of a broad section of the American electorate, as reflected in his front-running position in the public-opinion polls comparing him with the other Democratic candidates.

But the depth of Wallace's support may be deceptive. Rumblings are starting to be heard of growing disenchantment with the governor, even among blue-collar workers, one of the bulwarks of Wallace support. The very seriousness of Wallace's candidacy—it has gone far beyond a mere protest—may be hurting him, because he is now being judged, and found wanting, by different standards, a *Washington Star* analyst wrote Nov. 2. The Star story quoted a southern political veteran as saying, "He just plain wore out his welcome with a lot of folks. He's been around saying the same things too long."

The Health Problem

Even with all the expectancy of a well-financed and well-organized campaign, doubts linger about Wallace's health. He remains paralyzed from the waist down by an assassin's bullet fired in May 1972, while he was campaigning in the Maryland Democratic primary. When he speaks from a podium, he must be propped up. Apart from his paralysis, Wallace has a severe hearing problem, a carryover from spinal meningitis suffered during World War II.

But he aggressively asserts that his health difficulties are surmountable and will not deter his campaign activities. For the skeptical, he flexes biceps made firm by regular therapy. His two-week trip to western Europe in October was construed partly as a demonstration of his capacity to meet the rigors of the coming campaign.

"I'm known better," he said in a May 1975 newspaper interview. "I don't have to go as many places now. I don't

have to go out all the time. I can run as good a campaign as I used to, because I know how to pace myself now."

Wallace's campaign managers have said that the Alabamian intends to run in all 1976 presidential primaries but the first—New Hampshire's. But he expects to rely on television more than in the past.

The Message

In his announcement for a third term as governor, Wallace in February 1973 described himself as the voice of "the mainstream of American political thought." And as the buildup for his presidential campaign has continued since, he has made clear that in this fourth challenge, he will play a reprise on some past themes. The chief issue, he said, will be "big government."

That is hardly surprising. Ever since he has been a national figure, the former boxer has set himself up as the defender of the "average man," whom he has defined as "the taxi driver, the beautician and the steelworker," and he has been a persistent attacker of the federal government and the eastern establishment.

Wallace has gained respectability over the years, and his tone in this campaign probably will be less strident than in the past. But the message will be much the same, even if less shrill.

The tone was struck in the summer of 1974, when Wallace made a four-day trip west that gave every appearance of being a preliminary to the 1976 campaign. In a speech to the National Legislative Conference in Albuquerque, N.M., Wallace said at that time that Americans are tired of "a faceless, aimless government that today has more authority and power over our lives than we do ourselves."

"The average citizen," he continued, "has already found that the answer is not in a big national government. But this local control can be restored in a strong, viable, responsible state government that knows the needs and the wishes of the people it serves and is responsible to them."

Wallace's enemies scoff at his self-proclaimed fidelity to the common man, charging, rather, that he is more a protector of big business and the white middle class. His answer is that the people of Alabama would not have elected him governor three times if there were any merit to the accusations. "The ultra-leftists and their newspapers just can't stand the fact that I carried every county in Alabama in the last election—including counties that were over 90 per cent black—by a heavy vote," he said.

Whither Segregation?

His reference to blacks touched on another theme that has dominated Wallace's past campaigns—racial segregation. He gained notoriety as the man who "stood at the schoolhouse door" in 1963, confronting the federal officials who were trying to integrate the University of Alabama. Five months earlier, in his first inaugural address as governor, he had sounded the cry against the intruding northerners: "In the name of the greatest people who have ever trod this earth, I draw the line in the dust and toss the gauntlet before the feet of tyranny, and I say: Segregation now...segregation tomorrow...segregation forever."

Forever did not last long. By the fall of 1966, as Wallace was finishing his first term, 396 black students were enrolled in the University of Alabama system. Southern segregation was being swept aside by the power of the federal courts.

Less than a decade later, Americans in all parts of the country have discovered that a once-distant issue is now in their own schoolyards. Busing has come to Louisville and Detroit and Boston and many other cities. Segregation has lost its regionalism.

Thus Wallace was able to say in 1973: "I can remember a few years ago when candidates for the office of President might not have had kind words to say about Alabama. But now folks in both parties...are beginning to make speeches that sound like they were written in Alabama."

And now, striving to expand his base of support, he talks about "all the people." A black high school band and choir performed at his third-term inauguration in January 1975. In Tuscaloosa, he crowned a black homecoming queen at the university where he had stood in the doorway 11 years before.

Contributing to the softening of Wallace's reputation on the racial issue has been his growing acceptance with the public nationwide. And contributing to his acceptance have been visits to Alabama by such mainstream politicians as then-President Nixon and Democratic Senators Edward M. Kennedy of Massachusetts, Henry M. Jackson of Washington and Hubert H. Humphrey of

Minnesota. They all had the same message, he said: "How great thou art in Alabama."

Perhaps to Wallace the most gratifying visit was from Kennedy, the brother of the President and the attorney general who had forced integration on the South in the 1960s. Paying homage to Wallace at an Independence Day celebration in Alabama in 1973, the senator referred to Wallace as a man with whom he shared "the spirit of America."

In February 1975, one of Wallace's most stiff-necked foes, AFL-CIO President George Meany, allowed that Wallace had "mellowed somewhat" and altered his image "from that of an outright racist to something less than that." In mid-1974, a Harris survey found that Wallace no longer was considered an extremist by most people and was regarded as "a man of high integrity" by 61 per cent of those questioned.

Even some black leaders, including Charles Evers, mayor of Fayette, Miss., said they could live with Wallace on the national ticket in 1976. But the newfound obeisance does not convince all blacks.

Vernon E. Jordan Jr., executive director of the National Urban League, called Wallace the "symbol of segregation" in July 1974. He said: "[F]or national political leaders to make pilgrimages to Alabama, to lend their prestige to his cause and to publicly mention him as an acceptable candidate for national office is something that verges on the obscene."

Clarence Mitchell, Washington director of the National Association for the Advancement of Colored People, said: "I can't see a situation developing in this country where blacks would support a presidential ticket that included Gov. Wallace. I'm very certain that if the Democrats want to hand the election to the Republicans, all they've got to do is put Wallace on the ticket as vice presidential candidate, and you can be sure that blacks could put [in] a Republican administration."

Democratic Tenderness

Wallace has disclaimed interest in the vice presidency, even though some Democrats have mentioned it as a possible means of bringing the Wallace constituency into the party fold. This thought is repugnant to many others. "There's just no way it can happen," said one leader. "It's unthinkable, and we can't let it happen and we won't let it happen." The basis for that line of thinking is that, despite modified appearances, the root of the Wallace appeal is racism.

Whether or not Wallace repels them, the practical politicians who run the Democratic Party recognize acutely that they must try to find the best way to compete for his constituency in 1976. Many would agree with Wallace's own assessment in a 1974 speech to the Young Democrats' national convention.

The party lost in 1972, Wallace said, because "it refused to listen to the average citizen of this country and ignored their wishes completely. The people spoke in explicit language that they do not want the so-called New Left. The national Democratic Party will be foolish and doomed to defeat if it ignores the obvious lesson of 1972." Wallace said the average citizen feels aloof from his government and from the Democratic Party, which has "paid more attention to some of those who made all the noise but who had never worked a day in their lives."

Tacitly acknowledging the accuracy of those words, one of Wallace's opponents said: "We can't handle him with sweet talk. We have to go after his constituents on the issues."

"The trick," said a Democratic leader, "is to keep him in the tent as long as possible, to make him get used to being a Democrat, to make his followers feel like Democrats for as long as possible."

In the pre-campaign stages of the 1976 election, Wallace has stayed, if not "in the tent," at least close to it. He has a young, aggressive spokesman, Michael Griffin, on the executive committee of the Democratic National Committee. Wallace has made a point of having his views represented in party councils and at party meetings, including the 1974 off-year conference in Kansas City, Mo.

"If there was one thing we learned in '72," said Griffin in May 1975, "it was that we were not at the table when the rules were written, and they were stacked against us. This time we went to every function since the convention that the Democratic Party has had on writing rules for the [1976] convention."

What the relationship between Wallace and the national Democratic Party will be as the hour of deciding on a nominee approaches is anybody's guess. Wallace and his followers have dropped a few hints, however. "Gov. Wallace would like very much to support the ticket in 1976 if he is not on the ticket," said Griffin. "The one thing that he will not tolerate is being cheated out of what he deserves. If we win, we expect the party to support us. We expect to support the Democratic Party in 1976 if the Democratic Party reflects the average American."

Whether the party will accomplish that goal will be subject to interpretation by Wallace. At the summer meeting of the National Governors' Conference in 1975, he refused to sign a party loyalty oath because of the refusal of other candidates to pledge their support of him if he became the nominee.

The thorny if not insurmountable dilemma with which the Democrats must grapple is keeping Wallace's supporters in the tent, even if he leaves. In a statement that undoubtedly discomfited some Democratic regulars, Wallace said: "They need me—or the people I represent—more than I need them."

The Campaign

Wallace goes into the 1976 campaign in his strongest position ever. Long before most of his competitors were giving thought to the details of campaign organization, Wallace had his ongoing staff at work in its Montgomery, Ala., headquarters. The framework of grass-roots organizations was built up across the country.

A professional fund-raiser was hired to make mass mailings that bring in the small contributions that have been at the heart of all Wallace campaigns. Presidential primaries were scheduled for the first time in 1976 in six southern and border states—Arkansas, Louisiana, Mississippi, Texas, Kentucky and Georgia—which, in combination with other southern primaries, offered Wallace a good chance to bring a solid bloc of votes into the national convention.

Charles S. Snider, Wallace's national campaign manager, told Congressional Quarterly: "We see our strategy as going to the Democratic national convention with the least amount of physical effort and by spending the smallest amount of money."

Money seemed to be the least of Wallace's problems. Reports filed with the Federal Election Commission showed that in the first nine months of 1975, Wallace had

---

Wallace's Background

Profession: Attorney.
Born: Aug. 25, 1919, Clio, Ala.
Home: Montgomery, Ala.
Religion: Methodist.
Education: University of Alabama, LL. B., 1942.
Offices: Assistant state attorney general, 1946; state representative, 1947-53; Alabama circuit judge, 1953-59; governor, 1963-67, since 1971.
Military: Army Air Corps, 1942-45; discharged as flight sergeant.
Family: First wife, Lurleen, died May 7, 1968, while governor. Married Cornelia Ellis Snively Jan. 5, 1971; six children (four by Wallace's first marriage, two by Mrs. Wallace's).
Memberships: American Legion, Masons, VFW, Moose, Elks, Disabled American Veterans, Woodmen, Shrine, Eastern Star, Civitan.

---

collected some $2.5-million, more than any other candidate in either party, and had spent nearly $2-million. Snider said that Wallace would claim at least $2.6-million in federal matching funds in January, because 99 per cent of his contributions were below the $250 maximum required to qualify. The average gift to the Wallace campaign is $13.11, Snider said. And the money is still coming in.

In the early primaries, said Snider, Wallace will concentrate on the March 2 Massachusetts contest and the March 9 Florida race. In Massachusetts, the Boston busing dispute gives him an automatic issue. In Florida, a Wallace victory could knock a southern moderate, former Georgia Gov. Jimmy Carter (D 1971-75), out of contention.

Wallace has 45 paid workers in his national headquarters and another 13 in eight states. Snider said the campaign organization is studying each state carefully, with an eye to getting as many delegates as possible. "Within states, we will not go into districts heavily where we have little support," he said. "We'll concentrate in areas where we have strength."

Wallace's supporters emphasize only his candidacy as a Democrat and are reluctant to discuss alternate routes in the event that the party's nomination eludes him. "He's run for the last time for the sake of running," Snider told a newspaper interviewer late in October. Snider quoted Wallace as saying, "I'm not going to run unless I've got a chance to be elected President of the United States."

Apparently because he wants to be ready for any turn of events, Wallace is known to be in touch with a Washington-based, Republican-oriented organization called the Committee on Conservative Alternatives. And there is also the possibility of an eventual return to the banners of his American Party, which he founded in 1968 (as the American Independent Party) but with which he has had only tenuous relations in recent years.

The Early Years

Wallace can identify solidly with many of the working-class voters toward whom he directs his plain-spoken rhetoric, described by some observers as a variety of southern populism. He was one of four children of a poor farmer and local politician in Clio, Ala. In high school, he quarterbacked the football team and won his first boxing championship when he was 15. He was senior class president and a member of the school debating team.

Young George, his few belongings in a cardboard suitcase, arrived at the University of Alabama in the Depression year of 1937. His father died a few months later, and his mother, Mozelle Smith Wallace, went to work as a sewing supervisor in a factory to support the family. To stay in college, Wallace waited tables in a boarding house, clerked in the university registrar's office, drove a taxi and picked up extra cash boxing at local smokers.

He received his law degree in 1942 and went to work driving a state dump truck at 30 cents an hour. The same year, he enlisted in the Army Air Corps. In 1943, Wallace married Lurleen Burns, a dime-store clerk. He was shipped overseas and flew nine combat missions over Japan and other Pacific targets as a B-29 crew member.

At war's end, Wallace talked himself into a job as an assistant Alabama attorney general at $175 a month. In 1946, he won his first term in the Alabama House of Representatives as a Democrat in the one-party South.

An activist legislator, Wallace sponsored bills resulting in the building of several trade schools and in setting up scholarships for them, in covering city and county employees with Social Security, and in outlawing lotteries. He takes pride in his sponsorship of a law credited for many years with bringing new businesses into the state.

In his early political career, Wallace was relatively moderate on the race issue. As a legislator, he supported a bill banning the Ku Klux Klan from wearing masks in public in Alabama. At the 1948 Democratic national convention, most of Alabama's delegation walked out over the civil rights plank and helped form the Dixiecrat third party. However, delegate Wallace did not bolt the convention. He worked for the unsuccessful presidential candidacy of the late Sen. Richard B. Russell (D Ga. 1933-71).

Wallace was elected to a state circuit judgeship in 1952; he held the job until 1959. In late 1958, he clashed with U.S. District Judge Frank M. Johnson Jr. of Montgomery by refusing access to the voter registration files of two Alabama counties to U.S. Civil Rights Commission examiners probing alleged voting discrimination against blacks. Johnson cited Wallace for criminal contempt of court. The citation was later rescinded, but Wallace and Johnson remained bitter enemies.

The Governorship

While still on the circuit bench, Wallace ran his first and only unsuccessful race for governor, in 1958. The man elected was Democratic Attorney General John Patterson, who had the backing of the Ku Klux Klan and assumed the role of states' rights champion. After the unsuccessful election, loser Wallace reportedly made this ominous and often-quoted declaration: "They out-niggered me that time, but they'll never do it again."

In his winning race for governor in 1962, Wallace turned his full wrath on Judge Johnson, calling him an "integrating, scalawagging, carpetbagging, race-mixing, baldfaced liar." He declared, "This state is not going to be big enough for him and me running the schools." On that count Wallace was wrong. He and Johnson would clash again over other civil rights disputes. And Wallace would lose them all.

But Wallace had his issue for that gubernatorial race—and for future elections. He won the Democratic runoff, tantamount to election, with 56 per cent of the vote, campaigning as Alabama's "little judge" or "fightin' judge."

In effect, Wallace has presided over Alabama's destiny for 10 of the past 13 years. Prevented by the state constitution from running for a second consecutive term in 1966, he had his first wife, Lurleen, run. She won; during her abbreviated administration (she died of cancer in 1968, and George was out of power for three years), Wallace continued, from behind the scenes, to be the state's principal policy-maker. He returned to the governorship in 1971 and remained there, because of a constitutional amendment eliminating the one-consecutive-term rule in 1975.

The Wallaces expanded numerous state programs, paid for with higher taxes and higher indebtedness. *The Birmingham News,* in a 1970 analysis of the record up to that time, described Wallace's performance as more complex and paradoxical than his "simplistic populist approach to ballot box conquest" would indicate. The newspaper editorialized:

"...Somehow or other, probably through expert image-making, but more than likely through disproportionate emphasis on his manipulation of the racial issue, he is painted as a conservative.

"He is, in fact, no such thing, except for his purely reactionary stance on race. In all other commanding matters of politics and government, he is a decisive liberal.

"To produce a greatly-expanded public welfare program, to carry out massive roadbuilding, to build public projects all over the state, his administration and that of his late wife...put on vast new taxes and added enormously to the state's debt."

In his 1975 address inaugurating his third term as governor, Wallace said that Alabama had come far in the dozen years since the start of his first administration. Broadly ticking off advances in Alabama education, medicine, industrialization and human rights, he asserted: "We can look back with pride of accomplishment."

But in a long article May 5, 1975, *The New York Times,* which Wallace often has assailed as an ultra-liberal enemy, claimed that statistics are not on the governor's side. Drawing its figures "from public and private sources," the Times made an analysis of Alabama in the early 1960s and in the early 1970s—before and since the Wallace stewardship.

The Alabama profile shows, according to the Times, per pupil expenditure—50th among the states, down from 48th a decade earlier; percentage of draftees passing the armed forces mental test—48th, down from 47th; per capita income—49th, down from 45th; percentage of residents living above the poverty line—48th, down from 47th; infant survivability—48th, down from 45th; number of doctors per 100,000 residents—48th in both.

After Wallace had become a familiar figure on the national scene, he got the scare of his 30-year political life in 1970, when he challenged incumbent Democrat Albert Brewer (1968-71) for the governorship. Brewer, a onetime Wallace protege, had been elected lieutenant governor with Gov. Lurleen Wallace and had succeeded to the top office upon her death. Brewer was considered a moderate.

Wallace made no pretense of his eventual goal as he readied himself for the 1970 campaign. "If I run for governor," he said, "it will be to keep our movement [his drive for the presidency] alive."

Wallace directed his attack against outside influences in Alabama—President Nixon, big utilities, big banks and big newspapers. He told working men, "It's not George Wallace they are trying to get rid of. They're trying to get rid of you...." He claimed his victory in the primary "will force Mr. Nixon to give us back our schools."

In the runoff campaign, Wallace openly appealed to racial bias. Campaign propaganda proclaimed: "I'm for B and B—Brewer and the blacks." The election of Brewer, warned Wallace, would mean that the [black] "bloc vote would control politics in Alabama for the next 50 years." He barely pulled out a runoff victory, 51.5 per cent of the vote to Brewer's 48.5.

In contrast to his close call in 1970, Wallace's 1974 candidacy for a third term was a runaway. He paid scarcely any attention to his four primary opponents or to State Rep. Elvin McCary, the Republican who ran against him in the general election. Instead, Wallace concentrated on national issues. He won the primary with more than 64 per cent of the vote and the general election with more than 83 per cent.

The 1964 Campaign

"Stand Up for America" was Wallace's cry as he entered his first presidential race in 1964. In a short time, his segregationist stands had made his name, unlike that of any other Alabama politician in history, an American household word, *The Birmingham News* noted.

Announcing his candidacy amidst the great congressional and national debate on the 1964 Civil Rights Act, Wallace stated, "If six or seven states vote for neither [major party] candidate, we will have the balance of power. Then neither man can be President unless he enunciates the principles on which this country was founded." The statement implied that Wallace, by bolting the Democratic Party, would seek to win enough electoral votes to cause the election to be decided in the House of Representatives, where Wallace figured that southern Democrats could bargain for important concessions on civil rights.

Yet the two national parties looked upon Wallace as little more than a sectional candidate, albeit a noisy and aggressive one, with just one issue, segregation, which the parties thought was only a southern problem. Wallace showed them. Invading the North, Wallace said desegregation of public accommodations by federal law was an attack on private property and "is the forerunner of land reform in the United States...the beginning of a socialist state."

In each of three Democratic primaries, Wallace opposed either the state's sitting governor or one of its U.S. senators, all stand-ins for President Johnson. The Alabamian lost all three. But, in popular-vote counts, he made a much more respectable showing than national seers had anticipated—33.9 per cent of the vote in Wisconsin, long the home of liberal democracy; 22.9 per cent in Indiana, and 42.7 per cent in Maryland.

Wallace had put himself on the map of national politics. He also had unleashed a new phenomenon and put it into the lexicon of American political jargon: "the white backlash."

Just four days before the Republicans nominated Sen. Barry Goldwater (Ariz.) for President, Wallace withdrew. Goldwater had opposed the Civil Rights Act and espoused states' rights. Wallace declared, "I was the instrument through which the high councils of both major political parties had been conservatized."

The 1968 Campaign

In 1968, Wallace announced his third-party candidacy for President under the banner of his new American Independent Party. At a Pittsburgh press conference in February of that year, he set down seven conditions that he

would demand for his support if one of the major-party candidates failed to win an electoral vote majority. He would release his electoral votes to the candidate who promised to support:

● Criminal indictment of "people advocating a Viet Cong victory," which he also stated as "punish treason by putting some of these [Vietnam] dissenters in jail."

● Elimination of the federal anti-poverty program, which has "made a few people rich and done nothing to help the poor."

● A drastic curtailment of foreign aid, including an aid cutoff of all nations not assisting the United States in Vietnam.

● "A promise to make a strong stand for law and order."

● Abandonment of "any type of civil rights legislation."

● Appointment of "people differently oriented to the U.S. Supreme Court" and possible review of its decisions by a tribunal of the 50 state chief justices.

● "Turning back to the people of the states the right to control their democratic domestic institutions," including decisions affecting school and hospital integration, open-housing legislation, legislative reapportionment and congressional redistricting.

From this campaign emerged what became known as "the Wallace speech." He fully developed his baiting style, ever attacking his enemies, among them "the pointy-headed intellectuals and theoreticians who sit in their ivory towers looking down their noses at folks and drawing guidelines for trifling with folks' money and busing their little children from here to kingdom come when they can't even park their bicycles straight."

With neither Republican Richard M. Nixon nor Democrat Hubert H. Humphrey (Wallace called them "Tweedledum and Tweedledee") apparently able to muster a clear majority among the voters, the Alabamian's threatened emergence as the power broker frightened organized labor, among others. It was then that the AFL-CIO showed its muscle, calling its members' attention to Wallace's Alabama record, which the union claimed was anti-union and anti-poor man. That attack apparently worked, for, in the last days of the campaign, workers in northern cities, who liked Wallace's racial stand, began returning to their traditional Democratic vote.

In a close vote, Nixon won an electoral college majority. But Wallace, who had 45 electoral votes in five Deep

South states, came close to being the spoiler in one of the better third-party showings of the 20th century. The governor won less than 10 per cent of the non-southern vote, and analysts thought he hurt Nixon more than Humphrey. The supposition was that in a two-way race, Nixon would have carried the southern states that Wallace captured.

The 1972 Campaign

The Nixon-Agnew "southern strategy" appeared to gain some momentum from the Wallace style. But in 1972, Wallace declared that the Republican administration was not backing up its words with action. IIe launched his third presidential campaign, this time as a Democrat.

With seemingly adequate money and the support of an in-place staff, Wallace mounted a drive that, among other things, helped remove from the race Maine Sen. Edmund S. Muskie, long thought to be the front-runner for the Democratic nomination. Wallace walloped Muskie, who placed a poor fourth, and other Democrats in the crowded Florida primary. He made a good showing in Wisconsin and went on to win the Tennessee and North Carolina primaries.

In the Florida primary, there was a straw-vote referendum on a constitutional amendment to ban school busing. It was approved overwhelmingly. Two days later, President Nixon appeared on national television and asked Congress to approve a moratorium on all new busing orders by federal courts. Wallace said, "I knew the message from Florida would get to Washington pretty quick."

The Wallace march toward possible power looked increasingly menacing to both parties. Like no other candidate, Wallace could fill campaign halls with cheering, foot-stomping partisans.

But on May 15, on the eve of the Maryland primary, at a campaign rally at a shopping center in Laurel, a 21-year old social misfit from Milwaukee named Arthur H. Bremer pumped four bullets into Wallace. As Wallace began the fight for at least partial recovery from the crippling attack, his aides announced from a Silver Spring, Md., hospital that the campaign would continue.

On May 16, Wallace won both the Maryland and Michigan primaries. That marked the high point of his 1972 effort.

Two months later, a dispirited, partially paralyzed Wallace left the hospital to fly to the Democratic national convention in Miami Beach, Fla. Pushed to the rostrum in his wheelchair, he was alternately cheered and booed as he spoke for minority planks in the national platform. By that time, delegates supporting South Dakota Sen. George McGovern were in control, and the Wallace views were easily defeated.

Wallace had won five primaries, placed second in five others and won nearly four million votes in 17 state preference primaries. Yet, he drew only 385.7 votes on the first convention ballot which gave McGovern 1,715.35 votes and the nomination.

On July 29, Wallace refused to accept the American Independent Party's nomination a second time. He went home to Montgomery to concentrate on physical therapy and to fade, briefly, into the political shadows.

Positions on Issues

Wallace tends to address issues in general terms. Here are some of his positions:

Civil Rights

He has often characterized himself as "a segregationist, not a racist." He has described segregation as a "divine destination" and integration as a "Communist amalgamation." But in 1971, he said that "Alabamians have accepted a policy of non-discrimination."

Wallace has made it clear that, as President, he would do all in his power to take the federal government out of the business of legislating and enforcing integration.

The Economy

Wallace thinks that inflation is the country's chief economic problem, and he blames federal spending for it. Inflation, he has said, will result in the "radicalization of the great middle class."

He has advocated changing the tax structure. He believes that tax-free foundations should be taxed like ordinary businesses and that commercial property owned by churches should be taxed. He thinks that states should keep a greater share of tax revenues. In a 1974 speech, he said: "As long as the federal government continues to absorb such a disproportionate amount of the revenue that can be devoted to governmental purposes, states will remain the slaves of the national government."

Defense, Foreign Policy

Wallace's 1975 trip to Europe apparently was, in part, a response to criticism for his lack of experience in foreign affairs. He told reporters repeatedly that his message to the leaders with whom he met had been: "What's good for western Europe is good for the United States, and vice versa." Upon his return, he told an interviewer: "I've seen Europe on television, and thousands of Europeans, so really it was nothing new to me.... You can learn as much about going abroad by watching and reading news...."

During the Vietnam war, Wallace advised either winning through the all-out use of conventional weapons, or getting out. He supports a strong military and has decried proposed cutbacks.

At a controversial 1975 news conference with foreign journalists, he said he wondered whether the United States should not have been allied with Japan against Russia and China during World War II. "My foreign policy, if I were President, would be based on the fact you can't trust a Communist," he said. "You never have been able to trust them. I don't believe in confrontation. I believe in negotiation, and I believe in detente. But while I'm detenting, as they say, I wouldn't turn my back on them."

Crime

Wallace has blasted leniency toward criminals in the courts, saying that it is "false liberalism that brought us to a bottomless pit of taxation, heroin addiction, crime in the streets." He once said that he would make the streets of Washington, D.C., safe if, to do so, he had to station armed soldiers along them, 30 feet apart.

Election Reform

"It is important," Wallace said in 1974, "for the [Democratic] party to come up with some type of primary system such as regional primaries or maybe national primaries that would give the people a more active role in the selection of the candidate."

—By Ed Johnson

A SOLITARY CALL TO ABOLISH THE 2-PARTY SYSTEM

The road to the presidency has always been a lonely one for Eugene J. McCarthy. Now the former senator from Minnesota is making his third trip, and the going has never been lonelier.

Both times before, McCarthy sought the nomination as a Democrat. In 1968, at the head of a band of idealistic young followers, he and his anti-war message forced the resignation of an incumbent President of his own party. But the nomination escaped him that year and went instead to fellow Minnesotan Hubert H. Humphrey.

In 1972, his forces decimated and his message weakened by the impending end of hostilities in Indochina, his brief campaign for the nomination sputtered and died before it ever caught fire.

In 1975, at age 59, the tall, gray former senator has quit the Democratic Party and is running as an independent. The method is similar to the one he has always employed: understated, cerebral, sometimes enigmatic.

The message is a call for a total overhaul of the American electoral process. McCarthy would like to abolish the two-party system of nominating and electing Presidents. "What we have is undemocratic," he said in a newspaper interview in June 1975, "and it results in an unrepresentative presidency."

Evolving Concept

What McCarthy is telling the voters in 1976 is a natural evolution of what he was saying eight years earlier. Unlike many of his supporters in 1968, he did not see that year's election simply as a referendum on Vietnam. McCarthy opposed President Johnson's Vietnam policy; but, equally important, he opposed a system of government that was able to continue the war long after it had lost popular support.

McCarthy wanted to open up that system and make it more responsive. In pursuit of that goal, he saw his campaign as a challenge to the Democratic Party and the people who controlled it. In *The Year of the People*, his personal account of that turbulent campaign, McCarthy wrote: "It had from the beginning been my intention to test as thoroughly as I could the entire process of the Democratic Party...."

In today's speeches, mainly to college audiences, McCarthy points out that the founding fathers made no mention of political parties in the Constitution and that they intended for the electoral college to choose the President. McCarthy wants to return the election of future Presidents to a revised and expanded electoral college, which, he feels, can best represent the voters.

The Critical Lawsuit

But the former seminarian is confronted with more obstacles in trying to preach his gospel than are the purveyors of more conventional political doctrines. The system is tailored to the needs and customs of the two major parties. Five states—Utah, Idaho, Nebraska, Michigan and Kan-

sas—keep independent presidential and vice presidential candidates off their ballots. Ten others make no provision for independents.

More important, because it relates directly to the solvency of the McCarthy campaign, is the 1974 law that changed the rules for financing presidential campaigns. The law provides for public funding of party candidates, but it contains no provision for independents. McCarthy and others have challenged the law's constitutionality.

They claim the law favors incumbents at the expense of challengers, enshrines the two-party system by choking off minor parties and independents and creates a commission that violates the constitutional separation-of-powers doctrine.

At a press conference in August 1975, McCarthy said he was particularly disturbed by the law's attempt to suppress 1st Amendment rights of freedom of speech and assembly. "If this law had been in effect in 1776, George Washington, John Hancock and Gouverneur Morris would all have been criminals," he said. "They all contributed more than they should have. They put a large share of their fortunes into ensuring there would be freedom in this country."

On the more down-to-earth level of dollars and cents, the law's strict limit on individual donors makes it difficult for an independent candidate to compete. The Democratic and Republican presidential nominees will be eligible to receive $20-million each in public funds.

"The bill purports to reform electoral financing but in reality only is an insurance policy guaranteeing longer life for the doddering two-party system," McCarthy said in October 1974. He said later, "This comes at a time when a majority of American citizens identify themselves as independents, and the Republican Party by its own poll says it has only 18 per cent of the registered voters."

McCarthy's campaign manager, Ron Cocome, said that McCarthy does not believe in public financing of elections and would not accept public funds if they were available. But if the lawsuit were successful, McCarthy would be able to finance his campaign, as he did in 1968 and 1972, through one or two wealthy backers. His national fund-raising chairman, Jordan Miller, said, "We can't get into the big money, get those kind of commitments until the campaign finance law is overturned."

Whether or not that would happen was expected to be decided by the Supreme Court before the start of the election year. A federal appeals court ruled against McCarthy in August 1975.

McCarthy's Interest-Group Ratings

Americans for Democratic Action (ADA)—ADA ratings are based on the number of times a senator voted, was paired for or announced for the ADA position on selected issues.

National Farmers Union (NFU)—NFU ratings are based on the number of times a senator voted, was paired for or announced for the NFU position.

AFL-CIO Committee on Political Education (COPE)—COPE ratings reflect the percentage of the times a senator voted in accordance with or was paired in favor of the COPE position.

Americans for Constitutional Action (ACA)—ACA ratings record the percentage of the times a senator voted in accordance with the ACA position.

Following are McCarthy's ratings since Congressional Quarterly began publishing them in 1960, plus a composite score for 1955-59:

	ADA[1]	COPE[3]	NFU[3]	ACA
1970	72[4]	100	100	0
1969	83	100	92	0
1968	21	0	100	0
1967	62	100	90	5
1966	90	83[2]	100	0
1965	82	83[2]	77	8
1964	90	100[2]	88[2]	1
1963	94	100[2]	88[2]	0
1962	83	82[2]	100[2]	0[2]
1961	100	82[2]	100[2]	0[2]
1960	100	100[2]	90[2]	4[5]
1959	92	100[2]	90[2]	4[5]

1. Failure to vote lowers score.
2. Scores listed twice indicate rating compiled for entire Congress.
3. Percentages compiled by CQ from information provided by groups.
4. ADA score includes some votes from December 1969.
5. Score for votes on selected issues since 1955.

The 1976 Campaign

The McCarthy campaign considers the suit important enough to devote half of its research efforts to the case. Strapped for money and tied up with the lawsuit, the campaign got off to a late start in 1975. By autumn, the field organization consisted of a part-time field coordinator in Ohio. A national steering committee to select a vice presidential candidate was being formed. "We're about 2½ months behind where we would like to be," Cocome said in September.

Cocome said McCarthy would campaign actively in nearly all states but would concentrate on 15 states that he feels he must carry to win. The targeted states include the broad band of industrial states in the Northeast and Upper Midwest, plus Oregon and California on the West Coast and Iowa, Colorado and McCarthy's home state of Minnesota.

In keeping with his aloof style, McCarthy will not run a conventional campaign. His is not a bread-and-butter pitch to the various ethnic and economic groups. He will not attempt to regroup his former liberal Democratic supporters outside the two-party system. "The so-called knee-jerk, liberal, unwashed Democrats vote pragmatically," Cocome said. "When push comes to shove, they have to have a party."

Instead, McCarthy will look for support from disaffected voters of both parties, the 40 per cent of the electorate that say they are independent and, in Cocome's words, "the 61 per cent of the voters who didn't vote in 1972."

One thing in McCarthy's favor is name recognition. Unlike some other candidates, he does not have to wage a costly and exhausting media campaign to become known. And he has a small but dedicated core of supporters who have been working for him ever since 1968.

"We're looking for quality, not quantity," Cocome said. "It's not numbers that count but intensity of commitment. That's the kind of thing that made Wallace a strong candidate."

In 1976, McCarthy faces the same problem of convincing people he is serious that he faced in his two previous presidential campaigns. In announcing his candidacy, McCarthy stated that he would be a "deadly serious candidate for the White House." But after one of his lectures, a student told a reporter in what might have been a symptomatic observation: "I wonder how much of this is a serious effort and how much of it is a forum for a lecture series."

"Much of our strategy depends on who the major parties choose," Cocome said. "We have confidence they will pick the wrong people."

Aftermath of 1968

Despite the bravado of such statements, McCarthy has other problems, some dating back to 1968. He lacks an emotional, popular issue such as the war. His campaign committee is financed mainly by honoraria from McCarthy's speeches. He is short of followers as well as funds; a meeting at the University of Maryland in September 1975 to discuss the procedures for getting on that state's ballot drew only four people.

Moreover, McCarthy has alienated many of his original anti-war supporters and thereby has weakened his political base. After the 1968 election, McCarthy, a strong advocate of participatory politics, seemed to lose interest in the very issues that had brought him close to the Democratic presidential nomination.

In a move strongly criticized by some of his followers, McCarthy voluntarily relinquished his seat on the Senate Foreign Relations Committee to Gale W. McGee (D Wyo.), who supported administration policies in Vietnam. "Being on the Foreign Relations Committee," McCarthy said in response to his critics, "didn't change Vietnam. Going to New Hampshire did." McCarthy's strong showing in the March 1968 New Hampshire primary—42.2 per cent of the Democratic vote and 21 of 24 convention delegates—was critical to Johnson's decision, announced later that month to a stunned television audience, that he would not run for re-election.

McCarthy let other members of Congress become spokesmen for the anti-war movement. In a 1970 newspaper interview, he explained, "You can't do very much now. Presidential years are the years of decision on foreign policy."

In 1970, after two terms in the Senate, McCarthy declined to run for re-election. "He felt he was not accomplishing anything," Cocome told Congressional Quarterly. "McCarthy felt the Democrats were out to get him because of what he had done in 1968. He thought lending his name to a cause was more of a hindrance than a help."

Since then, McCarthy, a college sociology professor before his election to the House of Representatives in 1948, has returned to writing and lecturing. He taught, for one semester, a course in literature and politics at the University of Maryland and several political science courses at the New School for Social Research in New York City. His most recent book, *The Hard Years*, a look at contemporary America, was published in October 1975. Another, *America Revisited*, is scheduled for spring publication in 1976.

In his abortive try for the presidency in 1972, he campaigned actively against Maine Sen. Edmund S. Muskie in the Illinois Democratic primary, hoping to repeat his historic New Hampshire success of 1968. Despite a three-week campaign and a $200,000 media blitz, he finished second, polling 37 per cent of the vote against 63 per cent for Muskie. He did not contest the later primaries.

In 1974, McCarthy explored the possibility of running for the House of Representatives from Minnesota's 6th Congressional District, a sprawling, 22-county region in the central and southwestern part of the state.

During a four-day tour of the district, McCarthy told his listeners that he wanted to build "a more significant role" for the House, to restore it to the prestigious place it had occupied in the era of John Quincy Adams, who served 17 years in the House after leaving the presidency in 1829.

McCarthy was not warmly greeted. He met persistent criticism for his belated endorsement of Humphrey in 1968. The reception by local officials and rank-and-file members of the Democratic-Farmer-Labor (DFL) Party, McCarthy admitted, "wasn't exactly Palm Sunday." He did not become a candidate.

Watkins to Washington

McCarthy was born and raised in the small rural town of Watkins, Minn., in the 6th District. At 19 he was graduated with honors from St. John's University, a Catholic school in Collegeville, Minn., operated by the Benedictine order. He spent the next year as a novice in the order.

After leaving the novitiate, he taught social sciences in Minnesota high schools and courses in economics and education at St. John's.

McCarthy's Background

Profession: College professor.
Born: March 29, 1916, Watkins, Minn.
Home: Washington, D.C.
Religion: Roman Catholic.
Education: St. John's University, B.A., 1935; University of Minnesota, M.A., 1938.
Offices: House of Representatives, 1949-59; Senate, 1959-71.
Military: None.
Memberships: None.
Family: Separated from wife, Abigail Quigley; four children.

During the second world war, McCarthy worked as a civilian for the military intelligence division of the War Department. He returned to teaching in 1946 as acting head of the sociology department at the College of St. Thomas in St. Paul, Minn., in the state's 4th Congressional District.

His political involvement, he wrote later, "began almost by accident or default" that year. At the urging of a faculty colleague, McCarthy supported the drive of Humphrey, Orville L. Freeman and other liberals to purge the DFL Party of Communist influence.

Two years later, with the support of the DFL, McCarthy ran for the House of Representatives from the 4th District, defeating Rep. Edward J. Devitt (R 1947-49) by a margin of nearly 60 to 40 per cent.

In 1958, McCarthy ran for the Senate against incumbent Republican Edward J. Thye (1947-59). After a stiff fight for the DFL endorsement, McCarthy easily defeated his primary opponent, former Gov. Hjalmar Petersen (1936-37). In the general election, he polled 52.9 per cent. In 1964, McCarthy defeated Republican Wheelock Whitney with 60.3 per cent of the vote to win a second Senate term.

As a representative and senator, McCarthy compiled a liberal, internationalist voting record. He served on important committees—House Ways and Means, Senate Finance and Foreign Relations. But his name was associated with few major bills. Most of his original proposals were technical amendments to pending legislation.

One of McCarthy's most important contributions to the House was helping found the Democratic Study Group, an organization of liberal and moderate Democrats. (The actual start-up date of the group was in 1959, after McCarthy had gone to the Senate.) He has said that his efforts on behalf of the 1964 tax reduction and reform bill were "my most important achievement in the Senate."

In a book, *Nobody Knows*, Jeremy Larner, a McCarthy speechwriter in the 1968 presidential campaign, assessed McCarthy's congressional career in these words:

"He was for New Deal liberal aid programs, civil rights and civil liberties but never for anything that challenged interests, rocked the boat, or threatened institutional reform. He was comfortable with the orderly processes of Congress and its committee structure and there were many places where his liberal record reflected that comfort."

Rise to Prominence

McCarthy became nationally famous at the Democratic national convention in 1960 with a stirring,

McCarthy's CQ Vote Study Scores for Senate Years*

	1970	1969	1968	1967	1966	1965	1964	1963	1962	1961	1960	1959
Presidential												
support	16	29	5	56	68	62	79	84	81	58	38	31
opposition	24	43	2	12	17	4	6	2	13	10	49	55
Voting												
Participation	32	61	5	66	83	59	86	85	89	74	85	86
Party												
unity	43	53	4	49	81	51	80	88	86	69	76	85
opposition	1	12	—	7	4	4	9	—	4	5	14	5
Conservative Coalition												
support	—	12	—	13	3	7	14	0	24	9	4	2
opposition	47	55	7	45	86	38	76	93	74	71	72	87
Bipartisan												
support	18	44	3	56	62	57	69	68	83	70	66	69
opposition	8	15	2	16	20	6	9	14	6	2	15	13

Explanation of studies, p. 107.

last-minute appeal to the delegates to nominate Adlai E. Stevenson for the third time. He had served as cochairman of the Humphrey presidential campaign that year, and Johnson supporters later released an endorsement by McCarthy. But he felt Stevenson deserved a chance to be considered. McCarthy said the speech proved to be a handicap in later years. "People have expressed disappointment over subsequent speeches," he wrote.

He wanted the vice presidential nomination in 1964. Encouraged by various White House aides, McCarthy supporters opened a secret headquarters in Washington, D.C., early in the year. His supporters hoped that Johnson would balance the ticket by choosing a northern liberal Catholic for his running mate. But the people they looked to for help included conservatives such as Governors John B. Connally (D Texas 1963-69) and John J. McKeithen (D La. 1964-72) and Mayor Richard J. Daley of Chicago.

McCarthy stayed aloof from the campaign, although he did not discourage it. Humphrey, then the senior senator from Minnesota, campaigned actively for the vice presidency. The day before Johnson was to announce his running mate, after it had become clear that McCarthy would not be chosen, he withdrew in favor of Humphrey.

The 1968 Campaign

McCarthy's break with administration Vietnam policy came in 1966. He was one of 16 senators who urged President Johnson to continue a bombing halt then in effect, and he began to urge the United States to accept the idea of negotiating with the Viet Cong.

Despite McCarthy's growing outspokenness in opposing the war, the "dump Johnson" activists did not come to him first when they began searching for an alternative candidate for 1968. Their ideal choice would have been Sen. Robert Kennedy (D N.Y. 1965-68). McCarthy himself felt that Kennedy would be a better candidate. But while Kennedy equivocated, McCarthy announced his candidacy.

"I am hopeful that a challenge may alleviate the sense of political helplessness and restore to many people a belief in the processes of American politics and of American government," he said in his announcement statement on Dec. 4, 1967. "The issue of the war in Vietnam is not a separate issue but is one which must be dealt with in the configuration of problems in which it occurs. It is within this context that I intend to take the case to the people..."

McCarthy spent six weeks campaigning in New Hampshire, the first primary in the nation. An estimated 2,000 students poured into the state to ring doorbells and talk to voters personally on his behalf. The results of the March New Hampshire primary brought Kennedy into the race three days later. Before the month was over, Johnson announced he would not be a candidate for re-election.

But the euphoria of the McCarthy organization was short-lived. Kennedy's entry siphoned off some of McCarthy's anti-war vote. And McCarthy, whose wit and academic style appealed mostly to students and white-collar voters, could not compete with Kennedy's appeal to minorities and low-income groups. Before the June California primary, the once-lofty anti-war crusade had disintegrated into a bitter personality fight between the two peace candidates.

After Kennedy's assassination the night he had won the primary, McCarthy did not ask for the support of Kennedy's convention delegates, despite the urging of many of his advisers. Instead, McCarthy retreated from the race. In a newspaper interview, McCarthy conceded publicly, a full day before the nomination of the presidential candidate, that Humphrey would be the nominee.

Positions on Issues

For 1976, McCarthy says the essential issues are the "unfinished business" of 1968—militarism, the process of democracy and the "personalized presidency."

The Presidency

Long before the "imperial presidency" became a fashionable phrase, McCarthy proposed to start reforming the office by dismantling the fence around the White House and replacing the rose garden with a patch of cabbages and squash.

McCarthy is calling for a "back to basics" presidency. In April 1975, he said recent Presidents "have been distracted by the trappings of the office, have overpersonalized it and have overemphasized its military role." He said, "The next President must reduce the mystique and trappings of the office and return it to its constitutional role."

Foreign Policy

Although American troops have left Vietnam, McCarthy says the country has failed to learn the lessons of the war. "It was an excess of military power, combined with civilian leaders who were too eager to use that power, which led us into Vietnam," he said at the University of Chicago. "The great challenge today is to reduce our excessive military power and to renew the art of American diplomacy. We must develop a foreign policy which projects our internal strength and ideals, rather than one dictated by a militarism foreign to our traditions."

McCarthy has called on the United States to take the initiative in stopping the nuclear arms race. "We have agreements not to deploy nuclear bombs in outer space, in Antarctica or on the ocean floor," he said at the University of Washington. "It would be far better to have agreements not to explode them in places where people live."

In an interview with *The Washington Star*, McCarthy said his foreign policy would be based on "respect for the decent opinion of mankind." He said the United States had basic commitments to NATO, Japan and Israel but that much of the rest of the country's foreign policy needed to be re-examined.

Economic, Social Programs

McCarthy said that his domestic policies would include a poverty program to provide a "level of decent existence for everybody," a redistribution of work and an end to "wasteful production and wasteful consumption."

McCarthy Staff

Campaign manager: Ron Cocome, a former student at Kendall College in Evanston, Ill., who has worked for McCarthy in various capacities since 1968.

Fund-raising chairman: Jordan Miller, owner of a newspaper clipping service in Chicago.

Press secretary: Mary Meehan, a writer and researcher who has been with McCarthy since the 1968 campaign.

McCarthy, who chaired a special Senate committee on unemployment, says public service jobs will not eliminate unemployment. He says that unemployment has been structured into the economy and that work needs to be distributed.

"We have had some 30 years of technological growth and the spread of automation since the eight-hour day and 40-hour week were adopted as national standards," McCarthy told the Nucleus Club in Tucson. "Those standards are now outdated; they must be changed if we are to have any hope of providing enough jobs for Americans who want and need work."

He proposed shortening the work week from 40 to 35 hours to create new jobs for the unemployed. He said that if 23 million workers worked five fewer hours each week, more than three million new jobs would be provided. He called for tax credits for employers willing to shorten the work week and still pay their employees "approximately the same wages as they pay now."

McCarthy was calling for selective excise taxes and credit controls to curb excess consumption in 1972, before worldwide energy and commodity shortages. His particular target has been automobiles. In 1973, he wrote an article for *The Nation* titled, "We Cannot Afford Our Cars."

"The automobile threatens to destroy the economy of the country," he said in January 1975. If Karl Marx had foreseen the automobile, McCarthy said, he would have added a chapter to *Das Kapital* and written that capitalism would be destroyed either by foreign wars or its own auto industry.

—By Rochelle Jones

NO SHORTAGE OF HOPEFULS AWAITING THE CALL

In the tradition of American presidential election years, doors are being left open all over the place in 1976. Waiting to walk through them, from the shadows into the spotlight, are any number of politicians with varying motivations and ambitions.

They are not announced candidates. Most of them are not even in the front ranks of potential candidates who restlessly await some unforeseen dramatic development that will thrust them forward. They are members of both parties.

One who stands very much in the front ranks, in a category of his own, is Nelson A. Rockefeller. He informed President Ford in a letter Nov. 3, 1975, that he was withdrawing from the Republican ticket. At a news conference three days later, Rockefeller, who is anathema to party conservatives, admitted that "party squabbles" over his possible presence on the slate were behind his decision. But, despite his avowed support for Ford, he has resolutely declined to count himself out of the running if Ford is not the Republican nominee.

Another man in a category of his own is John B. Connally, the former Democratic governor of Texas who later became a member of President Nixon's cabinet and switched parties. Connally is keeping his options open, talking about playing some role in 1976 but not indicating exactly what it might be. He has even hinted at a third-party candidacy.

In a third category are the Republican moderates. These are senators who are concerned about the rightward drift of their party. They are sometimes considered as possible challengers to a conservative Republican—especially if Ford should lose the nomination to Ronald Reagan.

The names of three close Ford associates, all known to have political ambition, were added to the speculation lists early in November when the President made some major changes in his administration. They are Donald Rumsfeld, the White House staff coordinator who was nominated as secretary of defense; George Bush, the envoy to China, who was nominated to head the Central Intelligence Agency (CIA), and Elliot L. Richardson, the ambassador to Great Britain, who was nominated as secretary of commerce.

Finally, there are the Democrats. In this category are several men who are not candidates. But, because of their familiarity within the party, or the importance of the jobs they now have, or some other reason, they find themselves among those sometimes mentioned.

The list that follows has no pretense of being comprehensive. It deals only with some of the possibilities whose names turn up most often.

Nelson A. Rockefeller

Prodded persistently by reporters to state flatly that he would not seek the presidency in 1976, the 67-year-old Vice President just as persistently refused to do so. "I wouldn't have accepted the vice presidency," he said, "if I hadn't been willing to take the presidency should, God forbid, something happen to the President. So I am not going to kid you that I came down here with no thought of the presidency in mind. But I have no plans beyond what I said."

Rockefeller was even more blunt in a conversation with reporters Nov. 10 while flying to Austin, Texas, for a speech. "I'm just not freezing a position," he said. When asked why he would not rule out the possibility of running for President, he answered: "Because I might be President in '76. Some untoward circumstance might happen...that's the point of having a Vice President, so how can I rule myself out from that responsibility?"

Nelson A. Rockefeller

He said that he did not foresee the possibility of a Ford-Reagan convention deadlock.

The Vice Presidency

Ford chose Rockefeller as his Vice President Aug. 20, 1974. As Rockefeller recalled it in his letter to Ford, he accepted the post "based upon my concern to help restore national unity and confidence after the shattering experience of Watergate." The choice rankled conservatives and met with some delay in Congress, but the confirmation took place in December, and Rockefeller was off and running with his vice presidential duties.

Since then, Ford has met recurrent conservative complaints about the Rockefeller presence with statements of confidence in his choice and satisfaction with the work Rockefeller has done. Yet the President's own campaign manager, Howard (Bo) Callaway, said bluntly that Rockefeller would create problems for the Ford candidacy, and Ford himself consistently pulled up short from any assurances that he would not dump Rockefeller.

By late October, the question of Rockefeller's future was becoming ever more vital to Ford. The President's own campaign was in disarray, with the resignations of two major staffers, Lee Nunn and David Packard, and with dire warnings that the campaign was not jelling. Worse, speculation over a possible Reagan challenge firmed into a near certainty that the former California governor would announce in late November, and some Ford allies began to voice fears that Reagan could unravel Ford's candidacy as early as the primaries in New Hampshire and Florida.

Ford was confronted, as Rockefeller noted, with "difficult calculations" in mapping a campaign strategy to meet this growing challenge. Despite Ford's insistence that the decision was Rockefeller's, the consensus of reaction was that the move comported with Ford's own needs and electoral tactics.

Rockefeller fought for months to stay on the ticket, traveling to areas of the South where he is still seen as a liberal ogre, in order to quell opposition to him. Aides reminded the press that Rockefeller is an attractive campaigner who offers geographical and even ideological balance to the Ford candidacy. The Vice President did yeoman work in all tasks, from the menial to the sensitive, that the President asked of him. There was little in Rockefeller's conduct of the office that suggested he would refuse a sincere plea from Ford to remain on the ticket.

For the first time since the gregarious millionaire entered electoral politics in 1958, he is not a likely candidate for national office. He ran for the presidential nomination in 1960, 1964 and 1968. He reportedly was offered the second slot on the tickets of Republican Richard M. Nixon in 1960 and Democrat Hubert H. Humphrey in 1968. When he resigned after 15 years as governor of New York in 1973, it was clear to political observers that he had hopes of still another try for the presidency in 1976. Neither he nor anyone else foresaw the events that would lead him to abandon those hopes and accept President Ford's offer to join his new and unelected administration.

The Campaigner

Even Rockefeller's enemies concede that one of his shortcomings has never been lack of vigor. Early on, he proved to be a dynamic, folksy and effective campaigner. In the first gubernatorial campaign, he came from electoral obscurity and a 20-point deficit in the polls to defeat the aging but venerated incumbent, W. Averell Harriman (D 1955-59). In subsequent New York races, he overcame initially strong threats to win solidly. In 1970, he defeated his last and most eminent challenger, former Supreme Court Justice Arthur J. Goldberg, by 730,000 votes.

He proved willing to use his and his family's money liberally when needed to win those campaigns. He spent over $10-million in his 1966 re-election effort. His 1970 campaign cost $6.8-million, of which well over $4-million was said to be Rockefeller money. That year he even spent more than half a million dollars in the Republican primary, despite being unopposed. The effect of such large sums and the advertising they buy cannot be discounted, even when they support a concededly strong campaigner. Rockefeller critics frequently complained of the dangers of such money-dominated politics, but its success was clear.

Despite his great campaign assets and talents, Rockefeller's reaches for the presidency have been uniformly fruitless. From the moment of his 1958 gubernatorial upset victory, he sprang into the Republican consciousness as a formidable contender for the party's presidential nomination. But by 1960, he was well on the way toward alienating the more conservative elements of the national party. His late-hour combat against a firmly supported Vice President Nixon came nowhere near success.

Four years later, he was badly outdistanced by a superior Goldwater organization, and he irretrievably offended the conservatives by his tepid support of their ticket. He had by no means been forgiven when, in 1968, he again mounted an inadequate effort against a solidified Nixon candidacy.

Looking back on those campaigns, one Rockefeller associate now concedes that "it never was very well organized." Rockefeller enjoys a reputation as an organizer and a forward-looking planner, yet his presidential efforts simply were not sufficiently well conceived.

There were other liabilities. In 1960, the national image and support of an incumbent Vice President were too great to be pragmatically challenged. In 1964, Rockefeller's 1962 divorce and 1963 remarriage to a divorcée were lethal in the early primaries. And in any Rockefeller campaign, there are those, even among Republicans, for whom the "big-money" connotations of his name are a block to giving him their support.

Most important, Rockefeller's early record as governor of New York inescapably alienated him from the conservative Republican rank and file. He was enthusiastic in his support for the civil rights movement in the South as well as the North, aggressive in addressing social problems with state monies and programs, expansive in his brick-and-mortar public works.

Since the early years of his governorship, Rockefeller is thought by many to have transmuted himself from liberal to conservative, largely because of apparent frustrations at the inability of his programs to remedy their targeted ills. Among the specifics most often cited are his toughened attitudes toward welfare and crime.

Pre-elective Career

Rockefeller's philosophy has been shaped partly by his heritage as the grandson of the country's first billionaire, John D. Rockefeller, and as the son of its most famous philanthropist, John D. Rockefeller Jr. And it has been shaped partly by a lifelong fascination with international affairs and by appointments to important governmental positions.

Anecdotes abound that testify to young Nelson's "average guy" qualities during his years at Columbia's Lincoln School and at Dartmouth College, but his college studies included an examination of his grandfather's activities. He is reported to have remarked at the time, "My grandfather never broke a law, but a lot of laws were passed because of him."

Upon graduation in 1930, he married. His father's wedding present was a round-the-world honeymoon, replete with letters of introduction to business and governmental figures, including India's now legendary Mahatma Gandhi.

The next 10 years revolved around the myriad Rockefeller business enterprises. Nelson worked in the international offices of the Chase National Bank, was charged with finding tenants to fill the cavernous office spaces of the family's new Rockefeller Center, began his continuing interest in New York's Museum of Modern Art (a principal concern of his mother) and worked as a director of Standard Oil's Venezuelan subsidiary, Creole Petroleum. Rockefeller's activities in that country set the stage for the next decade of his life and for his first important jobs in government.

His early experience in Latin America suggested two things to him: that U.S. business was not utilizing fully the opportunities for trade and development in that region and that, as a consequence, the field was ripe for penetration by Nazi and other Axis agents. His initial response was to work within his own business community to alert people to the dangers and the possibilities presented by the Latin continent. In 1940, he also submitted a memorandum outlining his views to President Roosevelt.

Democrat Roosevelt heeded Republican Rockefeller's warnings and named him to the new position of inter-American affairs coordinator. Rockefeller held that position through most of World War II, from 1940 to 1944. He reported directly to Roosevelt, the first of five Presidents he has served in some capacity. From 1944 to 1945, he was assistant secretary of state for Latin American affairs and was involved in the drafting of the United Nations charter.

He left appointive office in 1945, only to return in 1950 for a stint as President Truman's International Development Advisory Board chairman. In that post, he was instrumental in developing Truman's Point Four program. In the interim between public offices, he pursued his interest in the developing countries as a private businessman, establishing the still-extant International Basic Economy Corporation, which does business in numerous developing nations.

Rockefeller's premise in all this work was that the strategic interests of the United States, in resisting first Nazism and then Communism, could mesh with the needs of the peoples in poorer countries. The meshing vehicle was to be international business investment. Rockefeller once stated: "In the past century, capital went where it could make the greatest profit. In this century, it must go where it can do the most good." Few developing countries would quarrel with that premise, but the practice has not always turned out so well. The Rockefeller holdings have not been exempted from the criticism and reaction aimed by developing countries at multi-national corporations, as witness the Venezuelan-forced sale of certain of their supermarket investments there and the upcoming nationalization of all of that country's oil production, including the wells of Rockefeller-founded Exxon.

Rockefeller did not confine his interests to the international sphere. He advised presidential candidate Dwight D. Eisenhower on government operations, and he crafted plans for coordinating the federal agencies spawned by Roosevelt's New Deal. One proposal that emerged was the creation of a new cabinet-level Department of Health, Education and Welfare (HEW). Rockefeller then served as under secretary of the new HEW, under Oveta Culp Hobby, in 1953-54. During the Eisenhower administration, he also chaired the Advisory Committee on Government Organization.

He kept his hand in international matters as special presidential assistant on foreign policy in 1954-55. In that post, he moved to the vanguard of those advocating the peaceful possibilities of atomic power, helping establish the cornerstone Atoms for Peace project.

After advising and working for three Presidents in such diverse areas, Rockefeller reportedly tired of the limitations of appointive office. He concluded that only elected officials had the direct mandate needed to accomplish anything of substance in the American system. Midway through the Eisenhower years, he left Washington and returned to New York state. The elective phase of his career was about to begin.

John B. Connally

Connally, 58, was, in 1973, considered a possible successor to President Nixon. The road seemed blocked in 1974, however, when he was indicted on charges of accepting a bribe from a milk industry lawyer in return for urging Nixon to raise price supports for milk. But, acquitted by a federal court jury early in 1975, he was once again on the campaign trail by the end of the year, apparently determined to follow wherever it might lead.

Heavily bankrolled by Texas friends and seemingly undaunted by his trial, the Houston lawyer and former governor (D 1963-69) was hedging his bets, suggesting himself as a possible Republican candidate if Ford is not nominated and weighing a third-party candidacy if he is. "Just because a man happens to occupy the White House is no sign that he ought to automatically get the nomination of his party," Connally said on NBC's "Meet the Press" in June 1975.

A few months later, he edged closer to a formal announcement of his candidacy by raising the possibility that he might run as a favorite son in the Texas primary May 1. "But not as a stand-in for anybody," he said. "I'd run on my own."

John B. Connally

Connally has met with William Rusher, publisher of the conservative *National Review*, who is chairman of the Committee for a New Majority, a group that is clearing a third-party line for a yet-unnamed presidential candidate on ballots in the 50 states. Connally says the project is "a good idea that could perform a very useful service."

Connally has said he will decide what political role, if any, to play in 1976 sometime after the first of the year. By then he will have completed a 60-day speaking tour that began in New Hampshire, home of the nation's first primary.

On a similar speaking tour two years earlier, the handsome Texan was greeted warmly by party professionals grateful for his conversion to the Republicans in the midst of the Watergate scandal. At a southern Republican conference in 1973, most of the 13 state party chairmen said he was their second choice, after Ronald Reagan, for the nomination. Sen. Henry Bellmon (R Okla.) even predicted that year that Connally would be the party's 1976 nominee.

Rebuilding that kind of enthusiasm among party officials after his indictment would be Connally's biggest challenge as a candidate. He says he does not consider the trial a substantial obstacle. "I was innocent before it started, and the jury said I was innocent. How does that hurt you?" he said. After his acquittal, Connally told friends in Texas, "I've survived a physical assassination and a political assassination." He referred to the bullet wounds he suffered while riding with President Kennedy on the day of the President's assassination in November 1963.

Political Career

Connally entered politics as a law student, managing Lyndon B. Johnson's first campaign for Congress in 1938 and later serving on his Washington staff. He became a successful Texas lawyer and a power in the state Democratic Party. In 1961, President Kennedy appointed him secretary of the Navy.

Barely a year after his appointment, Connally resigned to run for the governorship of his home state. He won —and was re-elected twice, despite the bitter internecine feuds in the Texas Democratic Party.

Connally was a successful governor of a conservative state. He supported some progressive legislation. Educational spending more than doubled during his administration, for example. But he fought legislation that would hurt the state's monied establishment, resisting efforts to enact either a personal or corporate income tax. And he vigorously opposed Medicare, the public accommodations section of the 1965 Civil Rights Act, federal aid to education and repeal of the right-to-work section (14-B) of the Taft-Hartley Act. He later reversed his positions on education aid, Medicare and much of the poverty program.

He accepted Nixon's invitation in 1970 to become his secretary of the treasury, becoming the only Democrat in the cabinet. With his charm, commanding presence and speaking ability, Connally quickly emerged as a dominant figure in an administration not known for strong cabinets.

Connally became Nixon's spokesman for domestic and international economic policy. He played a leading role in developing Nixon's economic policy, including the wage-price freeze, the import surcharge and the floating dollar on world currency exchanges.

Connally resigned in June 1972, 12 days before the Watergate burglary, to rejoin his Houston law firm, one of the country's largest.

Less than a year later, he switched to the Republican Party. "I believe that in our time the Republican Party best represents the broad view of most Americans whatever their formal political affiliations," he said. "I know that it now represents my own personal convictions."

Nixon, a strong admirer of Connally, considered nominating the new Republican for the vice presidency after Spiro T. Agnew resigned in 1973, but backed off because of warnings that Connally would have trouble being confirmed by Congress.

Republican Moderates

Baker

Sen. Howard H. Baker Jr. of Tennessee, 50, rose to national prominence as the ranking Republican on the Senate Watergate Committee. His repeated question—"What did the President know and when did he know it?"—became a dominant theme of the investigation. At the height of the hearings, a Harris Survey showed strong support for him outside the South. In a trial heat, he outran Sen. Edward M. Kennedy (D Mass.), 45 per cent to 44 per cent.

Baker was born into a political family. His late father was a Republican representative from Tennessee

Howard H. Baker Jr.

from 1951 to 1964. Howard Jr. married the daughter of the late Senator Everett McKinley Dirksen (R Ill. 1951-69). He was in contention for the vice presidential nomination in 1968. A year later, although only a freshman, he ran for Senate minority leader. Backed by conservative Republicans, he lost, 19 to 24, to the more liberal Hugh Scott (R Pa.), then the Senate whip.

In the year and a half after the Watergate hearings, Baker took exploratory soundings around the country. He said his travels were intended to find out "what the country thinks of Howard Baker, particularly what students think of Howard Baker." In February 1975, his Senate press

secretary said, "He's not ruling out running, even if President Ford decides to run." But the day after Ford announced his candidacy, Baker wrote to the President pledging his support and offering to help.

Baker said he intended "to carefully lay away my ambitions" until 1980. However, he did not say he had lost interest in the presidency, and he remains available for the vice presidency. "Sure I'd like to be Vice President," he said in a newspaper interview. "But that's not a viable option. Nobody runs for Vice President."

Baker, a criminal lawyer from eastern Tennessee, was first elected to the Senate in 1966. He defeated Gov. Frank Clement (1953-59, 1963-67) with 56 per cent of the vote to become the first Republican senator from Tennessee since Reconstruction. He was re-elected in 1972.

Percy

Charles H. Percy of Illinois was elected to the Senate in 1966, the same year as Baker. He defeated venerated Democratic incumbent Paul H. Douglas (1949-67). Before that, he had distinguished himself in business by becoming the president of Bell and Howell at age 30.

For a while, it looked as if 1976 would be the year Percy, 56, undertook a full-fledged campaign for the presidency. As a supporter of domestic welfare programs and a critic of the Vietnam war, Percy has had some liberal support. After Watergate, his independence from the Nixon administration was no longer a liability with rank-and-file Republicans.

When he began his exploratory candidacy in 1974, he told a Republican crowd, "Whether I actually make the race remains to be decided, but I'm not going to deny my interests nor conceal my preparations. I will not insult your intelligence by going through the motions of the non-candidate tango."

His preparations included a $215,000 campaign treasury and a six-volume political blueprint for winning the nomination, prepared by respected Washington, D.C., planning consultants. But in August 1975, Percy removed himself from the race, saying that President Ford had got off

Charles H. Percy

to an excellent start and that if he "continues to say and do the right things, he'll be nominated by acclamation" at the Republican convention. His own candidacy, Percy told reporters, had been put "on the back burner and maybe into the deep freeze."

But Percy will have time to revive his candidacy if Ford falters. The master plan, before it was abandoned, called for him to bypass the first few primaries in favor of the primary in his home state of Illinois April 16.

Mathias

Second-term Sen. Charles McC. Mathias Jr. of Maryland emerged as a possible presidential candidate in an appearance at the National Press Club in October 1975. In his speech, the 53-year-old Mathias criticized "President Ford's fascination with a very real threat on his right that is limiting debate among Republicans." He said, "The intraparty debate grows more and more tepid, and less and less relevant. A great creative force is wasted and dissipated at a time it is most needed." Answering a reporter's question, he hinted that he might consider running for the presidency to stimulate that debate.

Mathias, who comes from an old Maryland family with a tradition of public service dating back to revolutionary

Charles McC. Mathias Jr.

times, is a respected liberal. He antagonized many of his more conservative colleagues with his open criticism of the Nixon administration. He accused Nixon in 1971 of using hard-line rhetoric and "divisive exploitation" of social problems to be re-elected. In April 1973, as the Watergate scandal was breaking, he said, "The pursuit of truth is the only direction in which we can go in search of the way to preserve our loyalty to the Constitution and the laws."

For these and other apostasies, such as casting the deciding vote against L. Patrick Gray III's nomination as FBI director in 1973, Mathias was anathema to the Nixon White House. But he was easily re-elected in 1974.

Ford's Nominees

Richardson

The return from the Court of St. James' of Elliot L. Richardson, the 55-year-old Boston hero of the 1973 "Saturday night massacre," restored him to the list of possible presidential candidates. Richardson became something of a folk hero when he resigned as attorney general rather than follow Nixon's orders to fire Watergate Special Prosecutor Archibald Cox. This recognition elevated him to presidential contender status until he became ambassador to Great Britain early in 1975.

Richardson has not said he is interested in running for the presidency in 1976, but he has not ruled it out, either. "In the circumstances, I see no realistic prospect that I would be playing any active role on my own behalf in 1976," he said in a newspaper interview in June 1975.

But changing circumstances may revive his admitted interest in the presidency. In an earlier interview, when asked if he wanted to be President, he replied, "The only

Elliot L. Richardson

Donald Rumsfeld

honest answer I can give is that when I've thought about it, which is not often, I don't honestly think I don't want to be President."

Richardson is a skilled administrator who, *The New York Times* wrote when he was named secretary of commerce, has held almost every position in Washington except coach of the Redskins. In rapid succession, he was under secretary of state, secretary of health, education and welfare, secretary of defense and attorney general. He has held more cabinet posts than any other man in history.

But Richardson is perceived as more liberal than most of his fellow Republicans. While still secretary of HEW, he occasionally opposed Nixon administration positions. He differed with Nixon's views on school desegregation and busing, for example.

Another Richardson problem is his lack of a political base. His only elected positions, lieutenant governor of Massachusetts (1965-67) and state attorney general (1967-69), were held years ago.

Nevertheless, when Richardson left for Britain, columnist James Reston wrote, "In many ways, he is the most interesting figure on the American political scene today, maybe better qualified to be President in the last few years of the seventies than most candidates now in the race...."

Rumsfeld

Donald Rumsfeld, 43, has spent most of his adult life working for the federal government. After graduating from Princeton University in 1954 and serving as a naval aviator, he spent two years as an assistant to former Rep. David Dennsion (R Ohio 1957-59) and Sen. Robert P. Griffin (R Mich.). At age 29, he was elected to the House of Representatives from Illinois in 1962; he had been a Chicago stockbroker.

After serving three terms in Congress, he began to leapfrog from position to position in the executive branch. He was President Nixon's director of the Office of Economic Opportunity, White House counselor, director of the Cost of Living Council and then ambassador to the North Atlantic Treaty Organization.

He returned from NATO to become chief assistant to President Ford. As chief of staff, he won a reputation as a wily political infighter, an austere taskmaster and an efficient manager. He is a close confidant of Ford. He favors a strong defense posture and, as secretary of defense, is expected to fight hard against congressional slashes in the defense budget.

Although Rumsfeld, perhaps in deference to Ford, has never openly expressed an interest in the presidency, he is widely assumed to harbor presidential ambitions.

Bush

George Bush, 51, the first American envoy to the People's Republic of China, frequently has been mentioned as a candidate for high political office in the past. He was elected in 1966 and 1968 to the House of Representatives from Texas but lost two successive bids, in 1964 and 1970, for the Senate.

Bush spent two years as ambassador to the United Nations before being recalled to Washington in 1972 by President Nixon to head the Republican National Committee. As the Watergate scandals unfolded, Bush and President Ford, then the Vice President, formed a close bond. Shortly after assuming the presidency in 1974, Ford named Bush to head the United States liaison office in Peking.

Bush's nomination to the CIA immediately came under attack from congressional Democrats, who questioned the wisdom of having a professional politician in a sensitive position that traditionally has been non-partisan. He was called upon to disavow his interest in running for President or Vice President, and his confirmation hearings promised to be turbulent.

George Bush

The Other Democrats

McGovern

Since his defeat by Nixon in 1972, 53-year-old Sen. George McGovern of South Dakota has remained on the Democratic presidential sidelines, but he has indicated his willingness to enter the 1976 race if his party calls.

In a June 1975 letter to about 30 of his closest supporters, McGovern asked their advice on whether or not he

George McGovern

should again seek the presidency. While McGovern wrote that he did not intend to be a candidate "as things stand now," he said he was being urged to enter the primaries in Wisconsin, New Hampshire, Massachusetts and New York. Those are states where McGovern did well in 1972. The gist of the replies, according to McGovern's administrative assistant, George Cunningham, was: "We still love you, but this ain't the time—don't do it."

McGovern since has warned the Democratic Party against the nomination of a "no issues, centrist" candidate. In an October 1975 speech, he said, "The Democratic Party must demand of itself not merely how it may win but how it would govern." The speech was interpreted by many political observers as a rebuke to the announced presidential candidates and as evidence that McGovern might yet be persuaded to enter the race.

In 1974, the former political science professor was elected to a third term in the Senate. Since his re-election, McGovern has been active in the areas of food policy (one of his continuing legislative interests—he was President Kennedy's first director of the Food for Peace program) and foreign policy, traveling to Cuba to meet with Premier Fidel Castro and to the Middle East to meet with Palestinian leader Yasir Arafat.

Two Governors

Edmund G. Brown Jr. was elected governor of California in 1974. The same day, Hugh L. Carey was elected governor of New York. Traditionally, the governors of the two largest states automatically enter any presidential speculation involving a party out of power. But neither of these two Democrats could be considered more than an extremely dark horse as the year began.

The 37-year-old Brown may or may not be running. He has been noncommittal. In October 1975, an aide said, "I think it's about 50-50 right now."

Brown is enormously popular in his home state, where public-opinion polls in October 1975 showed him running ahead of all the announced presidential candidates in trial heats. And he has admitted a natural curiosity to see how he would do in a presidential primary without campaigning. In August 1975, he said that if his name appeared on a presidential primary ballot, he might leave it on. "I'm not kicking myself in or out of anything," he said.

Any call for national service may be a long time coming. Brown is far less popular with party professionals outside California than he is with the voters at home.

Since he took office in January 1975, Brown has emerged as an anomaly in California Democratic politics. During his gubernatorial campaign, Brown, whose father, Edmund G. (Pat) Brown, served as governor (1959-67), was viewed as a liberal. He since has startled Californians, however, with massive budget cuts and a tough, no-nonsense approach to many issues, including prison reform and poverty programs; he has called the latter "the last refuge of scoundrels."

Carey, 56, a former Democratic representative from Brooklyn (1961-75), has made no secret of his interest in a place on the ticket in 1976. But what he may do about it is not clear, and his hopes are undoubtedly diminished by his preoccupation with New York's fiscal crisis.

—By Barry Hager and Rochelle Jones

PAYING FOR ELECTIONS: NEW LAW UNDER ATTACK

The Watergate-spawned campaign finance law of 1974 is undergoing its first test under actual field conditions as politicians prepare for the 1976 presidential and congressional contests. The law (PL 93-443) is having the major impact on campaign financing that was expected at the time of its passage.

But, ironically, it is having side effects that may undermine the original intent of the bill's sponsors—to foster greater political competition and reduce the influence of "big money" in politics. For example:

● Instead of encouraging greater electoral competition, the law may tip the odds in favor of incumbents through its low spending limits.

● The law makes former President Nixon's 1972 Committee to Re-elect the President a model for future campaign organizations, in one sense, because of the premium it puts on accountants and managers instead of politicians to run campaigns.

● The law does not seriously lessen the influence and importance of special-interest groups and the President in raising political money. If anything, it has spurred business to become more politically involved and has created conditions that enhance the political influence of the President.

Growing awareness of these and other side effects has set off debate over how the American political system will be changed by the statute and whether the changes will be all for the good.

The law, which took effect Jan. 1, 1975, was one of the few legislative legacies of Watergate, the political and campaign finance scandal that forced President Nixon's resignation in August 1974. The first major overhaul of the campaign financing system in 49 years, it was passed ostensibly to rid politics of the evils associated with Watergate—the corrupting influences of big money and big special interests. It attempted to do that by going to the heart of the political system—money.

The campaign finance abuses of the 1972 Nixon re-election drive provided the backdrop of the law's enactment. The abuses occurred in two areas: spending and fund-raising.

The Nixon campaign spent $61.4-million seeking the President's re-election—more than double the previous high of $25-million reached in the 1968 Nixon-Agnew campaign. In contrast, Sen. George McGovern of South Dakota spent $42-million seeking the 1972 Democratic presidential nomination and running in the fall election. The total spending figures are only part of the story, however. Hundreds of thousands of dollars were spent secretly by the 1972 Nixon operation to carry out dirty tricks against Democratic opponents and to finance the break-in at the Democratic National Committee headquarters and its subsequent coverup.

Disclosures of fund-raising abuses were even more striking. The Nixon campaign undertook a massive effort to circumvent the Federal Election Campaign Act of 1971 (PL 92-225), which required full disclosure of political contributions and spending by collecting millions of dollars from illegal sources before the effective date of the measure—April 7, 1972.

The Nixon committee then fought desperately but unsuccessfully to hide its pre-April-7 contributors. Forced to disclose by Common Cause lawsuits, the Nixon fund-raisers acknowledged raising $19.9-million (one-third of all funds) before April 7. Of that amount, $16.3-million, or 81 per cent, was given by 105 contributors of $40,000 or more. Much of the money came from dozens of corporations and corporate officers who eventually would be found criminally guilty of using company funds for political contributions.

Three Approaches

The 1974 law tried to prevent the 1972-type abuses from occurring ever again by taking three approaches to regulating campaign financing. First, it required the strict disclosure of sources and uses of campaign money, to be policed by an independent, six-member Federal Election Commission. Second, it set strict limits on individual and organizational contributions to campaigns and on spending ceilings for House, Senate and presidential races. And third, it established the first public financing of presidential election campaigns, starting in 1976. The money will come from the presidential campaign fund set up in 1971 to finance presidential elections through a voluntary federal income tax checkoff.

The new law brought together in one package the principal approaches to regulating campaign finance that have been proposed since the Progressive era of the turn of the century. The problem with the earlier attempts at regulation was that they were riddled with loopholes and only rarely enforced.

The Federal Corrupt Practices Act of 1925, the basic campaign finance law for almost 50 years, was a classic case. It regulated campaign spending and disclosure of receipts and expenditures by congressional candidates. But

MILLIONS

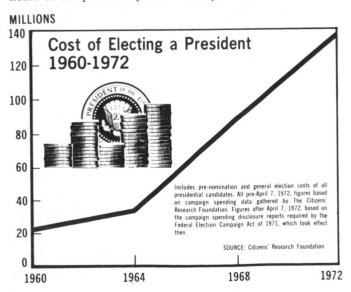

Cost of Electing a President 1960-1972

Includes pre-nomination and general election costs of all presidential candidates. All pre-April 7, 1972, figures based on campaign spending data gathered by The Citizens' Research Foundation. Figures after April 7, 1972, based on the campaign spending disclosure reports required by the Federal Election Campaign Act of 1971, which took effect then.

SOURCE: Citizens' Research Foundation

140

120

100

80

60

40

20

0

1960   1964   1968   1972

it covered only general elections, it did not require audits, and its spending limits could be evaded by claiming that certain expenditures were made without the candidate's "knowledge and consent." Furthermore, it was not enforced.

Congress moved to remedy the disclosure problem in the Federal Election Campaign Act of 1971. It repealed the meaningless contribution and spending limits of the 1925 law and required the most comprehensive disclosure of campaign contributions and expenditures in American history. It also imposed limits on spending for media advertising and on expenditures by candidates and their families. The 1971 statute proved to be an important tool in breaking open the Watergate scandal.

The 1974 law incorporated the strict disclosure requirements of the 1971 measure. But Congress faced a problem that went beyond disclosure when it took up new campaign finance legislation in the wake of Watergate. Could it pass a measure that would disclose not only how money was being used in politics but strictly regulate its use? Could it pass a law that would be enforceable? The 1974 statute provided tentative answers to those questions through its strict spending and contribution limits and the creation of the independent election commission.

Spiraling Spending

Regulation, however, was only half the question Congress considered. Public revulsion at what it perceived as big money in politics and exorbitant campaign spending began to take form in the late 1960s and early 1970s and reached a high mark after the 1972 election.

The public reaction is not hard to understand if one looks only at political spending figures. According to the Citizens' Research Foundation, total political spending in the United States at all levels of government rose by 13 per cent from 1956 to 1960 (from $155-million in 1956 to $175-million in 1960) and by 14 per cent in the following four-year period (up to $200-million in 1964). A sharp jump—50 per cent—occurred from 1964 to 1968. The 1968 total was $300-million. The 1972 spending figure of $425-million was 42 per cent higher than that of four years earlier.

The net effect of the 1974 law, its backers claimed when it was enacted, would be to foster greater political competition and at last to control the role of money in politics. There is little disagreement that the law has clamped down on spiraling campaign spending by candidates and has ended the dominance of large contributors. But the law is also having more subtle effects that extend through the whole fabric of American politics.

Constitutional Challenge

Although candidates are planning their campaigns to conform to the new campaign finance law, the law is under serious consitutional challenge and may be changed before the 1976 elections.

The day after the law took effect Jan. 1, 1975, Sen. James L. Buckley (Cons-R N.Y.), former Sen. Eugene J. McCarthy (D Minn. 1959-71), Rep. William A. Steiger (R Wis.) and the New York Civil Liberties Union filed a 34-count complaint in U.S. District Court in Washington, D.C., challenging every major provision of the act. A federal appeals court upheld the law's major provisions in an Aug. 14 opinion. But the Supreme Court was not expected to make a final decision until December.

"There aren't 33 primaries, but over 377 primaries."

—Robert J. Keefe, campaign manager for Henry M. Jackson

The challengers contend that the law violates the freedom of speech, equal protection and separation of powers clauses of the Constitution. In a brief filed June 2 before the U.S. Court of Appeals in Washington, they charged that the law constituted "a massive, unprecedented intrusion" into the political process that "strikes at the heart of democratic self-government."

Backers of the law acknowledge that in attempting to remedy "the evils that flow from excessive campaign giving and spending," Congress might have limited "rights and values" under the 1st Amendment and other sections of the Constitution. But they argued in their brief that the law, in the main, "fundamentally promotes rather than impairs First Amendment and other constitutional values."

"The Constitution," their brief stated, "is not an instrument for its own subversion. It does not condemn the nation to continue suffering old abuses that reached new extremes in the 1972 campaign."

The case, which some constitutional scholars consider one of the most significant in recent years, has six broad issues. As outlined in the court briefs and interviews with constitutional lawyers, they are:

● Disclosure. The challengers argue that the full public disclosure of contributions over $100 required by the law is too rigid and violates a contributor's 1st Amendment right to privacy. Such disclosures, they say, "may be required only of those contributors who may seek to influence government action unlawfully."

The law's defenders reply that "nothing but speculation supports plaintiffs' suggestion that disclosure will 'chill' contributions."

● Contribution limits. The limits restrict an individual's 1st Amendment right to freedom of speech, opponents charge. Because "every effective method of political communication requires the expenditure of money," their brief said, "to limit the expenditure is to restrict the communication."

Contribution limits "are plainly essential if we are to moderate undue influence of large contributors on candidates," the defenders replied, citing the Hatch Act and other legislation as earlier limits on political activity.

● Independent expenditure. The challengers claim that the $1,000 limit on individual political expenditures is a "stifling of the roles of individual citizens and independent groups" that is "patently unconstitutional."

Backers call the limits "a necessary and constitutionally permissible limitation to prevent wholesale evasion of contribution and expenditure limits."

● Spending limits. The government has "no compelling interest" to limit a candidate's campaign expenditures, the plaintiffs say. That discriminates, they argue, against the candidates challenging incumbents.

Highlights of 1974 Campaign Spending Law

Contribution Limits

$1,000 per individual for each primary, runoff and general election, and an aggregate contribution of $25,000 for all federal candidates annually; $5,000 per organization, political committee and state party organization for each election.

Candidate's and his family's contributions: $50,000 for president; $35,000 for Senate, $25,000 for House.

Individual unsolicited expenditures on behalf of a candidate limited to $1,000 a year.

Cash contributions of over $100 and foreign contributions barred.

Spending Limits

Presidential primaries—$10-million total per candidate for all primaries.

Presidential general election—$20-million.

Presidential nominating conventions—$2-million each major political party, lesser amounts for minor parties.

Senate primaries—$100,000 or eight cents per eligible voter, whichever is greater.

Senate general elections—$150,000 or 12 cents per eligible voter, whichever is greater.

House primaries—$70,000.

House general elections—$70,000.

Senate limits apply to House candidates who represent a whole state.

Repealed the media spending limitations in the Federal Election Campaign Act of 1971 (PL 92-225).

Limits increased annually based on the percentage rise in the cost of living index computed by the Labor Department's Bureau of Labor Statistics.

Party Spending

National parties permitted to spend independently $10,000 per candidate in House general elections; $20,000 or two cents per eligible voter, whichever is greater, for each candidate in Senate general elections; and two cents per eligible voter in presidential general elections. The expenditure would be above the candidate's individual spending limit.

Exemptions

Exempted from contribution and spending limits: expenditures of up to $500 for food and beverages, invitations, use of personal property and spending on "slate cards" and sample ballots.

Fund-raising costs of up to 20 per cent of the candidate spending limit exempted from spending limits. (That effectively increases the spending limits.)

Public Financing

Full optional public funding for presidential general elections; public funding of national party nominating conventions voluntary; matching public funds in presidential primaries of up to $5-million per candidate after meeting fund-raising requirement of $100,000 raised in amounts of at least $5,000 in each of 20 states or more and through contributions of $250 or less. All federal money for public funding of campaigns would come from the Presidential Election Campaign Fund. Proportional funding for minor-party candidates.

Congressional campaigns not publicly financed, but have to rely on private contributions.

Disclosure and Reporting Dates

Candidates required to establish a central campaign committee; bank loans treated as contributions; government contractors, unions and corporations permitted to maintain separate segregated political funds. Disclosure filing dates: 10 days before an election (postmarked no later than 12 days before the election), 30 days after an election and quarterly, unless the committee received or spent less than $1,000.

Enforcement

An eight-member, bipartisan, full-time supervisory board controlled by six voting public members. Two of the public members appointed by the House speaker, two by the president pro tem of the Senate and two by the President, all of whom are confirmed by Congress. The House clerk and the secretary of the Senate are ex officio members. The board has civil enforcement powers and is able to seek court injunctions. Criminal cases would be referred to the Justice Department for prosecution. House and Senate have veto power over regulations issued by the board within 30 legislative days.

Using campaign spending data for the 1972 and 1974 elections compiled by Common Cause, the defenders claim that only a few congressional candidates in 1972 and 1974 exceeded the new law's spending ceilings. "The President limits were exceeded in 1972—but that was the single campaign whose excesses most shocked the nation," their brief stated.

● Public financing. The challengers attack the law's public financing provisions for presidential elections. As they see them, the provisions discriminate against minor-party and independent candidates and give the major parties a preferred status.

The defenders respond that minor and new parties have to be treated differently as a matter of practical necessity. Equal protection of the laws, they add, "can hardly require more equality than circumstances make possible."

● Election commission. The Federal Election Commission is composed of four members appointed by Congress and two appointed by the President. That, the Justice Department and the challengers say, "appear[s] to violate the constitutional separation of powers," because the Constitution gives only the President the power of appointment. The make-up of the commission has turned it into a legislative body that would illegally exert powers reserved for the executive branch, they say.

Defenders say that Congress has broad powers to deal with elections and appoint officials to carry out quasi-judicial functions that fall within the purview of Congress.

Political Impact

Despite the constitutional challenge, the campaign finance law is an integral part of the politics of 1975 and 1976, and it will leave a lasting mark whether it stands or falls.

Politicians are planning the 1976 presidential campaigns on the assumption that they will have to operate under it. The message of Eddie Mahe, executive director of the Republican National Committee, is repeated whenever one talks with professional politicians. "We're telling people to forget the challenge and just go ahead full force," he said. "If it's going to change, fantastic. But don't count on it now."

The changes can be seen in the way the 1976 campaigns are being organized. They have made campaign planning and organization much more businesslike. And they have shown campaign managers the benefits of long-range planning and budgeting.

"Candidates and campaign managers will see the benefits of these changes," said Kent C. Cooper a staff member of the Federal Election Commission and former co-director of the National Information Center on Political Finance. "These are changes that will be with us for a long time, even it the law isn't."

All the prospective Democratic presidential candidates except Alabama Gov. George C. Wallace are planning to try public financing in 1976. Wallace aides have indicated they may reject matching public funds. They are so confident that they can raise the full $12-million that the law allows for campaigning for the nomination that their plan is to pass up the $5-million in matching federal money and use Wallace's independence as a political issue.

President Ford's top fund-raiser, David Packard, has said he hopes to avoid using matching money and instead raise the full amount authorized by the law for the primaries. By the end of the year, however, Ford aides indicated that the campaign would have to accept matching money because of its narrow fund-raising base.

Fund-Raising Patterns

W. Clement Stone, a millionaire Chicago insurance executive, will not be making $2-million contributions in 1976, as he did in 1972 to Richard Nixon's presidential campaign. Nor will Stewart Mott, an heir to the General Motors fortune, be able to give $729,000 to his favorite liberal presidential candidate in 1976, as he did in 1972 to George McGovern. The United Auto Workers Union will no longer be able to give $63,500 to a Senate candidate, as it did to Sen. Howard W. Metzenbaum (D Ohio 1973-75) in his unsuccessful 1974 bid for nomination to a full Senate term.

The new campaign finance law has put an end to that type of political money-giving by placing tight ceilings on contributions by individuals, organizations and political committees.

Contributions by individuals are now held to $1,000 for each primary, runoff and general election, with an annual aggregate $25,000 limit on contributors to federal candidates. Candidate-supporting organizations such as the liberal National Committee for an Effective Congress, political committees such as the AFL-CIO's Committee on Political Education (COPE) and the American Medical Association's Political Action Committee (AMPAC) and state party organizations may give no more than $5,000 to a candidate in any federal election.

"They don't have to feed him, they don't have to booze him. They just have to put his check in the bank."

—Eddie Mahe, executive director, Republican National Committee

Presidential Adjustment

The greatest adjustment to PL 93-443 is being made at the presidential level. "It's a funny law," said John T. Calkins, a political aide to President Ford, "because it makes it necessary to raise less money than before but forces you to think more about how to raise it."

The law sets a $10-million spending limit (with an additional $2-million set aside for fund-raising costs) on pre-nomination campaign activity—with one major hitch. It provides for partial public financing of presidential primary spending up to $5-million. To qualify for that money, a candidate has to raise $5,000 in each of 20 states in contributions of no more than $250, for a total of $100,000. Once he has raised that amount, contributions he receives will be matched dollar for dollar up to $250 per contribution.

That increases the strategic importance of fund-raising and requires much greater organization, planning and variety of approaches than in the past. Most of the presidential fund-raising activity by late 1975 had been on the Democratic side. It showed how candidates were adapting. For example:

● Wallace had used direct mail almost exclusively, relying on repeated small contributions averaging $11.70 from the 400,000 people on his contributor mailing list. Wallace used direct mail successfully in 1968 and 1972 to finance his presidential bids.

● Sen. Lloyd Bentsen (D Texas), on the other hand, had concentrated on raising $1,000 contributions in his home state while he prepared a limited direct-mail drive.

● Sen. Henry M. Jackson (D Wash.) was using a combination of direct mail and personal solicitation to collect his primary limit.

Fewer Fat Cats

The fund-raising strategy of Richard Kline, Jackson's finance chairman, shows how different 1976 will be from earlier presidential campaigns. Kline headed the fund-raising operation of Sen. Edmund S. Muskie's (D Maine) presidential campaign in 1972. "In May of 1971," he recalled, "a total of 40 contributors had put up money for Muskie's campaign. We had no mass fund-raising events, but we had raised about $600,000 from the $25,000 to $50,000 contributors." Muskie relied on the big givers to finance his campaign until he ran out of money after he began to falter in the presidential primaries.

The 1974 law has changed all that. "The fat cat who could give us $100,000 or $200,000 isn't as important today," Kline said. "Now the most important people are the fund-raisers, the men who know where to tap the $1,000 contributions. We try to find in every community one or two people who are respected by their peers and who work hard at raising money. The fund-raiser today is much like the precinct captain of old."

Candidates must have "access to a network they can plug into," said Eddie Mahe. "It not only cuts down on fund-raising costs but makes it possible for them to just walk up to a guy and ask him to help. They don't have to feed him, they don't have to booze him. They just have to put his check in the bank."

The new approach to fund-raising saves the candidate from pandering to the big contributor. But that means more work, because the candidate is dealing with more people to raise less money. Robert J. Keefe, Jackson's campaign manager, likened the new fund-raising demands to a voter registration drive. "It requires you to organize more directly," he said. "You can't worry about being extra nice to a few people."

The candidate who benefits most from the contribution limits and the matching system is Wallace. His top aides are open in expressing their delight. "The law is tailor-made for us," said Charles S. Snider, Wallace's campaign director. "We haven't had to change our operations substantially."

With its low contribution limits, the law encourages candidates to rely on small contributions to fund their campaigns. That fits in which the Wallace strategy of the past two years of building up a massive mailing list of contributors who will give small amounts regularly. The Alabama governor financed his 1968 and 1972 presidential campaigns through small contributions generated by direct mail and raised $2.5-million in small contributions during the first nine months of 1975, the largest amount gathered by any of the presidential contenders in that period.

Wallace gets an added bonus from the law. Because practically all of his contributions are under $250, he has a chance to receive more matching money than the other candidates. Four $250 contributions that he receives are nearly twice as good as one $1,000 gift, because all four of the smaller donations are eligible for matching.

Impact on Special Interests

Special-interest groups, including labor unions and education, business, health and dairy political action committees, are affected, especially at the Senate and presidential levels, by the lower contribution limits. Although they traditionally have given less than $5,000 each to House candidates, they have contributed much more to Senate and presidential candidates. *(Chart, p. 100)*

Those groups, nevertheless, are expected to encounter little difficulty in meeting the law's new requirements. It is ironic and instructive that labor, one of the groups the law would be expected to check, had no complaints with the $5,000 contribution limit on political committees. Neal Gregory, former codirector of the Center for Public Financing, an organization that lobbied for the law's passage, reported that the $5,000 limit was checked with the AFL-CIO before it was put in the bill. "There was no opposition to it," he said.

That lack of opposition stems from the fact that labor unions and other organizations with many affiliates will be able to get around the limit by having more contributions funneled through their state and local organizations.

While special-interest political contributions are expected to be more decentralized, spokesmen for several politically active unions said that more money would be spent in 1976 on internal union political activity. "The con-

---

T.R. and the New Law

The 1974 campaign financing law works against the stability of minor parties by allowing a presidential candidate who qualifies for public financing in one election to take the money with him if he switches parties in the next election.

If the new law had been in effect in 1912, for example, Theodore Roosevelt, the Progressive Party candidate that year, would have become eligible for full public financing in 1916, because he polled 27 per cent of the vote with his "Bull Moose" campaign. Winning more than 25 per cent would have given him major-party status.

In the same election, the Republican Party, under whose banner Roosevelt had served as President from 1901 until 1909, collected only 23 per cent of the vote and thus would have been a minor party in 1916 and would have had only partial public financing.

But if Roosevelt had rejoined the Republicans and been their candidate in 1916, they would have taken the full public funding away from the Progressives.

---

tribution limits will free more money for other things like political education work," said Sam Fishman of the United Auto Workers in Detroit. "We'll also have free money around to put staff guys into campaigns. We hope to register more members to vote, get a higher percentage of members voting for union-endorsed candidates and get a higher vote turnout from union members."

Ideological fund-raising organizations such as the American Conservative Union's Conservative Victory Fund, George Agree's Senate campaign fund and the liberal National Committee for an Effective Congress are expected to be hard hit, because they raise money by direct mail. They do not have local chapters to raise money and thus increase the number of contributions they can make.

"It may be possible for these groups to set up West Coast and Rocky Mountain units, mail separately and keep separate bank accounts," said Agree, who raises money by direct mail for liberal Democratic Senate candidates. "But it's going to involve very great additions to the cost of the operations. I probably won't engage in it, and others won't."

Agree criticized the contribution limits for organizations as discriminating against national groups. "In a democratic society, a limitation ought to be related to individuals or, in the case of groups, to the number of individuals involved. An association of 100,000 members ought to be treated differently than an association with 1,000 individuals," he said. "The limits work against associations that are not highly structured like the American Medical Association and the dairy groups. They operate against associations of poorer people and in favor of associations of a few wealthy people."

The law has activated business as a force in political fund-raising. Corporations are now specifically allowed to form political action committees (PACs) to make contributions, a hazy area that in the past deterred them from making above-board contributions. Corporations and businesses have seized on that change to become increasingly involved in political fund-raising. The National Association of Manufacturers, the U.S. Chamber of Commerce and the Republican National Committee are urging businesses to form their own PACs.

Mahe, who calls business PACs a "United Fund for Republicans," sees them as rich, untapped sources of Republican money. "They will regularize contributions and bring them in on an on-going basis," he said. "Once people sign a payroll deduction plan for political contributions, it just happens. You get the automatic deduction every month, and every month the corporation takes out their $3 or their $2 or whatever it is. And you don't have to resolicit them, you don't have to do anything. You do it once and you're through. And just once a year, you go by and scoop it out." In the past, business contributions frequently were made through individual giving by top executives of corporations.

Individual Expenditures

The law hits the well-heeled candidate who in the past has been able to bankroll his own campaign. Vice President Nelson A. Rockefeller self-financed his 1964 and 1968 presidential bids, and Rep. Richard L. Ottinger (D) contributed a great deal of money to his own 1970 New York Senate campaign. But for 1976, presidential candidates are limited to a $50,000 contribution to their own campaign, Senate candidates to $35,000 and House candidates to $25,000.

The individual contribution ceilings are weakened, however, by a provision allowing individuals to spend up to $1,000 on behalf of a candidate. There is no aggregate limit on these independent political expenditures.

The law also allows independent political expenditures, in deference to the constitutional guarantee of freedom of expression. The practical effect is to double the individual contribution limit, because a contributor could give $1,000 to a candidate outright and then spend another $1,000 on his own newspaper ad or billboard on the candidate's behalf.

"In certain situations," said Agree, "ways may be found to make these [broad] expenditures. For example, an individual of great means could buy a billboard in every congressional district in the country backing all Democratic or Republican candidates. There's a large loophole here for the flow of money."

Individual contributors get another break through a provision in the law that exempts from candidate spending limits expenditures of up to $500 for food and beverages, invitations and unreimbursed travel expenses by volunteers. This allows a fund-raiser to absorb up to $500 in travel expenses while collecting contributions.

Strengthening The Parties

Democratic and Republican professionals see the law as giving the established parties new life. The additive is the independent expenditures parties are allowed to make for House, Senate and presidential candidates. "The law would be a great deal worse than it is without that," acknowledged Mahe.

The national and state parties each can spend $10,000 per candidate in House general elections; $20,000 or two cents a voter, whichever is greater, for candidates in Senate general elections, and two cents a voter in presidential general elections. What makes those expenditures so attractive is that they are above the candidate's individual spending limits.

Finding the Funds

Both parties, however, have to raise the money to cover their independent expenditures, a prospect that is causing headaches. "The national committee is allowed to spend $9-million on candidates next year," said Rod Smith, deputy treasurer of the Republican National Committee.

Excess 1972 Contributions Over New Law's Limits

The chart below lists the contributions made by four groups of special-interest committees to federal candidates in 1972 that would have exceeded the limits of the 1974 law as it applies to the 1976 elections.

The figures, covering the period April 7, 1972, through Dec. 31, 1972, do not include contributions from national, state or local party-related committees.

CONTRIBUTOR	RECIPIENT			TOTAL
	President or Vice President	Senator	Representative	
Health-Related Committees	$0 (of $2,750 given)	$10,274 (of $158,628 given)	$13,500 (of $828,464 given)	$23,774 (of $989,842 given)
Ideological and Miscellaneous Committees	$0 (of $15,957)	$267,988 (of $584,394 given)	$138,977 (of $995,418 given)	$406,965 (of $1,595,769 given)
Business-Related Committees*	$321,835 (of $574,813 given)	$144,800 (of $822,175 given)	$28,450 (of $1,638,325 given)	$495,085 (of $3,035,313 given)
Labor-Related Committees	$824,400 (of $1,136,196 given)	$222,546 (of $1,285,616 given)	$129,234 (of $2,654,161 given)	$1,176,180 (of $5,075,973 given)
TOTAL	$1,146,235 (of $1,729,716 given)	$645,608 (of $2,850,813 given)	$310,161 (of $6,116,368 given)	$2,102,004 (of $10,696,897 given)

* Figures do not include the large amounts of money contributed by business before April 7, 1972, when the reporting rules of the Federal Election Campaign Act of 1971 took effect. Most of the money was given to President Nixon's 1972 re-election campaign.

SOURCE: Citizens' Research Foundation

"But it might cost us $3- to $4-million to raise the $9-million, which means the national committee can expect to spend only $6-million. Also, we've never engaged in that type of fund-raising ourselves before."

Nor have the parties had to spend money on campaigns before. Under the law, the party cannot give the money to the candidate. It has to spend it on behalf of the candidate on items such as political advertising. Officials at both national committees say that will require much more work by political staffers and much greater involvement in campaigns than before.

Minor-Party Presidential Candidates

Minor-party candidates for President in 1976 will receive no public financing at the start of their campaigns. Under PL 93-443, they first have to receive more than 5 per cent of the vote and finish up the campaign with debts in order to get a proportional share of public money after that election. A candidate with more than 25 per cent would receive full public financing in the next election, and any candidate who received over 5 per cent of the vote in the preceding election would be entitled to a proportional share of public funds at the beginning of the next presidential election campaign. The law does not cover minor-party candidates for Congress.

Some political observers, including George Agree, see the delayed financing of third parties in presidential elections as patently discriminatory. "Usually third parties are one-shot deals under our system," he said. "Protest is not deferred for four years."

Political scientist Nelson Polsby, however, fears that the minor-party financing mechanism in the law will institutionalize and perpetuate them. "Third parties have an ebb and flow," he said. "But if they get 5 per cent in one election, they will get money in the next election far after they reach their peak. This can perpetuate third parties long after they've served their purpose and only splinter the party system."

Businesslike Tactics

Professional politicians at the national level agree that corporate techniques will play a more important role in campaigns because of the new finance law.

Although the misuse of some of these techniques earned a bad reputation for CREEP, the pejorative acronym for the Committee to Re-elect the President, "CREEP was a masterfully done political re-election job despite Watergate," said Calkins, Ford's adviser. "CREEP is an indication of the management and accounting organization needed for future campaigns."

Candidates are planning their 1976 budgets to make sure that they stay within the spending limits without paring activities too sharply. "You now have a level of accounting sophistication in politics you've never had before," said Rod Smith. "The treasurer has been elevated to the key person in the campaign because of the need to keep track of all the money."

Money is not spent as casually as in the past. Robert Keefe said, "You might be more restrained on trying things. Now you're forced to evaluate in such a way to do things right the first time. You can't apply dollars against your mistakes, which has been the case in the past."

The professionals are divided over the impact of the corporate practices. The tighter accounting requirements

"The law, far from shortening the campaign cycle, is going to lengthen it."

—George E. Agree, political fund-raiser

required by the contribution and spending limits were a major goal of the law's sponsors. They wanted not only an accounting of where campaign money came from and was spent but greater accountability by campaign officials and candidates on how they raised and used political money.

To David L. Rosenbloom, a student of congressional campaign financing and director of the Parkman Center for Urban Affairs in Boston, the new law will have a salutary effect on campaigns by forcing candidates to tidy up their operations and stop wasting money. The law will moderate the conduct of elections," he predicted. "People will more carefully budget their money and work through organizations that can mobilize people."

But some political figures and campaign finance experts fear that control of campaigns by accountants, managers and lawyers will hamstring the conduct of campaigns, exclude local and state political groups from presidential politics and open the possibility of campaign financing abuses.

Candidates might lose their freedom of action in handling issues that arise late in a campaign. "You need to have money at the end to deal with late issues and marginal areas," said David W. Adamany, the Wisconsin secretary of revenue. "But when you budget down to the last detail as the law requires, it precludes a candidate from dealing with events over which he has no control. Inflexible budgeting prevents politicians from being part of what is happening in society at any given moment."

The fact that all expenditures have to be approved by the candidate's national headquarters to make sure that they fit within the spending limits means a new relationship between presidential campaigns and local politicians, with the local politicans playing a much-reduced role. "Local politicians can't set up independent operations as they did in the past," said Richard Kline. He likened the new relationship to "the negotiating process between a national office and its local plant managers. You have to weigh local decisions against a national picture. They'll have to realize that their state or local operation has to take second place to national needs and the national operation. This will change the old relationship between states and national campaigns and will affect politics immensely."

Herbert E. Alexander of the Citizens' Research Foundation, one of the nation's leading campaign finance experts, is worried that the law's emphasis on centralized campaign direction "may tend to inhibit local political activity. Local committees that cannot obtain authorization to purchase a newspaper ad or buy a radio spot will not feel their activities for federal candidates are meaningful," he said, "and so may focus increasingly on state and local campaigns."

The corporate emphasis may also create serious potential political problems by divorcing the financial functions from the political functions of campaigns. "This is a matter of some concern," warned Alexander, "since financial accountability and responsibility cannot be guaranteed apart from political accountability and responsibility. The Nixon campaign in 1972 well illustrates the hazards of trying to separate financial from political functions."

The Presidential Dilemma

Prospective presidential candidates, particularly the out-of-power Democrats, face a common dilemma as they lay their plans for 1976: How many primaries can they afford to run in? They, more than anyone else, will feel the impact of PL 93-443.

The question defies an easy answer. As the cost of running for President is being pushed up by the proliferation of primaries, campaign spending has been restricted. More than 30 states, including the 10 largest, will have presidential primaries. Primary campaigns alone could cost a candidate more than the over-all pre-nomination campaign spending limit of $12-million (including $2-million for fund-raising) set by the law, in the opinion of some experts interviewed.

Kline, Jackson's finance chairman, predicts that his campaign will be able to spend no more than $7.5-million on the spring primaries. "We're setting aside $2-million for headquarters and travel costs," he said, "plus another $500,-000 for the convention. That leaves $7.5-million for every one of these primaries. That's very little money."

The Democrats' proportional representation rules for the 1976 convention encourage candidates to enter as many primaries as possible. "You no longer have a situation where delegates are selected by convention in the key states, as in 1960," said Mark Siegel, executive director of the Democratic National Committee. "Then a few wins in key primaries like Wisconsin and West Virginia would influence the convention states like Pennsylvania. Now candidates will have to nickel and dime it from primary to primary, picking up delegates where they can."

Primary campaign costs may be kept down by the selection of delegates by congressional district. Most of the big primary states already have or are expected to adopt that system.

"There aren't 33 primaries, but over 377 primaries," said Robert Keefe. "We're planning on that basis. The new finance law comes into play, because we'll target by congressional districts rather than by states. We'll spend money on districts that have higher odds."

General Election Costs

Once a candidate is nominated, he will be able to spend $20-million in the general election, about two-thirds of what was spent for Democrat George McGovern in his losing bid in 1972 and more than half of the record $40-million spent for Richard Nixon. But several observers warned that the general election limit is too low and will increase the advantages of the incumbent President at the expense of his opponents. "You need a minimum of $30-million to run an adequate national campaign," said Adamany.

Proponents of the law argue that the expenditure limit will end extravagant campaign spending and force candidates to be creative in trying to reach the electorate. But inflation will take its toll. "Compared to 1972," said Calkins,

"the $20-million limit in real dollars will be $15-million to $16-million."

While the Democratic and Republican candidates are guaranteed full public financing for the general election, minor-party and independent candidates will have to pay for their campaigns themselves, at least in 1976.

Wallace aides are confident they could raise the $20-million to pay for a general election campaign if Wallace bolted the party, as he did in 1968. "I don't have any reservations about financing a third-party effort," said Snider. "In fact, getting no public money then could help us. That could stimulate the public, since they would know we were running against $20-million in public money."

Other prospective candidates, however, are not in such a fortunate position. Many will have trouble collecting enough money to get past the crucial start-up point. And it is a certainty, as it is before every presidential election year, that the field of aspirants will be substantially smaller when campaigning begins in earnest.

The big, unsettling change in presidential politics is the new matching system to partially finance pre-nomination campaigns with public money. The system was created to reduce the reliance on private money in presidential primaries by matching the first $250 of a contribution. But it also established a new set of hurdles that a candidate has to surmount before he can start his campaign. These hurdles may, in the end, limit who can run and, ultimately, who can win.

Under the old system, most presidential candidates started their campaigns with a few wealthy backers who put up the seed money. Candidates raised money from primary to primary, relying on an earlier victory to generate money for the next primary campaign. The $100,-000 fund-raising threshold, intended to weed out fringe candidates and force the others to demonstrate that they had a broad base of support before they could be eligible to tap the public till, has changed all that.

But the effects of the threshold may go even further, according to several observers. The 20-state rule works against governors and regional candidates seeking the presidency, said Wisconsin's Adamany. "Governors traditionally start as a state or regional candidate. Now they'll have to go national from the start if they're going to have a chance," he said.

The threshold encourages the early starter. "The law, far from shortening the campaign cycle, is going to lengthen it," said Agree. "It's easy to understand. The earlier a guy starts, the better chances he has."

The statute may set up barriers to late entries. If the law had been in effect in 1968, Vice President Hubert H. Humphrey and the late Sen. Robert F. Kennedy (D N.Y. 1965-68) would have had great difficulty entering the presidential campaign a scant four months before the Democratic national convention. They would have had little time to meet the threshold and then raise enough money under the $1,000 and $5,000 contribution limits.

The net effect of the threshold requirement, according to several observers, is to tip the balance toward candidates who are nationally known, who have strong ideological followings and who raised a great deal of money early. "Wallace has an advantage because he has a constituency, a place to begin from," said Mahe. "Humphrey would have it if he decided to run. Muskie would have it. Kennedy would have it. Anybody that has had national exposure and visibility is put miles ahead of a newcomer."

—By Bruce F. Freed

REFERENCE BIBLIOGRAPHY

Books

Amrine, Michael, *This is Humphrey*, New York, Popular Library, 1964.

Anson, Robert S., *McGovern: A Biography*, New York, Holt, Rinehart and Winston, 1972.

Boyarsky, Bill, *The Rise of Ronald Reagan*, New York, Random House, 1968.

Brown, Edmund G., *Reagan and Reality: The Two Californias*, New York, Praeger, 1970.

Cannon, Lou, *Ronnie and Jesse: A Political Odyssey*, Garden City, N.Y., Doubleday, 1969.

Cleveland, Martha, *Charles Percy: A Strong New Voice from Illinois; a Biography*, Jacksonville, Ill., Harris-Wolfe, 1968.

Crawford, Ann F., *John B. Connally: Portrait in Power*, Austin, Texas, Jenkins Publishing Company, 1973.

David, Lester, *Ted Kennedy, Triumphs and Tragedies*, New York, Grosset and Dunlap, 1972.

Desmond, James, *Nelson Rockefeller: A Political Biography*, New York, Macmillan, 1964.

Dougherty, Richard, *Goodbye Mr. Christian: A Personal Account of McGovern's Rise and Fall*, Garden City, N.Y., Doubleday, 1973.

Edwards, Lee, *Reagan: A Political Biography*, San Diego, Calif., Viewpoint Books, 1967.

Ford, Gerald R., *Selected Speeches*, Arlington, Va., R. W. Beatty, 1973.

Frady, Marshall, *Wallace*, New York, World, 1968.

Gervasi, Frank H., *The Real Rockefeller: The Story of the Rise, Decline and Resurgence of the Presidential Aspirations of Nelson Rockefeller*, New York, Atheneum, 1964.

Governing New York State: The Rockefeller Years, New York, Academy of Political Science, 1974.

Greene, Bob, *Running*, Chicago, Regnery, 1973.

Harris, Fred R., *Alarms and Hopes: A Personal Journey, a Personal View*, New York, Harper, 1968.

Harris, Fred R., *The New Populism*, New York, Saturday Review Press, 1973.

Harris, Fred R., *Now is the Time: A New Populist Call to Action*, New York, McGraw-Hill, 1971.

Hart, Gary W., *Right from the Start: A Chronicle of the McGovern Campaign*, New York, Quadrangle, 1973.

Hersh, Burton, *The Education of Edward Kennedy: A Family Biography*, New York, Morrow, 1972.

Herzog, Arthur, *McCarthy for President*, New York, Viking, 1969.

Honan, William H., *Ted Kennedy, a Profile of a Survivor; Edward Kennedy after Bobby, After Chappaquiddick, and After Three Years of Nixon*, New York, Quadrangle, 1972.

Jackson, Henry M., *Fact, Fiction and National Security*, New York, Macfadden-Bartell Corporation, 1964.

Jones, Bill, *The Wallace Story*, Northport, Ala., American Publishing Company, 1966.

Kennedy, Edward M., *Decisions for a Decade: Policies and Programs for the 1970s*, Garden City, N.Y., Doubleday, 1968.

Kennedy, Edward M., *In Critical Condition: The Crisis in America's Health Care*, New York, Simon and Schuster, 1972.

Kurland, Gerald, *George Wallace: Southern Governor and Presidential Candidate*, Charlotteville, N.Y., Sam Har Press, 1972.

Kutz, Myer, *Rockefeller Power*, New York, Simon and Schuster, 1974.

Larner, Jeremy, *Nobody Knows: Reflections on the McCarthy Campaign of 1968*, New York, Macmillan, 1970.

LeRoy, Dave, *Gerald Ford, Untold Story*, Arlington, Va., R. W. Beatty, 1974.

Lewis, Joseph, *What Makes Reagan Run: A Political Profile*, New York, McGraw-Hill, 1968.

Lippman, Theo, *Muskie*, New York, Norton, 1971.

Liston, Robert A., *Sargent Shriver: A Candid Portrait*, New York, Farrar, Straus, 1964.

McCarthy, Eugene J., *Eugene J. McCarthy on the Record: Excerpts from his Writings and Speeches*, New York, Coalition for a Democratic Alternative, 1968.

McCarthy, Eugene J., *First Things First: New Priorities for America*, New York, New American Library, 1968.

McCarthy, Eugene J., *The Hard Years: A Look at Contemporary America and American Institutions*, New York, Viking, 1975.

McCarthy, Eugene J., *A Liberal Answer to the Conservative Challenge*, New York, Praeger, 1965.

McCarthy, Eugene J., *The Limits of Power: America's Role in the World*, New York, Holt, Rinehart and Winston, 1967.

McGovern, George S., *An American Journey: The Presidential Campaign Speeches of George McGovern*, New York, Random House, 1974.

McGovern, George S., *McGovern: The Man and His Beliefs*, New York, Norton, 1972.

Morris, Joe A., *Nelson A. Rockefeller: A Biography*, New York, Harper, 1960.

Murray, David, *Charles Percy of Illinois*, New York, Harper, 1968.

Muskie, Edmund S., *Journeys*, Garden City, N.Y., Doubleday, 1972.

Nevin, David, *Muskie of Maine*, New York, Random House, 1972.

Ognibene, Peter J., *Scoop: The Life and Politics of Senator Henry M. Jackson*, New York, Stein and Day, 1975.

Percy, Charles H., *Growing Old in the Country of the Young*, New York, McGraw-Hill, 1974.

Prochnau, William W., *A Certain Democrat: Senator Henry M. Jackson; a Political Biography*, Englewood Cliffs, N.J., Prentice-Hall, 1972.

President Ford: The Man and His Record, Washington, D.C., Congressional Quarterly, 1974.

Reagan, Ronald, *The Creative Society: Some Comments on Problems Facing America*, New York, Devin-Adair Company, 1968.

Reeves, Richard, *A Ford Not a Lincoln*, New York, Harcourt Brace Jovanovich, 1975.

Rockefeller, Nelson A., *The Future of Federalism*, Cambridge, Mass., Harvard University Press, 1962.

Rockefeller, Nelson A., *Unity, Freedom and Peace: A Blueprint for Tomorrow*, New York, Random House, 1968.

Rodgers, William H., *Rockefeller's Follies: An Unauthorized View of Nelson A. Rockefeller*, New York, Stein and Day, 1966.

Schwarz, Thomas J., *Public Financing of Elections: A Constitutional Division of the Wealth*, Chicago, Special Committee on Election Reform, American Bar Association, 1975.

Sherrill, Robert, *The Drugstore Liberal*, New York, Grossman, 1968.

Sidey, Hugh, *Portrait of a President*, New York, Harper and Row, 1975.

Stavis, Ben, *We Were the Campaign: New Hampshire to Chicago for McCarthy*, Boston, Beacon Press, 1969.

Ter Horst, Jerald F., *Gerald Ford and the Future of the Presidency*, New York, Third Press, 1974.

Symposium on Campaign Financing, Chicago, Special Committee on Election Reform, American Bar Association, 1975.

Udall, Morris K., *Education of a Congressman, the Newsletters of Morris K. Udall*, Indianapolis, Ind., Bobbs-Merrill, 1972.

Vestal, Bud, *Jerry Ford, Up Close: An Investigative Biography*, New York, Coward, McCann and Geoghegan, 1974.

Wallace, George C., *Hear Me Out*, New York, Grosset and Dunlap, 1968.

Weil, Gordon L., *The Long Shot: George McGovern Runs for President*, New York, Norton, 1973.

White, Theodore H., *The Making of the President, 1960*, New York, Atheneum, 1961.

White, Theodore H., *The Making of the President, 1964*, New York, Atheneum, 1965.

White, Theodore H., *The Making of the President, 1968*, New York, Atheneum, 1969.

White, Theodore H., *The Making of the President, 1972*, New York, Atheneum, 1973.

Articles

Adamany, David, "Election Campaign Financing: The 1974 Reforms," *Political Science Quarterly*, Summer 1975, pp. 201-220.

"Age of Rockefeller," *New Republic*, Aug. 30, 1975, pp. 3-4.

Alexander, S., "Panic to Reform: Opposition to the Campaign Reform Act by J. Buckley and E. McCarthy," *Newsweek*, Jan. 20, 1975, p. 84.

"Another Man from Texas with Eyes on the White House: L. Bentsen," *U.S. News and World Report*, Aug. 4, 1975, pp. 49-50.

Ashmore, Harry S., "Electoral Reforms: All Qualified Candidates Should Have Equal Access to the Voters," *Center Magazine*, November/December 1975, pp. 14-19.

Barnes, P., "Fred Harris Starts from Scratch," *Nation*, Feb. 8, 1975, pp. 145-147.

"Bentsen: No Chasing of Rainbows," *Time*, Sept. 29, 1975, pp. 31-32.

"Big Chance for Church," *U.S. News and World Report*, June 30, 1975, p. 15.

Bode, Ken, "The Democrats' Wallace Problem," *New Republic*, Oct. 25, 1975, pp. 6-9.

Bode, Ken, "Primary Politics," *New Republic*, Sept. 6, 1975, pp. 8-10.

Bonafede, Dom, "Ford's Positions Show Ambivalence," *National Journal Reports*, May 3, 1975, p. 657.

Bruno, H., "Big John on Ford and Himself," *Newsweek*, June 16, 1975, p. 22.

Buckley, William F., "Reagan for Challenger," *National Review*, Sept. 12, 1975, p. 1008.

Buckley, William F., "Rockefeller and the Twenty-Fifth," *National Review*, Dec. 20, 1974, p. 1481.

"Carey: An F.D.R. from Brooklyn," *Time*, Nov. 18, 1974, pp. 10-11.

Carney, F., "Riddle of Governor Jerry Brown," *Ramparts*, April 1975, pp. 34-37; July 1975, pp. 31-33.

Castelli, J., "Digging up the Rose Garden: McCarthy Challenges the System," *Nation*, Aug. 30, 1975, pp. 142-145.

"Chasing New Hampshire: Presidential Primaries," *Time*, April 28, 1975, p. 26.

"Cozying Up to Wallace," *Nation*, June 21, 1975, pp. 740-741.

Dennis, J., "Jimmy Carter's Fierce Campaign," *Nation*, May 17, 1975, pp. 592-596.

"Election '76: The Race for President Is Up for Grabs," *Senior Scholastic*, April 24, 1975, p. 19.

"Electoral Reform: Discussion," *Center Magazine*, November/December 1975, pp. 25-33.

"Eternal Democratic Majority: Passage of the Campaign Reform Act," *National Review*, Jan. 31, 1975, p. 88.

Foley, T. J., "In His Own Words: Wallace on Key Issues," *U.S. News and World Report*, May 26, 1975, pp. 48-49.

"Ford and Wallace," *Nation*, July 5, 1975, pp. 5-6.

"Ford Campaign," *Nation*, June 21, 1975, pp. 739-740.

"Ford's '76 Game Plan," *U.S. News and World Report*, July 21, 1975, pp. 11-12.

Freed, Bruce, "Financing Elections: New Law Under Attack," *Congressional Quarterly Weekly Report*, June 14, 1975, pp. 1239-1248.

Freed, Bruce, "This Time Everybody's Got a CREEP," *Washington Monthly*, November 1975, pp. 31-36.

"From Defeat Rises a Free Spirit: H. Humphrey," *Time*, Aug. 18, 1975, p. 13.

"From House to White House: Udall Aims for the Big Jump," *U.S. News and World Report*, Aug. 18, 1975, pp. 39-40.

Furlong, William B., "The Adlai III Brand of Politics," *New York Times Magazine*, Feb. 22, 1970, p. 28.

"George Wallace: Man to Beat in '76?" *U.S. News and World Report*, May 26, 1975, pp. 47-49.

Goldman, P., "Fastest Tortoise? H. M. Jackson," *Newsweek*, Feb. 10, 1975, p. 18.

Goldman, P., "New Money Rules," *Newsweek*, June 16, 1975, pp. 26-27.

Goldman, P., "President Faces 1976," *Newsweek*, May 5, 1975, pp. 48-49.

Goldman, P., "Ready for Teddy?" *Newsweek*, June 2, 1975, p. 22.

Goldman, P., "Ready on the Right: R. Reagan," *Newsweek*, March 24, 1975, pp. 20-22.

Goulden, J. C., "Bentsen: Money Man from Texas," *Nation*, March 8, 1975, pp. 267-272.

Grasmick, Harold G., "Rural Culture and the Wallace Movement in the South," *Rural Sociology*, Winter 1974, pp. 454-470.

Gwirtzman, M. S., "Who's on First: Democratic Candidates," *New York Times Magazine*, March 23, 1975, p. 14.

Hadley, A., "Morris Udall: Can a Congressman from a Small State Out West?" *Atlantic*, December 1974, p. 91.

Harrison, G. A., "Eugene McCarthy," *New Republic*, Sept. 21, 1974, pp. 12-13.

Healy, P., "Donald Rumsfeld: President Ford's Ring-master," *Saturday Evening Post*, September 1975, pp. 42-43.

"Heat on Wallace," *National Review*, June 6, 1975, p. 594.

Hobbs, C. D., "How Ronald Reagan Governed California," *National Review*, Jan. 17, 1975, p. 32.

Humphrey, Hubert H., "Guaranteed Jobs for Human Rights," *Annals of the American Academy of Political and Social Science*, March 1975, pp. 17-25.

Humphrey, Hubert H., "Planning Economic Policy," *Challenge*, March/April 1975, pp. 21-27.

"Issues that Will Decide the '76 Elections," *Nation's Business*, November 1975, pp. 22-36.

"Jackson: Running Hard, but Hardly Moving," *U.S. News and World Report*, June 9, 1975, pp. 20-22.

"Jimmy Who?" *Newsweek*, Dec. 23, 1974, p. 24.

Johnson, L., "Idaho Yahoos: Frank Church," *Nation*, Oct. 19, 1974, pp. 358-360.

Karnow, S., "Dilemma of the Dark Horses: The Democratic Nomination in '76." *New Republic*, June 15, 1974, pp. 13-16.

Karnow, S., "Elliot Richardson," *New Republic*, May 17, 1975, pp. 14-16.

Kraft, Joseph, "The Cast: Democratic Candidates," *New York Times Magazine*, Nov. 17, 1974, p. 32.

Lawson, Herbert G., "Recycled Reagan? California Governor Elected as Liberal Surprises His Backers," *Wall Street Journal*, April 29, 1975, p. 1.

McCarthy, Eugene J., "Electoral Reform: It Is a Closed System and One Suspects It Was Meant to be Closed," *Center Magazine*, November/December 1975, pp. 20-22.

McWilliams, C., "Scenario for '76," *Nation*, Feb. 1, 1975, pp. 98-100.

Miller, Norman C., "Jimmy Carter's Plan," *Wall Street Journal*, July 7, 1975, p. 1.

Miller, Norman C., "Man in the Middle? Lloyd Bentsen Tries to Please all Sides," *Wall Street Journal*, July 30, 1975, p. 1.

Moscow, A., "Nelson Aldrich Rockefeller," *Readers Digest*, November 1974, pp. 105-108.

Mott, Stewart R., "Electoral Reform: Needed a Disclosure Law to Reveal the Quo in Quid pro Quo Politics," *Center Magazine*, November/December 1975, pp. 23-24.

"The New Governor's Agenda for California," *California Journal*, February 1975, pp. 59-60.

"Nostalgia and Fatigue: Looking to Humphrey," *Nation*, Sept. 6, 1975, p. 162.

Osborn, John, "Ford's First Year," *New Republic*, July 26, 1975, p. 6.

Osborn, John, "Report on Rocky," *New Republic*, Nov. 8, 1975, pp. 8-9.

Phillips, K. P., "Reagan-Wallace Ticket," *Newsweek*, May 19, 1975, p. 13.

Pierson, John, "State of Neglect? Alabama Languishes as Wallace Focuses on Presidential Drive," *Wall Street Journal*, April 28, 1975, p. 1.

Pinsky, M., "Sanford: Everyone's Second Choice," *Nation*, Feb. 22, 1975, pp. 210-213.

"Playing It Cool as Vice President," *U.S. News and World Report*, May 19, 1975, pp. 26-28.

"Poll of Democratic Leaders: It Looks Like Humphrey," *U.S. News and World Report*, Nov. 17, 1975, pp. 24-27.

"Reagan's Quandary," *New Republic*, March 1, 1975, p. 4.

Reeves, Richard, "Carey versus Wilson," *New York Times Magazine*, Oct. 27, 1974, p. 17.

Reeves, Richard, "How Does the Governor of California Differ from a Shoemaker?" *New York Times Magazine*, Aug. 24, 1975, p. 8.

Reston, James, "Talk with George Wallace," *New York Times Magazine*, April 27, 1975, pp. 44-48.

"Rockefeller Issue," *Nation*, Dec. 21, 1974, pp. 643-644.

"Rockefeller's Record," *American Libraries*, November 1974, p. 538.

"Rock's Turn to the Right," *Time*, May 12, 1975, pp. 27-28.

"Rocky Learns to Whistle Dixie," *Time*, Sept. 8, 1975, pp. 7-8.

Rosen, G. R., "Democratic Businessmen Like L. Bentsen," *Duns*, March 1975, pp. 66-69.

Rumsfeld, Donald H., "Now the Constituency Is the Nation: An Run: An Interview with Donald Rumsfeld, Assistant to the President," *U.S. News and World Report*, March 17, 1975, p. 8.

Rumsfeld, Donald H., "Now the Constituency Is the Nation: An Interview," *Time*, Jan. 20, 1975, p. 16.

Salman, S., "Long, Long Road: L. Bentsen," *Newsweek*, Feb. 24, 1975, p. 20.

Salzman, Ed, "The Greening of Governor Brown: What's his Philosophy? What Has He Accomplished? Who Are His Closest Advisors?" *California Journal*, May 1975, pp. 149-152.

Scheer, R., "Why You Should Think About Scoop Again, and Again, and Again," *Esquire*, September 1975, p. 93.

"Scoop Jackson: Running Hard Uphill," *Time*, Feb. 17, 1975, pp. 11-12.

Shearer, D., "Down on Jerry Brown," *New Republic*, Sept. 13, 1975, pp. 8-10.

Shearer, Lloyd, "Don Rumsfeld: He's President Ford's Number One," *Parade Magazine*, Feb. 2, 1975, pp. 4-7.

Sherrill, Robert, "Senator Jackson Enters Right," *Nation*, Feb. 1, 1975, pp. 105-111.

"Shriver: Is He Kennedy's Stalking Horse?" *U.S. News and World Report*, Nov. 3, 1975, pp. 24-25.

Stocker, J., "Why Udall Wants to Run," *Nation*, Feb. 15, 1975, pp. 17-23.

"Terry Sanford: Another Spirit for '76," *Newsweek*, June 9, 1975, p. 26.

"Two Governors Full of Surprises: Brown of California: More Tightfisted than Predecessor Reagan; Carey of New York: Liberal in Congress, Budget-Cutter in Albany," *U.S. News and World Report*, June 2, 1975, p. 52.

"Wallace's Revisionism," *Time*, May 10, 1975, p. 16.

Walters, R., "Millions for Third Parties? the 1974 Amendments to the Federal Election Campaign Act," *Ramparts*, July 1975, p. 14.

Watson, R., "Rocky and the Right," *Newsweek*, March 3, 1975, pp. 17-18.

Wieck, P. R., "Fred Harris: The Oklahoma Preacher," *New Republic*, June 21, 1975, pp. 27-29.

Wieck, P. R., "Henry Jackson's Way with Money," *New Republic*, Feb. 15, 1975, pp. 14-15.

Wieck, P. R., "Long Shot Jimmy Carter," *New Republic*, April 12, 1975, pp. 16-19.

"With Rockefeller Out, A Wide Open Choice," *U.S. News and World Report*, Nov. 17, 1975, p. 23.

Documents

U.S. Congress, House Committee on House Administration, *Federal Election Campaign Act Amendments of 1974, Report, Oct. 7, 1974*, Washington, D.C., Government Printing Office, 1974.

U.S. Congress, House Committee on House Administration, *Federal Election Campaign Act Amendments of 1974, Report, July 30, 1974*, Washington, D.C., Government Printing Office, 1974.

U.S. Congress, House Committee on House Administration, *Federal Election Reform, Hearings Oct. 2, 1973*, Washington, Government Printing Office, 1973.

U.S. Congress House Committee on House Administration, *Proposed Legislation to Reform the Conduct and Financing of Federal Election Campaigns, March 27, 1974*, Washington, D.C., Government Printing Office, 1974.

U.S. Congress, House Committee on the Judiciary, *Confirmation of Gerald R. Ford as Vice President of the United States, Dec. 4, 1973*, Washington, D.C., Government Printing Office, 1974.

U.S. Congress, House Committee on the Judiciary, *Confirmation of Nelson A. Rockefeller as Vice President of the United States*, Dec. 17, 1974, Washington, D.C., Government Printing Office, 1974.

U.S. Congress, House Committee on the Judiciary, *Debate on the Nomination of Nelson A. Rockefeller to be Vice President of the United States*, Washington, D.C., Government Printing Office, 1975.

U.S. Congress, House Committee on the Judiciary, *Nomination of Gerald R. Ford to be Vice President of the United States, Hearings, Nov. 15, 16, 19-21, 26, 1973*, Washington, D.C., Government Printing Office, 1973.

U.S. Congress, House Committee on the Judiciary, *Selected Issues and Positions of Nelson A. Rockefeller, Nominee for Vice President of the United States: An Analysis*, Washington, D.C., Government Printing Office, 1974.

U.S. Congress, Senate Committee on Rules and Administration, *Federal Election Campaign Act Amendments of 1974, Report, Feb. 21, 1974*, Washington, D.C., Government Printing Office, 1974.

U.S. Congress, Senate Committee on Rules Administration, *Federal Election Campaign Laws*, Washington, D.C., Government Printing Office, 1975.

U.S. Congress, Senate Committee on Rules and Administration, *Federal Election Reform, Hearings, June 6, 7, 1973*, Washington, D.C., Government Printing Office, 1973.

U.S. Congress, Senate Committee on Rules and Administration, *Nomination of Gerald R. Ford of Michigan to be Vice President of the United States, Hearings, Nov. 5, 7, 14, 1973*, Washington, D.C., Govenment Printing Office, 1973.

U.S. Congress, Senate Committee on Rules and Administration, *Nomination of Gerald R. Ford of Michigan to be Vice President of the United States, Report, Nov. 23, 1973*, Washington, D.C., Government Printing Office, 1973.

U.S. Congress, Senate Committee on Rules and Administration, *Nomination of Nelson A. Rockefeller of New York to be Vice President of the United States, Hearings, Sept. 23-26, 1974*, Washington, D.C., Government Printing Office, 1974.

U.S. Congress, Senate Committee on Rules and Administration, *Nomination of Nelson A. Rockefeller of New York to be Vice President of the United States, Report, Dec. 3, 1974*, Washington, D.C., Government Printing Office, 1974.

Explanation of Vote Studies on Members of Congress

In an attempt to provide students of Congress with a meaningful but nonpartisan analysis of record voting, Congressional Quarterly conducts several annual studies. Following are the ground rules for the studies included in this book's chapters on members of Congress who are prospective presidential candidates in 1976:

Presidential Support and Opposition

This study is designed to show the extent to which each member of Congress supports or opposes the specific legislative requests or stands of the President. The key step is the choice of roll calls for inclusion in the tabulation. Only those votes are included on which the President has publicly indicated a position, either in messages or statements, before the vote was taken. This method results in the inclusion of some non-controversial votes as well as the exclusion of certain important roll calls on which the President's own position was not publicly clear at the time the vote was taken. Any departure from the method used, however, would lead to a subjective weighting of issues, the results of which would be open to serious challenge.

Voting Participation

This study is designed to show the extent to which each member actually casts "yea" or "nay" votes—the only kind that can determine the legislative outcome—on roll calls for which he or she is eligible. Relatively few members score 100 per cent, because absences due to illness, committee sessions and travel are common. Voting participation is not, however, a record of absenteeism as such. It is a measure of the relative extent to which members make effective use of their voting privilege.

Party Unity

This study is designed to show the extent to which each member votes with the majority of his or her party when that majority is opposed by a majority of the other party. Thus, by definition, roll calls included in the tabulation of party unity scores are selected automatically according to the numerical outcome of the vote.

Conservative Coalition

This study examines all the votes in which a majority of voting northern Democrats and a majority of voting southern Democrats took opposing positions, and the southern majority sided with a majority of voting Republicans, thus forming a "conservative coalition." Individual coalition support scores are listed, as well as opposition scores.

Bipartisan Voting

This study examines the votes on which a majority of voting Democrats and of voting Republicans voted in agreement. Among the elements highlighted by the study are the "independent" voters—those who voted most consistently against the majorities of both parties.

INDEX

Adamany, David W.
   Campaign finance law - 101, 102
Adams, Don - 9
AFL-CIO. *See also* Interest-Group Ratings.
   Committee on Political Education (COPE)
      Campaign spending - 98, 99
      Wallace 1968 campaign - 82
Agnew, Spiro T. - 10
Agree, George
   Campaign spending law - 99, 100, 101, 102
Albert, Carl (D Okla.) - 73
Alexander, Herbert E.
   Campaign finance law - 101, 102
American Conservative Union
   Conservative Victory Fund
      Campaign spending limits - 99
American Independent Party - 80, 82
American Medical Association
   Political Action Committee (AMPAC)
      Campaign spending limits - 99
Americans for Constitutional Action (ACA). *See* Interest-Group Ratings.
Americans for Democratic Action (ADA). *See* Interest-Group Ratings.
Anderson, John B. (R Ill.)
   Campaign reform - 73
Arnall, Ellis - 29

Baker, Howard H. Jr. (R Tenn.)
   Prospective candidate - 92
Baker, Michael Jr. - 67
Bayh, Birch (D Ind.)
   Background (box) - 19
   Campaign strategy - 17, 18
   Interest-group ratings (box) - 18
   Issue positions - 19-21
   Kennedy plane crash - 52
   Primary issues - 2
   Senate campaigns - 18
   Staff, advisers (box) - 21
   Vote study scores (box) - 20
Bell, Daniel
   Post-industrial society - 1
Bellmon, Henry (R Okla.) - 59, 91
Bentsen, Lloyd (D Texas)
   Background - 23, (box) 24
   Campaign strategy - 22-23
   Fund-raising strategy - 98
   House career - 23
   Interest-group ratings (box) - 23
   Issue positions - 25-26
   Senate campaign, 1970 - 24
   Senate career - 25
   Staff, advisers (box) - 26
   Vote study scores (box) - 25
Bishop, Neil S. - 58
Bliss, Ray C. - 7
Boggs, Hale - 73, 74
Borah, William E. - 33
Brewer, Albert - 81
Bridges, Styles - 8
Bracy, Terry - 73

Broderick, Raymond J. - 66
Brooke, Edward W. (R Mass.) - 8
Brown, Edmund G.
   Reagan threat - 13
Brown, Edmund G. Jr.
   Governorship - 13
   Possible candidate - 94
Brzezinski, Zbigniew
   Post-industrial society - 1
Buckley, James L. (Cons-R N.Y.)
   Campaign finance law - 96
Burch, Dean - 7
Burke, Carl
   Church candidacy - 31
Bush, George
   CIA appointment - 34, 94
   Possible candidate - 89, 93
   Senate campaign, 1970 - 24
Bushell, Gary
   Bentsen campaign - 25, (box) 26
Busing. *See* Civil Rights.
Butz, Earl L. - 46
Byrd, Robert C. (D W.Va.) - 54

Cain, Harry P. - 44
Calkins, John T. - 98, 101, 102
Callaway, Howard H. (Bo)
   Ford campaign - 5, 6-7, (box) 10, 89
Campaign Finance Law (1974)
   Constitutional challenge - 96
   Cost of electing a president, 1960-72 (graph) - 95
   Excess 1972 contributions (box) - 100
   Highlights of law (box) - 97
   McCarthy challenge - 84
   Minor party candidates - 101
   Public financing - 97, 102
   Special interests, impact on - 99
   Udall funds - 73
Campaign Reform
   Bentsen amendments - 26
   Harris and new law - 36
   Kennedy position - 55
   Udall efforts - 73
Capehart, Homer E. - 18
Carey, Hugh L.
   Possible candidate - 94
Carr, Billie - 23, 25
Carswell, G. Harrold
   Bayh attack - 17
Carter, Jimmy
   Background (box) - 29
   Campaign strategy - 27
   Governorship - 29-30
   Gubernatorial races - 29
   Issue positions - 30
   Party, national attention - 30
   Primary prospects - 28, 72
   Staff, advisers (box) - 28
   Wallace problem - 28
Case, Clifford P. (R N.J.) - 34
Casey, Robert P.
   Shapp governor race - 65
Casper, William - 67
Center for Public Financing - 99
Chisholm, Shirley (D N.Y.) - 62

Church, Frank (D Idaho)
   Background (box) - 31
   CIA inquiry - 34
   Interest-group ratings (box) - 34
   Keynoter, 1960 Democratic convention - 32
   Prospective candidacy - 31
   Senate campaigns - 32, 33
   Senate career - 31, 32, 33-34
   Staff, advisers (box) - 34
   Vote study scores (box) - 32-33
Civil Liberties Union, N.Y.
   Campaign finance law - 96
Civil Rights
   Bayh position - 17
   Bentsen position - 26
   Ford position - 10, 11
   Harris position - 36, 38
   Humphrey views - 42
   Jackson position - 50
   Kennedy position - 54
   Reagan position - 16
   Sanford position - 61, 63
   Udall and Mormonism - 77
   Wallace position - 79, 82, 88
Clark, Dick (D Iowa) - 55
Clement, Frank - 92
Cleveland, James C. (R N.H.) - 7, 8
Cocome, Ron
   McCarthy campaign - 85, 86, (box) 88
Cohen, William S. (R Maine)
   Muskie Senate seat - 56
Cohn, Roy - 45
Committee for the New Majority - 4, 91
Committee on Conservative Alternatives - 80
Committee on Political Education (COPE). *See* AFL-CIO; Interest-Group Ratings.
Connally, John B.
   Bentsen Senate campaign - 24
   Prospective candidate - 91
Constitution, U.S.
   Bayh work on amendments - 19
   Campaign finance law - 96
Cooper, John Sherman (R Ky.) - 34
Cooper, Kent C.
   Campaign finance law - 98
Cox, Archibald - 93
Cramer, William C. - 9
Crane, Philip M. (R Ill.) - 9
Cranston, Alan (D Calif.) - 55
Crime
   Bayh and youth programs - 19-20
   Bentsen legislation - 26
   Kennedy legislation - 55
   Reagan position - 16
   Shapp position - 67
   Shriver position - 71
   Wallace position - 83
Cross, Burton M. - 58
Cunningham, George - 94

Daley, Richard J.
   Shriver ties - 70

   Stevenson candidacy - 94
Defense Policy. *See* National Defense.
Democratic Party
   1976 candidate outlook - 4
   Economic election issues - 3
   Proportionality rule - 2
   Wallace relationship - 79
Democratic Study Group
   McCarthy founding - 86
   Udall support - 73, 74
Dennison, David - 93
Devitt, Edward J. - 86
Dirksen, Everett McKinley - 10, 92, 94
Dole, Robert (R Kan.)
   Ford campaign - 6, 7
Douglas, Paul H. - 92
Drinan, Robert F. (D Mass.) - 48, 67
Durkin, John A. (D N.H.) - 8, 12

Eagleton, Thomas F. - 69
Eastland, James O. (D Miss.) - 53
Economy
   Bayh position - 20
   Bentsen views - 3, 25
   Carter policies - 30
   Election issue, 1976 - 3
   Ford position - 10, 11
   Jackson position - 50
   McCarthy policies - 88
   Muskie budget role - 59
   Reagan position - 15
   Sanford position - 63
   Shapp position - 67
   Shriver position - 71
   Udall proposals - 3, 76
   Wallace position - 83
Education
   New Class issue - 3
   Reagan's California record - 15
   Shapp views - 67
Education Commission of the States
   Sanford role - 63
Edwards, Edwin W. - 23
Ehrlichman, John D.
   Carter attack - 30
Election, 1976
   Campaign finance law - 95
   Candidate emotional appeal - 2
   Economic issues - 3
   Independent candidates - 4
   Nomination paradox - 2
   Outlook: post-industrial politics - 1
   Party campaign strategy - 4
   Primary schedule (table) - 3
   Voter party affiliations (box) - 2
Elicker, Charles W. - 44
Employment. *See* Economy.
Energy
   Bayh position - 20
   Bentsen plan - 26
   Carter position - 30
   Ford policy - 11
   Harris position - 39